TELEVISION GOES TO THE MOVIES

Television and film have always been connected, but recent years have seen them overlapping, collaborating, and moving towards each other in ever more ways. Set amidst this moment of unprecedented synergy, this book examines how television and film culture interact in the 21st century.

Both media appear side by side in many platforms or venues, stories and storytellers cross between them, they regularly have common owners, and they discuss each other constantly. Jonathan Gray and Derek Johnson examine what happens at these points of interaction, studying the imaginary borderlands between each medium, the boundary maintenance that quickly envelops much discussion of interaction, and ultimately what we allow or require television and film to be. Offering separate chapters on television exhibition at movie theaters, cinematic representations of television, television-to-film and film-to-television adaptations, and television producers crossing over to film, the book explores how each zone of interaction invokes fervid debate of the roles that producers, audiences, and critics want and need each medium to play. From *Game of Thrones* to *The TV Set*, *Bewitched* to the Marvel Cinematic Universe, hundreds of TV shows and films are discussed.

Television Goes to the Movies will be of interest to students and scholars of television studies, film studies, media studies, popular culture, adaptation studies, production studies, and media industries.

Jonathan Gray is Hamel Family Distinguished Chair in Communication Arts at University of Wisconsin-Madison. He is author of *Dislike-Minded: Media, Audiences, and the Dynamics of Taste*, *Television Studies* (with Amanda D. Lotz), *Show Sold Separately: Promos, Spoilers, and Other Media Paratexts*, *Television Entertainment*, and *Watching with The Simpsons: Television, Parody, and Intertextuality*, and co-editor of numerous books including *Keywords for Media Studies* (with Laurie Ouellette) and *A Companion to Media Authorship* (with Derek Johnson).

Derek Johnson is Professor of Media and Cultural Studies in the Communication Arts Department at the University of Wisconsin-Madison. He is the author of *Transgenerational Media Industries: Adults, Children and the Reproduction of Culture* and *Media Franchising: Creative License and Collaboration in the Culture Industries*. He has also edited or co-edited several books, including most recently *From Networks to Netflix: A Guide to Changing Channels* and *Point of Sale: Analyzing Media Retail* (with Daniel Herbert).

TELEVISION GOES TO THE MOVIES

*Jonathan Gray and
Derek Johnson*

Routledge
Taylor & Francis Group

NEW YORK AND LONDON

First published 2021
by Routledge
52 Vanderbilt Avenue, New York, NY 10017

and by Routledge
2 Park Square, Milton Park, Abingdon, Oxon, OX14 4RN

Routledge is an imprint of the Taylor & Francis Group, an informa business

Library of Congress Cataloging-in-Publication Data
A catalog record for this title has been requested

ISBN: 978-1-138-47643-1 (hbk)
ISBN: 978-1-138-47644-8 (pbk)
ISBN: 978-1-351-10597-2 (ebk)

Typeset in Bembo
by codeMantra

CONTENTS

ACKNOWLEDGMENTS

We'd both like to begin by thanking the Wisconsin Alumni Research Foundation and the University of Wisconsin-Madison for supporting some of the research behind this book through an H.I. Romnes Faculty Fellowship and a Vilas Mid-Career Investigator's Award. We are also grateful to the Hamel family for their generous support of our research.

The funds from these sources allowed us to hire three superb research assistants. Jennifer Smith and Nicholas Benson each logged two summers worth of watching media about media and adaptations, respectively, and their brilliant notes and observations undergird Chapters 2 and 3. Laura Schumacher also contributed by seeking out other touchpoints where film and television clash or are at least imagined to clash. We offer our profuse thanks to all three.

Much of this book was written, though, while locked down during the COVID-19 pandemic, so we'd like to direct most of our remaining thanks to those who kept us company (and only a little insane) during hard times. For Jonathan, that means Monica Grant and Abigail Gray; for Derek it means Colleen, Dahlia, and Annika Johnson, as well as stalwart, socially distanced running buddy Jeremy Morris; while for both of us it means the wonderful porch pals and cocktail connoisseurs Jason Kido Lopez, Lori Kido Lopez, and Mimsy. Knowing that Eric Hoyt was only a message away helped too. New puppy Captain did very little to speed this book to its conclusion, but he was appreciated nonetheless.

Together we'd like to dedicate the book to Michele Hilmes, someone we wish we could've spent our lockdown with (even if that would've constituted a flagrant violation of Bruce's "three hour" rule). Michele has been our teacher, mentor, colleague, friend, ace bartender, confidante, and role model, and though we know that we could never balance our ledger of thanks with her, we'll try here nonetheless.

INTRODUCTION

On May 19, 2019, the final episode of *Game of Thrones* (2011–2019), "The Iron Throne," aired on HBO. Over its eight-year run, *Game of Thrones* had regularly been called "cinematic" or even "the most cinematic television show ever made" (Epstein 2016), a sentiment echoed when HBO Chairman and CEO Richard Plepler spoke of the final season as much more like "six movies" (Littleton 2019), and when showrunner David Benioff shared that the production team had always considered the show like a "73 hour movie" (Hibberd 2017). *Game of Thrones* was not the only major finale that week in the United States, though, as Marvel's *Avengers: Endgame* (2019) was still in cinemas everywhere. For all its $2.8 billion command of the box office and for all the sweeping effects that its $356 million budget bought it, though, in structure and style *Endgame* felt very much like a television series finale, complete with the tour through past episodes, return of past characters, and sad diegetic goodbyes standing in for presumed sad real-life goodbyes. That week in May thus focused how loosely the labels of "film" or "television" may sit on their wearers, and focuses a feeling many of us have probably had of late, that television and film might be a lot more alike than we have been told was the case. Television and film critics—and television and film professors—can prove overfond of pitting the two media against each other as if rival sports teams, with each new major achievement in either medium being read as a step closer to winning a bowl, cup, or medal. Especially as critics, academics, and the public at large have increasingly noted a "Second Golden Age" of television, an era of "peak TV" in which television has finally begun to shake off its identity as the "idiot box" or the "boob tube," there is a sense of zero-sum competition in which the plaudits enjoyed by one medium might come at the expense of another. But they still have a lot in common, and the pathways between the media are both well-traveled and multiplying.

Hit films old and new are being adapted to television, in the form of high-budget, critically acclaimed shows such as *Fargo* (2014–), *Hannibal* (2013–2015), and *Bates Motel* (2013–2017). Film, meanwhile, has regularly drawn from television's creative pool to produce franchises such as *Transformers* or *Mission: Impossible*. Marvel comic book characters (owned by Disney) move back and forth from television to film in its ever-expanding universe. Each such movement requires a host of behind-the-scenes work, from licensing and lawyering to ambitious projects of co-authorship, broader corporate strategy of timed releases, and more. Many film-to-television or television-to-film moves, moreover, happen wholly within a corporate family, reminding us in the process that film and television are hardly "competing" in any true sense. Instead film and television represent horizontally integrated components within a media corporation's diversified portfolio. And beyond the texts and industries, people are moving between film and television all the time, as many of the film industry's most successful actors, writers, and directors cross over to work in television with previously unrivaled frequency.

Television Goes to the Movies is set amidst this odd drama of unprecedented synergy mixed with competitive, comparative discourses that run throughout everyday media encounters. We see this as an especially good time to ask questions of what the two media mean to their viewers, to those who create them, to their self-appointed guardians, and to each other. At this historical conjuncture, how are film and television related, how are they seen to be related, and how do they interact in ways that tell us about their places in contemporary mediated culture? *Television Goes to the Movies* addresses these questions. We focus on how television *shows* and *stories* go to the movies through exhibition, on how television as *medium* goes to the movies as the subject of adaptation, and on how television *personnel* situate their careers across and between television and film. In doing so, though, we ultimately ask how television *culture* has "gone to" the movies—how the meanings, practices, rituals, and identities of film and television have collided in specific contexts of experience—and how *discourses* of television, what it is, and what it does interact with discourses of film, what it is, and what it does. *Television Goes to the Movies* focuses on the boundaries and passages between media, identifying them as porous, while revealing the significant efforts made—across the levels of exhibition, discourse, adaptation, and labor—to build them back up again. As television goes to the movies, it nevertheless participates in a counterintuitive process of calcifying the boundaries felt and experienced as media are produced and consumed.

Shifting and Reinforcing Boundaries in Film and Television

Understanding the relationships between these media requires a grasp of their relative orbits to one another and how those orientations might be perceived and experienced. At the turn of the millennium, film and television in the

United States seemed to be moving closer together. Spurred by media owner-ship deregulation, five of the big six Hollywood studios—Disney, Paramount, 20th Century Fox, Universal, and Warner Bros.—had joined or would soon join corporate families that included the top US television networks ABC, CBS, FOX, NBC, UPN, and WB, alongside many cable offerings. Sony, a company perhaps best known for making television sets, owned the sixth stu-dio, Columbia, since 1989. The 1990s had also seen the rise of so-called "qual-ity television," and as the 2000s began, the networks would be challenged by a slew of cable channels and eventually streaming services offering their own high-prestige channels. Two of them even had names that situated them be-tween film and television—with its slogan that it's "It's Not TV, It's HBO," HBO promised a "home box office," while Netflix began as a service send-ing DVD "flix" to your mail box, before transitioning to its current position as the world's preeminent streaming television service and lead producer of television content globally. Regardless of these positionings, the online sub-scription services that define the "streaming wars" brought the libraries of film and television studios alike together in their efforts to attract potential cus-tomers with interest in both. Encouraged to do so in part by these changes, personnel increasingly moved between the film and television industries: many creative personnel now regularly go back and forth between film and tele-vision, while the rise of franchising and transmedia storytelling has required many producers to keep one foot planted firmly in each medium in order to structure deals for entities that know no media boundaries. Meanwhile, high-definition televisions achieved near-ubiquity at speed, and soundbars, surround sound systems, and other acoustic treats came down in price and spread far and wide, allowing more people to approximate the pleasures of a movie theater in their own living rooms (Klinger 2006). Crossing similar boundaries, movie theaters started replacing their stadium seating with lounge chairs and added alcohol and food service to approximate the pleasures of watching at home in the theater (Benson-Allott 2021). The theatrical experience came to in-clude advertisements, too, with companies such as Before the Movie packaging these consumer appeals as part of pre-shows that evoke the sequential pro-gramming "flows" (Williams 1972) of broadcast television. And an increased amount of viewing of both film and television was happening on multiple other screens altogether—on phones and tablets, on airplane seat backs, on computer screens—where film and television were often separated only by menu options. Thus, while film and television had always been intimately connected, the 2000s brought them even closer together in many ways.

This is not to say, however, that boundaries between film and television have no longer been felt in the 21st century. Few examples make this clearer than the impact of the COVID-19 pandemic on the entertainment industries. As the needs of social distancing brought production of both film and television content to a standstill in early 2020, Hollywood calculated its exposure as a loss that would span both sectors (Lang, Vary, and Donnelly 2020; Littleton and Low 2020). As early as March 2020, analysts estimated that the shutdown of the production operations shared across film and television combined would cost Hollywood as a whole some $20 billion (Siegel, Kit, and Goldberg 2020). And yet, the pain of the pandemic was not necessarily felt equally across industry sectors still distinguished as film and television. In the face of social distancing policies, theatrical exhibitors were forced to close as anticipated blockbuster film releases like *Mulan* (2020), *No Time to Die* (forthcoming), and *Black Widow* (forthcoming) were repeatedly and indefinitely delayed. Unlike the public entertainment of the cinema, television appeared better suited to adapt to the crisis, given its status as a domestic medium tied to privatized devices and viewing spaces. Undoubtedly, both film and television faced similar supply problems as the production shutdown limited the amount of new content in the pipeline; yet at the level of distribution and exhibition, television could still deliver programming to consumers isolated in their homes in a way film could not. In fact, this existential threat to theatrical modes of exhibition was arguably a boon to domestic forms of programming delivery long associated with television. With socially distant consumers isolated in their homes, domestic forms of entertainment enjoyed a captive audience eager for social connection and windows to the outside world. Television could pick up the slack as public forms of entertainment faltered.

Early reports from the Nielsen Company thus revealed that there could be winners as well as losers in the crisis engulfing Hollywood. As stay-at-home orders and other social distancing policies took hold in the United States in March 2020, ratings data revealed a potential 60% increase in television viewership (Spangler, "Quarantine" 2020). Clearly, there was an opportunity here. Streaming services like Netflix and Disney+ found that the isolation of consumers at home helped to drive up subscription rates. Between January and April 2020, Netflix added almost 16 million subscribers globally, helping to increase the market value of the company by another $50 billion (Lee 2020; Spangler, "Netflix" 2020). In the second quarter, that growth slowed, but still added another 10 million subscribers. The biggest challenge facing Netflix was the fear that thanks to the pandemic, everyone who might ever want a subscription might now already have one (Alexander 2020). Disney+, too, stood to benefit from the pandemic. By March 2020, the service was already in half of US households with children ten years old or younger, but Disney anticipated even further growth given parents' interest in occupying children stuck at home (Spangler, "Disney" 2020). By August, strong performance for the streaming service was credited as the lone "bright spot" enabling Disney to maintain its value during the pandemic (Jenkins 2020).

One way to read these successes is to focus on delivery technology and affirm the greater advantages television held in this crisis as a domestic medium, compared to the public medium of film. However, the advantages enjoyed by

Netflix and Disney+ could be equally understood as a function of the persistent interrelationships between the two media. In Netflix's case, the service may have been delivered domestically; yet it would be a mistake to say it only brought television to its subscribers. During the first six months of the pandemic in the United States, Netflix was one of the very few outlets providing consumers with new feature film releases featuring recognizable Hollywood stars. While theatrically exhibited films sat in standstill, subscribers could still see the Charlize Theron superhero vehicle *The Old Guard* (2020), the goofy Will Ferrell romantic comedy *Eurovision Song Contest: The Story of Fire Saga* (2020), the action thriller *Extraction* (2020) starring Chris Hemsworth, and many more. Netflix thrived in the pandemic in part because it provided a means of continuity for the cinema, not because it stood outside of it. Similarly, while Disney sometimes resisted using the domestic delivery service of its streaming platform to bring its film content to viewers, it redirected planned film releases like *Hamilton* (2020) and (eventually) *Mulan* to Disney+. Yet in some contrast to Netflix, the success of Disney+ in the domestic realm long dominated by television had to be understood in relationship to the company's persistent investment in public entertainments. Plaudits that Disney+ received for helping the company to retain its value represented somewhat damning praise at a corporate level; while Disney+ represented one bright spot, it only offset all the losses that the company continued to face in theatrical markets and theme park operations. So when analysts called Disney the "bellwether of the industries' resistance to the virus" (Lang, Vary, and Donnelly 2020), it was out of recognition that the worlds of domestic and public entertainments remained intimately connected. By contrast, Netflix could be described as "virus proof" because it was non-diversified, having gone all-in on a single service perfectly suited to the dynamics of social distancing (Lang, Vary, and Donnelly 2020). Yet in that single service, film and television remained fundamentally linked as equivalent choices for the isolated consumer browsing the Netflix menu.

The COVID-19 pandemic thus intensified the boundaries felt between film and television even as the mode of their delivery blurred those same boundaries. Even at the level of production, television could be observed to recover differently than film. While both film and television production largely shut down at the same time in 2020, the latter recovered more quickly. As domestic delivery had been unbroken, television distributors had continued to burn through their program supply at a quick rate (whereas many films simply sat in limbo awaiting the reopening of theaters). Given that, television distributors faced a greater demand for content sooner, and began developing new socially distant strategies for making television. To continue production of *Full Frontal with Samantha Bee* (2016–), the eponymous comedian enlisted her family to serve as crew and resume production in her backyard. Other late-night hosts, including Stephen Colbert and Trevor Noah, began filming from their own homes and using digital communication tools like Skype and Zoom to connect with their guests. Channels like Nickelodeon began signing YouTube influencers to produce "made-from-home" series (Tuchow 2020). All these strategies worked to get the supply of television flowing again while big-budget films continued to wait for release. In adopting aesthetics and production strategies borrowed from YouTube and other spaces of amateur production, "made-from-home" strategies seemed to highlight television's difference from the blockbuster spectacles of film. Yet this transformation of television form equally revealed the ways in which the boundaries around media are rarely fixed or stable. Just as television began to transform, analysts predicted that film, too, would change in response to the pandemic (Zeitchik, "Pandemic" 2020). In their forms and in their delivery, film, television, and new media are highly fluid, and that dynamism allows them to frequently overlap and converge with one another even as the experience of them can unfold in very specific and divergent ways.

All this is to say that there is no reason that the boundaries we see around "film" and "television" are natural or inevitable. They have to be made to seem so.

And yet, in spite of the changes that have often put these media into closer relationship in the 21st century, film and television are still regularly depicted as rivals or antagonists—at best distant relatives and at worst, it now seems, differently evolved entities adapting to cataclysm on the basis of their inherited traits. Perhaps precisely because the real boundaries between the two media have been crumbling, many film or television watchers, makers, and funders have worked to reinforce the *discursive* boundaries, to insist that film and television are wholly different meaning systems and experiences, with vastly different claims to the status of art, vastly different modes and spaces of experiences, vastly different roles to play in society. Even as most of us probably engage in the watching of both film and television, discursive boundary maintenance can suggest two different types of viewers, posing the differences in spectatorship or audiencehood as if they are as disparate as the acts of sleeping and running a race.

A recent eruption of this discursive boundary maintenance occurred in August 2019, when the Academy of Motion Picture Arts and Sciences' Board of Governors met to discuss whether Netflix movies should be eligible for Oscars. Steven Spielberg missed the meeting, but offered his thoughts nonetheless. In particular, he noted:

> I feel people need to have the opportunity to leave the safe and familiar of their lives and go to a place where they can sit in the company of others and have a shared experience—cry together, laugh together, be afraid together—so that when it's over they might feel a little less like strangers. I want to see the survival of movie theaters. I want the theatrical experience to remain relevant in our culture.
>
> *(Pedersen 2019)*

Such a statement offers no *explicit* criticism of television; indeed, Spielberg preceded it by insisting that "Big screen, small screen—what really matters to me is a great story and everyone should have access to great stories" (Pedersen 2019). Rather, he framed his comments as concerned only with the continued vitality and viability of movie theaters. However, a lot more is being said *implicitly*. First, his comments gently imply that living rooms across the globe are not also places in which people sit in the company of others and have a shared experience, crying together, laughing together, being afraid together, and that the Internet's and social media's various discussion forums are not also places that could allow viewers to share their thoughts about films and feel a little less like strangers. Second, one might ask whether movies weren't already benefiting from such living rooms and digital discussion forums significantly; whether experienced on VHS, DVD, or now streaming video platforms, certainly a vast number of audiences have been just as enchanted and beguiled by Spielberg's films as those who watched them in theaters. Third, as critic Mike Fleming, Jr. argues, theatrical exhibition is hardly the context in which Academy members make their evaluative judgments: "most of you [Academy] voters bound to protect the sanctity of the theatrical release are making decisions based on watching screeners on our television sets. Isn't there a bit of hypocrisy here?" (Bart and Fleming 2018).

Above all, though, the threat being posed seems outlandish: how would movies being screened on Netflix becoming eligible to win Oscars lead to the shuttering of movie theaters? The logic that connects this cause and effect involves a steep slope wherein the movie industry's preeminent award is seen to play an important role in validating what is and isn't a movie; should that validation be given to movies intended for home viewing, the Oscars would contribute to the fatal devaluation of the movie theater. On one hand, therefore, an overestimation of the Oscar's powers envelopes these comments. But on the other hand, and looking past that quaint reputational inflation, Spielberg clearly sees home viewing as threatening to movie theaters. In purely financial terms, this argument is specious—home viewing has added billions in revenue to Hollywood's coffers for many decades, creating a thriving "secondary" market for films across broadcast or cable exhibition rights, VHS, DVD, downloads, and streaming that regularly eclipses the supposedly "primary" market of the movie theater and its box office. But Spielberg only alludes to the financial, instead framing the issue as one of experiences, wherein the romanticized vision of a theater full of viewers leaving as brothers and sisters is held up over the presumed alternative, and calls out for the Academy's defense. The statement is more than a little paternalistic, moreover, in posing that the Academy may need to protect audiences and the industry from themselves, withholding Oscars so that producers withhold movies so that audiences are forced still to frequent movie theaters rather than giving in to their urges to stay at home. Spielberg's statement doesn't name television, but television looms large as the plucky threat nipping at film's heels, not financially but culturally and experientially.

Admittedly, Spielberg's comments met a mixed response, but they had many defenders, and were echoed repeatedly in the critical galaxy. Among the defenders was *Variety*'s Owen Glieberman (2019), who opined grandiosely that the "Spielberg vs. Netflix battle" was "A Preview of the War for Cinema's Future." Spielberg, Glieberman insisted, "is trying to isolate and hang onto the DNA of cinema—to preserve an essential definition of what movies are, as distinct from what we watch on television." Media *essence* is invoked, and far from welcoming Netflix as a movie company, Glieberman oozes contempt for the company's own public statement that they "love cinema," instead quickly classifying them as a television company. And he builds up to a rhetorical question that scoffs at the idea that television could ever be good enough to deserve to be classified alongside "true" Oscar fare:

> Is the technology of streaming now going to redefine what movies are? Because if a movie just streams, then what *makes* it a movie? Why not allow hundreds of films that are made for television to qualify for the Oscars?

Palpable in both men's concern about Netflix is that television is invading movies, not as business but as cultural and aesthetic system.

Certainly, Spielberg was just scratching an itch that had bothered many filmmakers, cultural critics, and observers for a while. Earlier debates about Netflix's eligibility for Oscars had surrounded both *Mudbound* (2017) and *Roma* (2018), rehearsed at Cannes too. What's interesting in reading through many think pieces, columns, hot takes, and tweets about Netflix's award eligibility, though, is how rarely anyone asks the seemingly just-as-prescient question of what Netflix's movies means for television awards. *MediaPost*'s Adam Buckman (2019) is one of very few critics to ask why *Roma* isn't eligible for an Emmy, and yet even then he offers the question as a hypothetical, exhibiting no need to offer an answer or opinion. When in 2016 Netflix's *Beasts of No Nation* (2015) won a Peabody Award, an award given for television, radio, and electronic media, the award was reported by all the usual trade press outlets; yet none balked at movies invading television or worried that either the televisual experience or television's essence was in jeopardy. And thus as television and the movies grow closer together, numerous voices express loud concern that television is threatening the movies, but few conversely appear to worry that movies are threatening television.

One could in theory see the story of Netflix as one of the movies threatening television. Between the above-noted trends driving the industries, their personnel, and their audiences together, and with the rise of streaming platforms known as much for their movie selections as for their television selections, a centripetal force drives the two media closer together. And yet culturally, few have characterized this shift as one of the movies going to television, and fewer still have felt the need to insist, defensively, that the movies are not going to television. Rather, we're constantly hearing either that television is going to the movies or impassioned boundary maintenance insisting that it is not. This book thus focuses on this moment: on how the ways in which television goes to the movies reveal the maintenance of boundaries between media as well as the system of values attached to those boundaries.

Going with Television

Given our choice to follow television's role in crossing all of these boundaries, it is useful to reflect on the meanings and politics of "going" across these lines. What exactly does it mean for television to go to the movies? One can go to a place with no intent to return, whether as migrant or intended conqueror. One can go as a visitor, whether on a holiday, for purposes of academic study, to attend negotiations, as a trader, as a guest, or perhaps even as a spy. The distance traveled may be short, as when one pops over to a neighbor's house, or long, as when one voyages across the globe. Going can be purposive, but wind, waves, or currents might also cause unintended drift. Going may be transformative too, a merger or becoming. And some goings are envisioned to be spiraling collapses into failure (going down), while others are promotions or evolutions (going up).

Within these pages, we hope to examine a wide range of goings (and comings) related to television's voyages to the movies. *Television Goes to the Movies* offers a travelogue of those voyages, tracing the journey as television encounters film in different cultural and industrial contexts. More specifically, Chapter 1 considers television exhibited at movie theaters, with television as product going to the movies as a physical place. In this case, television goes to new spaces of consumption beyond the space of the living room or other domestic, private spaces in which it is more commonly envisioned to exist. Chapter 2 considers films about television, with television as subject and the movies as representing medium. Here, television goes into the world of the cinema by becoming the content of its representational practice. Chapter 3 considers a transformation of form and style as television shows are adapted into movies, but also considers television going to the movies as if the movies were a well or resource, conversely adapting movies into television. And Chapter 4 considers television personnel going to work in the movies, examining the case of former television producers developing writer-director credits in film. These creative professionals go across industry lines and in doing so both disrupt and reinforce the spheres of film and television. But along the way we'll consider other passages, too, and we'll consider barriers and obstacles to movement, in the form of discursive attempts to insist upon divergent ontologies. Rather than pontificate on what it means *to us* for television to go to the movies, therefore, our primary interest lies in examining what that motion has meant, represented, and portended in wider 21st-century cultures of media production and consumption. Examining multiple sites at which television and the movies interact, at which television goes to the movies, we study what these tell us about broader societal evaluations of each media individually and of what relationship they are perceived to have to one another.

To put our cards on the table, we come to both media with an awareness of their considerable possibilities to earn positive and negative evaluations alike. If lazy critics have fashioned clickbait out of arguing which medium is best, which is worst, we believe that in absolute terms the task of ranking them is absurd. We take the position that by almost any fair metric one would care to propose, each of television and film has produced some truly excellent work, and some truly abysmal work. Both produce beautiful, important, socially relevant, moving, and brilliantly written texts, just as both produce drivel. To some audiences, movies are Heaven-sent, television infernal, while to others television elevates them and film drags them down. To many more, we suspect, each medium succeeds at some points, fails at others, and that is where we find ourselves. We are each more regularly classified as "television studies" scholars, and hence may seem devious in posing neutrality, but we are neutral because we find the battle tedious. Television and movies are not perpetual combatants in a never-ending, Sisyphean little league baseball championship series. But since they are often posited as such, both by some on the field and by self-fashioned parents yelling from the stands, this book focuses on why, and on the natures of their discursive positioning and the discursive odds placed upon this championship. Indeed, in tracing television's journeys to and through the cinema, we aim not to choose a team, but to problematize our perception of fixed sides.

Identifying (with) Film and Television

Despite these goals, our book cannot move forward without acknowledging all the side taking that defines television's journeys into cinematic realms. If television going to the movies apparently worries or disturbs considerably more commentators than it delights, and if movies going to television don't even register, television would actually seem to have been winning the most recent innings of its mythic competition with film. But from the outset we note that often discursive capitulations and professions of momentary defeat betray a larger belief in overall victory, and thus we will be careful to attend not just to the score of such a competition, but to the commentary that accompanies it. Doing so reveals how the opposition imposed between these media does more than facilitate score keeping and comparative competition; it also supports a form of identification in which texts, spaces, and people accrue meaning, value, and social position. The journey by which television goes to the movies is one that determines who and what has value, in what ways, in relation to whom.

Witness, for instance, the slate of columns and think pieces that insist television is better than film. These include prominently James Wolcott (2012) of *Vanity Fair*'s "Prime Time's Graduation" and Gavin Polone (2012) of *Vulture*'s "The Main Reason TV Is Now Better Than Movies." Both seemingly declare that television is winning, yet their titles already equivocate. If prime time is "graduating," clearly it was envisioned to be still taking instruction, and film's status as fully educated adult is presumed, while Polone delineates that the winning is only recent—"now"—and hence yields that earlier television was by no means winning. Moreover, while both offer compliments to some television, their judgment is clearly swayed by their joint belief not so much that television is winning as film is losing. Consider Wolcott's comment that

> Movies will never die, not as long as a director like Terrence Malick can make every green blade of grass sway like the first dance of creation, but TV is where the action is, the addictions forged, the dream machine operating on all cylinders,

which allows film the status of sublime beauty and art, while television forms addictions, and is likened to a great big factory machine. And if film is losing, to Wolcott, it's because of its own factory machine in the form of franchising:

> for those of us who have fallen out of romance with movies, its franchise blockbusters seem to be leeching off the legacy of pop culture and cinema history, squandering the inheritance with endless superhero sequels and video-game emulations that digitize action stars into avatars and motion-capture figures, a mutant species with an emotive range running strictly in shades of bold.

Film comedy, meanwhile,

> has become a plague, a blight, and an affront to humanity. The gross-out element in film comedy (puke, poop, sperm, breast milk—any bodily fluid with projectile possibilities) has gotten so prevalent and predictable that it's as if filmmakers had their heads diapered.

To Wolcott, the film industry has lost its willingness to take risks, to strive to be or surpass its better self (even if the Malicks are boldly fighting the fight), and thus if television has caught up, it's largely because most film isn't even trying any more.

On this point Polone concurs, answering his implied titular question by stating, "The most significant reason TV is favored has to be the overall malaise that has taken hold of the movie audience, which is illustrated by the oft-heard phrase, 'There is nothing out worth seeing.' " A.O. Scott (2010) of *The New York Times* treads a similar path in an article whose title asks, "Are Films Bad, or Is TV Just Better?" worrying about whether audiences still care about film. Little of Scott's article even mentions television, as it serves more clearly as a hand-wringing warning about film. And echoes of these worries are heard elsewhere, as in Brian Rafferty (2016) of *Wired*'s tellingly titled "Could This Be The Year Movies Stop Mattering?" We thus see a familiar gambit of film critics using the semblance of praise for television to in truth bemoan the state of film. Even if we take that praise at face value as authentic, the critics in question are still clearly bothered that film is losing, since to them it should be winning. Their articles, complete with provocative titles (admittedly perhaps authored by provocative editors), aim to shame film, shock it from its slumber, by the mere suggestion that television is winning.

Even with such a seemingly obvious rhetorical purpose, these articles, though, provoked many a response from other film critics insisting that, no, television was still losing in spite of it all. In "Why Movies Still Matter," for instance, *The New Yorker*'s Richard Brody (2016) responds directly to Rafferty by suggesting that if television is talked about, this is largely due to a combination of critics creating an echo chamber and the medium cynically yet unartistically playing for that alone. "Many series," Brody sneers, "seem to exist only to present topics in ready-to-debate form; they are built to give rise to 'think pieces,' which have become the dominant, if easily parodied, critical mode." Television incessantly and annoyingly demands attention, he suggests, but is artless and, worse yet, inspires bad criticism (unlike his and his film critic colleagues' own cerebral work, it is implied). Or *Slate*'s David Haglund (2013) offers a more pointed, if rather childish, plea, his title imploring "Stop Saying That TV is Better Than Movies These Days," while then pivoting to suggest that "sophisticated viewers" should know better.

Within this genre of provocative insistences on film or television being better, much of the discussion is about film. When the critic mentions television, too often it's to quickly compliment an assortment from within the very restricted list of *The Sopranos* (1999–2007), *The Wire* (2002–2008), *Mad Men* (2007–2015), and *Breaking Bad* (2008–2013), then either to leverage those to shame the current state of film or to note how the medium as a whole is still relatively debased (Newman and Levine 2011). We find ourselves, though, empathizing with Melissa Maerz, who in a staged debate on the topic, "Are TV Shows Better Than Movies Right Now?" for *Entertainment Weekly* with Chris Nashawaty, begins with evident frustration, "Do we really have to argue that television is better than film? Can't we just agree that this is a golden age for both?" (Maerz and Nashawaty 2015). The battle is always staged for specific rhetorical purposes, often to do with the clucking of the critic's tongue at film for allowing television to rival it in any way, but why must we choose a winner for something that shouldn't be a battle?

Paul Young suggests that much pitting of film against other media occurs not so much to declare one medium champion but to police a specific, classicist notion of what film should and must be, serving as "an ongoing institutional defense of classical form, address, and spectatorship" (2006, xxviii). Young examines what he calls film "fantasies" and "phobias" of other media—and hence we'll return to Young in Chapter 2—but refutes that these are based on economic rivalry, or "the sour grapes argument," as he dubs it. Young points to a wealth of work by scholars such as Michele Hilmes (1990), Janet Wasko (1994), Christopher Anderson (1994), and William Uricchio (1998) that shows how close and interdependent the two media have been since television's infancy. Instead, he argues, "If Hollywood films exude suspicion about TV—and they do so constantly—whatever relationship these films have to the industry's self-definition must be more complex than economic fear and loathing" (2006, xviii), and sees such films, and the discourse of film as television's superior, as "rhetorical defenses of classicality against those newer media rivals that offer very different, more deliberately *social* forms of reception to their users" (2006, xxvii). We might add, as Young only implies, that the defense is also against other *films* that eschew classical style and veer toward more deliberately social forms of reception. And applying Young to the many debates of whether film or television is better, we'd note how often television's "water cooler effect" of being talked about proves central to critics' anxieties about and disapprovals of television's cultural ascension (as with Brody above). Even the nominated examples of television's successes—the holy quaternity of *The Sopranos, The Wire, Mad Men,* and *Breaking Bad*—work well for such critics inasmuch as they operate within a more classicist style (where, we ask, is the column that posits *Sesame Street* [1969–] or *General Hospital* [1963–] as television's pinch-hitters in its little league match against film?). Hence these programs can be held up as doing classicist film style better than the superhero films and other blockbuster fare that such critics see as forfeiting the game to television.

While seeing a lot in Young's explanation, we think these discussions point to more than just a defense of classicist film style. Young's discussion of fantasies and phobias delves into the psychological, almost to offer a psychoanalysis of a medium and its struggle for identity. But what of the identities of the actual people? Behind the discourse of film's and television's supposed battle for supremacy, we see a performance of identity, by those making films, those criticizing them, those consuming them. Thus while finding Young's explanation compelling in ways, we propose shifting the focus from style to identity.

On a basic level, the battle for medial supremacy is very Bourdieu-ian. Sociologist Pierre Bourdieu conducted survey work in France in the 1960s asking about people's cultural preferences, favorites, and dislikes, and in *Distinction: A Social Critique of the Judgement of Taste* (1984), he concluded that taste performed class. Bourdieu saw class as burrowing into taste, so that it could avoid being tied to money alone, and saw taste as a realm in which "cultural capital" was instead created, with the bourgeois passing down, and in some cases recalibrating, a system of preferences that would mark the speaker or feeler of such preferences as either a nobler or baser type of person. Bourdieu's system stumbles in being attached to social class alone, not allowing that tastes perform multiple other forms of identity too—think of the disdain for young women singers that performs masculinity, for instance, or of other dislikes that perform race, sexuality, nationality, generation, or more. His system also allows for few other reasons for like or dislike, taste or distaste (see Gray 2021). But a central point that scholars have rescued from *Distinction*—that taste can perform superiority—can obviously be applied here.

This loosely Bourdieu-ian schema allows us to revisit the political economist's fear that corporate consolidation would lead to all parts of a conglomerate working together in synch by instead reasserting the role of humans in that system. First, fear of conglomerate functionality is somewhat naïve to the many logistical challenges faced by any organization of the size of Disney or Comcast, as much as they might want all divisions to be working in synch. Cross-promotion, for instance, may be a dream of any conglomerate, but in practice making it happen can be hard (Copple Smith 2012). Second, though, in any conglomerate, we should expect to see thousands of staffers who work not just at the pleasure of the CEO, but also to fashion their own careers, identities, and senses of self. Especially in industries such as film and television in which many personnel at all levels will likely work for multiple companies across a career, and in which all have front row seats to the very obvious performances and careful, planned construction of star images, we should expect individual performances of identity to be heavily infused in, or outright driving, many decisions and moves. From a purely political economic standpoint, film and television *should* be working together, each other's best friend and closest economic colleague, but the humans in the system often have other ideas, scripts for identity, and notions of what they should and shouldn't be doing. Sometimes these will be classed, per Bourdieu, as the language of what is and isn't "classy" can pervade comparisons of, say, "cerebral" movies and "trashy" reality shows and their presumed audiences. But at other times the performances will simply be of superiority writ large.

At this point, one might wonder, though, why film producers, critics, and fans seem to care so much more about performing a distinction between film and television than do television producers, critics, and fans. Of course, some might respond with their own performance of identity—because "film is better"—so television producers, critics, and fans are well served by being placed alongside film in a cultural pantheon, enjoying an unearned promotion. We pose, instead, that on one hand, television was born on a lower rung on the cultural hierarchy ladder than film, so the medium, its producers, critics, and fans have lived their lives under film's shadow, a position which may irk them but that means they have heard and seen all the performances of superiority already, many times over. On the other hand, film has regularly identified itself with a rhetoric and aura of magic, as evident, for example, in Spielberg's above-quoted romantic notion of strangers coming together in Theater 11. Moreover, as Spielberg's comments (and the reasons behind him offering them in the first place) also show, that aura of magic has been tightly articulated to the space of the movie theater. We don't mean to be cold-hearted observers either, as certainly we both feel that aura at times. But film's proposed identity and ontology therefore rely more centrally on distinction, and on superiority, than does television's or video games', comics', radio's, or mobile media's, for that matter. That identity needs defense, and heightened defense against the barbarian at the gate that is television, unless it is to give way to another identity. And thus we see why even conglomerate CEOs may either endorse or tolerate the performance if they regard their movie division as selling not just movies but the aura of movies, even if that performance comes at the expense of continual derision of television, especially since television has thrived in (spite of) that cultural shadow.

Our book focuses on the performances of identity that swirl around the discursive boundary maintenance between film and television. When television goes to the movies, what cultural work is being done to variously construct or break down the discursive barriers between movies and television, to perform superiority and identity, to keep the two realms forever distinct?

Let's Go

The story we tell is decisively an American one. That is not to say the story isn't exported across the globe, like so many other American products and discourses. But our focus is on American films, filmmakers, and critics, and on American television, television creators, and critics, with only a few exceptions. Performances of identity, after all, are always situated within many other performances, cultural scripts, and specific social settings. Even when American discourses and performances export to other countries, therefore, we avoid assuming they will function in the same way, and instead are cognizant that they will likely interact with other scripts in interesting ways.

In particular, we note that the aura of magic that surrounds theatrical exhibition that is in turn key to the creation of identity for American film, likely requires significant cultural translation in other settings. Certainly, the hand-wringing from the likes of Spielberg, the Academy, or American film critics about the threat that Netflix supposedly poses to that aura assumes a setting in which films regularly have been released theatrically before becoming widely available by other means. But a history of staggered release windows and/or regulatory regimes that otherwise delayed release dates, wherein Hollywood films wouldn't find themselves playing in a cinema in Melbourne, Kunming, Chennai, Cairo, Sao Paolo, or elsewhere until months after they had screened in the United States, was a history that created a thriving network of global piracy. The knowledge that one could get a film on VHS, DVD, or later online for a fraction of the cost, and the knowledge that the film was arriving six, eight, or twelve months "late" at one's local movie theater—even while discussion of the movie had continued and in many cases ebbed in the popular press or online—surely dispelled some of the magic of seeing a movie on "opening" weekend for much of the world. Theater quality, too, ranges from country to country, town to town. In many places, a "theater" was and is a room fitting 20 to 40 with a television hooked up to a VCR or DVD player. Viewing contexts vary in other ways, too, as theaters in some places have served as vibrant meeting places, with no expectation of silent, reverential viewing. And of course local film and television industries grew around the world from various starting points, in ways that might radically or subtly shift the terms of engagement between film and television, and between film, television, and other media. Movies and movie theaters may well hold many other auras of magic around the world, as might television, but we cannot assume they are constant between countries. These other contexts and tales should be held in mind when considering statements about the ontologies of film and television by Americans and American films, since they remind us that those ontologies are never set, always variable. But practically for this book, we therefore eschew a universalist mode, and underline here that our focus is on discourses of boundary maintenance in the United States, offering a consideration of what happens when American television goes to the American movies.

Our awareness that television and the movies are different beings in different countries also strengthens our refusal to see one or two media's "essence" as in any way responsible for this story. While Marshall McLuhan surfed his way to public intellectual status amidst a wave of aphoristic declarations that each medium has a determined character—"the medium is the message," he pronounced (1964)—we follow Raymond Williams' (1974) eschewal of such technological determinism. Technologies certainly offer affordances, but those affordances will change with context—a different regulatory system, a different structuring of the industry, a different audience, a different set of creators, and many other factors can always re-write a medium's destiny in any particular social setting, and might operationalize some affordances while rendering others hard. As a result, absolutely any statement one might care to offer about what television or the movies "are," now and always, will immediately rub up against exceptions, counter-examples, or at least alternate futures, pasts, and existences. If a medium seems to "be" something at a specific point in time, that is not only because it has been fashioned as such by particular industries, policies, audiences, and creators, but also because it is still being fashioned. Discourse, and how we talk about media—what we see as their possibilities, nature, goals, and best and worst instances—is one of the key elements that fashions, hence our focus here upon American discourses of television and the movies in the last 20 years or so across a variety of sites.

We begin our journey by turning to the space of exhibition, exploring a few of the moments in which television content has been repurposed for theatrical exhibition. Chapter 1 reveals how industry strategies construct the boundaries that define media, but at the same time suggests how practices of exhibition that extend from those strategies have often destabilized those distinctions. It explores the theatrical screenings that have served to promote home video releases for television series like *Game of Thrones* and *Star Trek: The Next Generation* (1987–1994), and, in doing so, offers insight into what kinds of programs are deemed valuable enough, to whom, and in what ways, to make the journey into cinematic spaces. As a point of historical comparison, the chapter also explores the theatrical exhibition strategies used to reposition US television in film releases during the late 20th century, revealing how the discourses that define these boundaries are both geographically and historically contingent. With that fluidity in mind, it turns to more recent instances in which the value of theatrical exhibition has been challenged, and, in the face of the COVID-19 pandemic, reworked in significant ways. When the idea of "going to the movies" loses its magic, television movement into that space necessarily takes on new meanings and identities.

From there, we turn next to what happens when television enters the space of film storytelling as the subject of its representations and narratives. If the first chapter zeroes in on where television might be exhibited in relationship to film, Chapter 2 reflects on what the cinema presents television to be. Film texts have generated a complex, ongoing discourse that works to define television, shaping and eliminating its potential identities and values. In other words, film does significant discursive work to shape our perceptions of television. To explore how film does this, the chapter analyzes a large body of films that take television and the worlds of its production and consumption as their subjects. The result of this process is regularly a highly critical perspective on television that is suspicious of its materiality and its supposed artlessness in favor of commercial interests. While this is perhaps not surprising given all the competitive dynamics already explored here, the chapter reveals a significant imbalance in the way that television seems comparatively disinterested in building a critique of the cinema (even as many television programs look inward to question the values undergirding their own medium). In highlighting that imbalance, we can see how the journeys of crossing boundaries between media are not neutral or equal in comparison to one another. Instead, they reflect the power and positionality of the fields being crossed.

Continuing this focus on the content of the film and television industries, Chapter 3 turns to the question of adaptation and the way that television becomes not just the subject matter of film, but also a resource to be manipulated and transformed via cinematic forms. These adaptations grapple with questions about what essential qualities define each medium, and in doing so reinforce the very boundaries that they cross. Once again looking for patterns across a wide body of movies and television shows, this chapter explains how the adaptation of television series into film projects, and vice versa, reconfigures the importance placed on stardom and celebrity in media marketing. Similarly, it provides significant data to show how filmmakers adapting television series assume that the process of adaptation must turn on action, spectacle, and an amplification of adult appeals in order to transform the televisual into something more cinematic. Meanwhile, adaptations of film to television back away from such qualities, seeing in television a medium better suited to more personal stories situated in the private realm, and adaptations of comics into film and television similarly betray a sense of film and television each being able to cope best with certain types of stories told in certain ways. Whether it is film adapting television, television adapting film, or either medium adapting comics, the adaptive process says much about the assumptions that media makers have about film, television, and their supposedly essential qualities.

Chapter 4 moves away from exhibition strategies and the construction of media texts to consider journeys between the work worlds of film and television. Although media convergence has led to significant overlap between personnel working in each industry, movement between these industries is not entirely fluid. Given how unequal the values and identities surrounding these media are, the ability to move between them professionally often depends on the status and privilege necessary to allow it. At the core of this chapter is an investigation of the Marvel Cinematic Universe and the way in which its production has often relied upon directors who trained in the realm of television production. An analysis of the industry conversations surrounding these hiring practices demonstrates that television has fostered a culture of creativity that positions some kinds of creators—typically white men—for a perceived permanent promotion to the supposed big leagues of film. At the same time, however, the chapter reveals how the improved valuation of television in these industry narratives opens the door for professional identifications with television that resist the idea of a permanent transformation. Instead, many television creators, including women and people of color, work across film and television in fluid ways without this investment in a permanent transition to film work. In the process, the hierarchies of value in which film and television are embedded could be challenged rather than reaffirmed. At that final leg in television's journey of going to the movies, we can see how the distinctions at the heart of this relationship articulate to the identities of specific communities.

Having offered these case studies in border crossings and border maintenance, we then offer a brief Coda asking whether it is high time to let go of these entrenched distinctions between film and television.

It's common to bring a lot of stuff with us when we go to the movies. We might bring our friends and loved ones. We might bring some money to buy an $18 Manhattan and some snacks, or sneak in our own from home. We bring the concerns and feelings that occupy us throughout the day. And we bring certain anticipations and expectations for the experience based on what we saw in trailers and in other promotional material. No matter what, we bring some kind of cultural, social, and industrial baggage with us. And when we leave, we bring things home with us too—memories of the parts we liked, conversations with our filmgoing companions, or even just the ticket stub that serves as a memento of the experience or a receipt of the transaction.

It is not that dissimilar when television goes to the movies. The journey is wrapped up in the cultural, social, and industrial hierarchies in which television circulates, and we cannot explain the relationship between these media without reflecting on the baggage that is brought into and out of the encounter. These moments are shaped by assumptions going in about what television is, who television viewers are, why television does (or does not) have value, and more. Coming out, both television and film can be transformed. Their interaction might reshape what we perceive to be the essential formal qualities of a medium, the proper spaces and technologies in which it should be experienced, and the identities of who might produce and consume it. The encounter between film and television is one in which we see the calcification of assumptions about media cultures; but it is also where we might see them reimagined and transformed.

1

TELEVISION PROGRAMS GO TO THE MOVIES

Crossing Boundaries in Exhibition Spaces

One of the most fundamental distinctions levied between television and cinema centers around the place in which we experience each medium. To many, our sense of what these media are depends significantly upon the technological means of content delivery and the site to which that content is being delivered. The cinema, in particular, has often been defined with a rather singular focus on the site of theatrical exhibition with its projected images and sounds. Even as mechanical projection of film canisters that physically travel the globe has given way to digital projection of films sent from distributors' servers, the theater persists as the cinematic *sin qua non*. Of course, the content we recognize as film circulates beyond those spaces, too, moving through a number of release windows across television, home video, and online streaming. And yet theatrical exhibition enjoys a pride of place in this sequence, as the primary and initializing moment of that distribution chain. No example makes this clearer than the Oscars, the awards granted by the Academy of Motion Picture Arts and Sciences in recognition of outstanding achievement in the medium. To win this ultimate validation of cinematic achievement, one's work must be intended for theatrical exhibition. By contrast to this insistence on public exhibition, television has been significantly understood by reference to the domestic and individualized settings of its private consumption. Television devices have certainly changed—from set-top boxes that receive signals from antenna or cable to laptops and phones that stream content from the internet—but even when taken out of the space of the family room, the "mobile privatization" of television (Williams 2003/1974) creates a sense of viewing while being at home in a comfortable space to which viewers are individually attached (Maly-Bowie 2019). Where we watch seems to matter a great deal to a great many, and our sense of what we watch is often shaped by that sense of where we are.

However, rather than reinforce this perception of fundamental differences, this chapter seeks to interrogate it, denaturalizing the discourses that suggest that cinema and television have essential characters defined by their context of exhibition. To do so, it explores some of the instances in which television has been exhibited as cinema as well as, by contrast, cases in which cinema has been brought into the realm of the television. Through that effort, it will become clear that neither television nor film can be understood in isolation from one another by a distinction based in location: instead, these media frequently overlap in their exhibition and consumption. Just as movies can come home on television, home video, or Netflix, television can literally go to the movies as programs are slated for theatrical exhibition as part of industry experiments in making these media work together. On the one hand, then, the presence of television in the spaces of theatrical exhibition reveals that place-centric definitions of media essence are tenuously constructed and problematic in that construction. On the other hand, the persistence of these definitions as part of the production of value and prestige in each medium demonstrates the continued power of these ideas as well as the need for them to be confronted and better understood in media theory. So when television programs go to the movies, we have an opportunity to reflect on the way in which media industries and media cultures push against the very boundaries often deployed to define and limit them.

In an age of media convergence (Jenkins 2006) in which the boundaries between media are regularly rendered blurry, there are no shortages of examples in which "film" content is distributed and viewed via television, and in which "television" content manifests in cinematic forms. The history of film distribution in the second half of the 20th century and beyond has turned centrally on its relationship to television industries, as studios and networks weighed their competing and collaborative interests (Hilmes 1990), content came to be valued for its cross-promotional functions (Anderson 1994; Wasko 2001), distribution strategies increasingly accounted for ancillary markets (Balio 1990), and film libraries could be resold across media lines (Hoyt 2015; Kompare 2005). Somewhat less prominent, however, has been attention to the ways in which the history of television has been shaped by its ability to serve as cinema. Perhaps most notably, Michael Newman and Elana Levine (2011) interrogate the way in which the increasing legitimation of television in the 21st century has depended in significant part on its identification as a "cinematic" medium that eschews the look, feel, and taste cultures of so much broadcast history. Newman and Levine reveal television as a medium constructed in significant part by reference to its overlap with the cinema—the partial nature of which prompts important political questions about what cultures, which viewers, and whose tastes are and are not perceived to have value in the hierarchies into which media like film and television can be placed. Building on this interrogation of the politics of television's convergence with film, this chapter moves beyond the question of how television is described as cinematic to explore how television is exhibited as cinema. In doing so, it reveals productive linkages between film historians' interest in the contexts of distribution and exhibition with the perspectives of television scholars focused on the meanings, values, and assumptions that undergird the convergence of media.

To these ends, the chapter first unpacks recent industry strategies in which television programming has been reallocated and transformed for exhibition in theatrical venues. By developing a deeper understanding of the industrial strategies behind the theatrical exhibition of cult hits like *Star Trek: The Next Generation* (1987–1994) or *Game of Thrones* (2010–2019), we can understand what television is deemed worthy and viable of going to the movies, and by extension, what television remains decidedly more difficult to bring to the cinema. This analysis can reveal how and why television industries look to the cinema as an exhibition partner, as well as why cinema operators would look to television to diversify their offerings to patrons.

Second, this chapter will consider the ways in which television's capacity to go to the movies is imagined within the frameworks of national film cultures, and how investment in the difference between cinema and television in one local context need not extend to another. Some television series that have not appeared on the cinema screen in the US context, for example, have transformed into cinematic fare far more freely when traded on the international marketplace. By looking at the ways in which US television programs find abroad the theatrical exhibition that is denied them in their domestic market, the chapter reveals that the lines between cinema and television are not essential characteristics of the medium, but instead culturally specific constructions. In fact, when failed US television program *Battlestar Galactica* (1978–1980) found exhibition as cinema throughout the globe, these industry practices proved quite revealing: first, they showed that definitions of the cinema based in theatrical exhibition may not be universal throughout the globe; second, they demonstrated that hierarchies of value between media are not essential and vary with values, tastes, and assumptions articulated to different populations.

Finally, while the history of film exhibited on television is far too complex to attend to in any real depth, this chapter will look to an extreme example of film's reliance on television exhibition as a limit case. In the wake of the 2020 COVID-19 pandemic, industrial models that treat the public space of theatrical exhibition as a cornerstone were shaken to the core. While the move to theatrical exhibition used to be a calculus of the value accrued to television programming, during the pandemic content produced for the cinema migrated to Netflix, video-on-demand, and other digital television platforms to mitigate the lost value of theatrical release. Strategies that turned on theatrical release were rethought, or at the very least suspended indefinitely, and in that context television emerged as a platform in which the potential failure of film projects might be recalculated. Moreover, when going to the movies lost its appeal, the crisis the pandemic created for the film industry invites us to reconsider television's potential to be exhibited theatrically, too. In short, this disruption of the distributional hierarchies and cultures of exhibition in film and television reveals the contingent and fragile nature of any essential boundaries between media—even as media institutions quickly seek to repair those walls. Ultimately, what all these case studies reveal is the way in which media industries construct the boundaries in which they operate through the very strategies and practices with which they operate. Yet that process also undoes these boundaries, both through concerted efforts to welcome television into the spaces of film exhibition, and in crises of disruption that present television as a potential alternative to film exhibition.

Theatrical Event Television

In the contemporary television industries, it is rare but not at all unheard of for television programming to be exhibited in the theatrical spaces of cinematic exhibition. Many exhibitors, for example, have made their theater screens available for viewing live television sporting events. Film festivals, too, have served as sites of exhibition for television programming. Many television mini-series and specials from around the world often end up showing at international exhibitions, as has, for instance, Lars Von Trier's mini-series *Kingdom* (1994–1997). The theatrical exhibition of television programming inevitably raises a question of timing: only in rare cases like sports and other live programming do theatrical screenings unfold simultaneously with television presentation. On some occasions, theatrical exhibition has preceded the debut of programming in broadcast, cable, or online channels of distribution as part of promotional events meant to create publicity and prestige for forthcoming television series. At other times, these exhibition practices have sought to create new opportunities for unique viewing experiences that only come after release in these more traditional television venues. The HBO series *Game of Thrones* offers instructive examples of both cases, having been exhibited theatrically at times both before and after its television debut.

On the one hand, HBO used a very limited form of theatrical exhibition to build up hype for the premiere of new seasons, including the eighth and final season in 2019. These "red carpet" events served as celebrations for professionals working in the television industry, rather than public screenings for general audiences. Held at Radio City Music Hall in New York City, the April 3 premiere event served as a gala under which to gather the cast of the series and parade them before onlookers in the entertainment, celebrity, and fashion presses. Publications like *Bazaar* and *Elle* could then feature photo albums of images from the event, providing a glimpse into how stars like Emilia Clarke, Sophie Turner, and Maisie Williams were attired (Bowenbank 2019; Dibdin 2019). Such stories focused exclusively on the on-screen talent behind the series, featuring 30-some images each of cast members from across all eight seasons who had been invited to the event. From this perspective, this one-night showing of the Season Eight premiere existed as an excuse to hold step-and-repeat photo shoots on the red carpet in order to maximize the visibility of the series in the world of celebrity fashion.

A parallel report in *Insider*, however, suggests that the function of this theatrical premiere went beyond capturing the fashion choices of on-screen stars: the red carpet was only the first stage in this carefully curated event. *Insider*'s Kim Renfro (2019) documents an hours-long event that continued into the screening room in which HBO programming president Casey Bloys, showrunners David Benioff and DB Weiss, and author George RR Martin addressed their colleagues and collaborators, "paying tribute to the hard work and faith of the entire HBO and 'Game of Thrones' family." Renfro further relays that following the speech, the curtain on stage parted to reveal the fully assembled cast of former and present actors that had attended the event that night—implicitly revealing that despite the fashion press' focus on on-screen talent, the audience for this screening consisted of a much wider population of industry professionals and their guests. *Insider*'s photo captions estimate an audience of 6,000 in attendance, and while Renfro refuses to offer spoilers, she nevertheless reports on the screening as one that elicited both cheers and moments that were "deadly silent, focused on the unfolding spectacle." In this account, the experience of having seen the episode, even for an audience largely of television professionals, was no mere formality, but a visceral, powerful, and potentially unruly form of engagement with television content. Having debuted the Season Eight premiere in this theatrical setting almost two weeks ahead of its forthcoming premiere on April 14, HBO now sought to manage the power of the audience to share their response. HBO distributed to this audience buttons with a photo of *Game of Thrones* spymaster Lord Varys that read "keep the secrets," while Sophie Turner and Maisie Williams announced that if spoilers did spill from this event, master assassin Arya Stark would step from the screen to "f------ kill" the assembled crowd (Renfro 2019). Of course, the event did not end here, and the audience (or at least some part of it) gathered at the Ziegfeld Ballroom for an after-party featuring a replica Iron Throne, "Cold Fashioned" cocktails, and more opportunities for celebrity watching.

Taken as a whole, then, such theatrical premieres for television content represent a form of entertainment industry event that both creates publicity valued by the hype machine of promotional departments and enables a form of community building and celebration within the television business itself. Theatrical exhibition serves in these multiple ways to create new value for television programs. In some ways, these opportunities are entirely unremarkable if we compare the hoopla around *Game of Thrones*' eighth season to the red-carpet events held regularly for every major Hollywood film release. Part of the mythology of the US film industry centers on the glamour of movie premieres held at venues like Grauman's Chinese Theater on the Hollywood Walk of Fame. From the theatrical screening itself to the after parties, these television-focused events are hardly any different from their cinema counterparts—with the exception, of course, that no theatrical run is scheduled to follow such a premiere, and the wider public release of the content will be via broadcast, cable, or streaming services. Thus, not only exceptional programs like *Game of Thrones* have enjoyed theatrical premieres; in 2019–2020 alone, similar events surrounded the world premiere screenings for the first season of *Star Trek: Picard* (2020–), the third season of *Westworld* (2016–), the second season of *Big Little Lies* (2017–), the second season of *Killing Eve* (2018–), the first season of *The Mandalorian* (2019–), the limited HBO series *Watchmen* (2019), and many more.

This is not to suggest, however, that all television content has access to this kind of value creation via theatrical performance. It is no coincidence that HBO series like *Game of Thrones*, *Big Little Lies*, *Watchmen*, and more all debut through this promotional and celebratory detour to the film theater. HBO has long traded in the value of television that is perceived to be more "cinematic" than its competitors in the broadcast and cable arenas (McCabe and Akass 2008; Newman and Levine 2011; Santo 2008). Streaming services like Netflix challenged HBO by laying their own claims to the quality distinctions of the cinema (Tryon 2015), and that pattern has continued as services like Amazon Prime Video, Hulu, and more join the fray. These claims to quality all rely on distinguishing select services and programs from the larger pool offered by the television industries. Thus, while association with film brings added value to television, this articulation works only if it is a limited set of television programs that enjoy that cinematic status. It is not surprising, then, that it is the high production value, scripted television projects produced for premium services, where budgets rival those in the film industry and claims to cinematic quality pervade, that more often make their world debuts in theatrical settings replete with red-carpet treatment and celebrity news coverage. In fact, that attention helps to render television actors more clearly as "stars," which—as discussed in the next chapter—can announce and establish cinematic status contra television. By contrast, few, if any, reality series screen content theatrically; even juggernauts like *The Bachelor* (2002–) franchise that center on premiere events do so in ways that embrace the liveness of television in contrast to the idea of a film screening. While celebrities gather in a theater to screen the final, "in the can" cut of *Game of Thrones*, *The Bachelor* gathers audiences in a studio setting to participate in season-ending live reveals. Even *Survivor* (2000–), which stages its finales in large theatrical spaces, stops short of presenting the reality TV experience as a cinematic one. Instead of emphasizing its potential as an exhibition space for filmed footage, the theatrical space is used to assemble the cast, their family members, and a cheering crowd to watch the live drama that unfolds on a set onstage. The reality TV auditorium is more a stage for theater than watching filmed entertainment. So while the theatrical debut is increasingly a significant promotional event and professional ritual in the television industries, it has been unevenly applied within the medium, focused on spaces in which overtures to cinematic style, stardom, and prestige are already in play.

Beyond these invite-only, staged red-carpet events, the television industries have also looked to theatrical exhibition as a way of directly engaging audiences in new forms of public participation and new kinds of media transactions. Here, too, *Game of Thrones* provides a useful example. In 2015, select movie theaters throughout the United States, including some operating under the AMC chain, offered cinemagoers a "Game of Thrones IMAX Experience"—a very limited engagement screening that made two fourth season episodes available for theatrical exhibition. Selected were the last two episodes of the season, starting with episode nine, "The Watchers on the Wall," a spectacle-driven episode that depicts one uninterrupted battle as Jon Snow and the Night's Watch protect Castle Black from invading Wildlings. Following this was "The Children," a season finale that changes focus to characters like Bran, Tyrion, and Daenerys in other locations in the fictional world. These episodes had already aired on HBO seven months prior in June 2014; yet for one night only on January 30, IMAX patrons could see them on the big screen. The selection of these episodes is not surprising; the series had developed a reputation for memorable and spectacular penultimate episodes each season, and "Watchers on The Wall" represented a significant investment in resources to deliver a visceral combat experience. As described on the website, the episode boasted "one of the fiercest and most intense battle scenes ever filmed for television" (AMC 2015). Implicit in this summary is an argument that the worthiness of the episode for the big screen treatment lies in a scope and a production value that exceeds televisual norms. AMC treated "The Children" more descriptively, but here too the selection of this episode had strategic value beyond continuity with its predecessor. With the premiere of the fifth season only three months away, this most recent episode served to prime viewers to soon return to the narrative threads left unanswered.

However, as a one-night event accessible only to theater-goers who had access to IMAX screening venues, the Game of Thrones IMAX Experience may seem limited as an attempt to generate significant visibility or revenue for the series. The special event itself would most likely have been designed to serve the superfan willing to seek out special viewing opportunities and pay the premium ticket prices to see content they had likely already paid for via their HBO subscription. After all, a theatrical screening of the 39th and 40th episodes of a highly serialized television series hardly bears potential for building new interest; if attracting new fans was the aim, HBO would have been better off releasing the first two episodes in this IMAX format. Instead, the primary intent here seems to have been to offer a novelty to existing fans, and to do so by seizing on the single episode most likely to prove compatible with the norms and expectations of cinematic presentation—the biggest, loudest, most epic spectacle that the series had yet produced, where the norms of television storytelling based on ensemble casts are even suspended in one of the selected episodes in favor of a more singular focus on one setting and one protagonist. However, in supporting this claim to cinematic status, the event also had some power to build value and interest in the series beyond this one-time screening. Any other filmgoers present that evening who saw posters and witnessed other cinemagoers gathering to watch *Game of Thrones* could have had their interest piqued. Meanwhile, the promotion for the event, and fan discussion of it, could live on online and in social media posts, amplifying the notion that HBO programming like *Game of Thrones* warranted this cinematic treatment.

This was not the last experiment with theatrical exhibition of *Game of Thrones*. After organizing special theatrical screenings of the Season Six premiere, HBO developed for the seventh season a strategy that made somewhat clearer the value that theatrical release did and did not have for its television business. Because of the intensive labor that went into the production of the eighth and final season, fans suffered a 20-month wait for new episodes after the conclusion of Season Seven. It was during this time in December 2017 between the release of seasons that HBO organized a limited number of event screenings of "The Spoils of War"—billed as the "most action-packed episode of Season 7 getting the big screen treatment," echoing the criteria by which previous episodes made their way into cinematic spaces. Although reports suggested that these special events were meant "to distract us from our clock-watching," the scope of the "us" invoked in that claim proved to be quite select indeed. HBO organized eight screenings in only three cities: New York, Los Angeles, and Chicago. If all of these screenings had been held in venues that rivaled the largest in the world (Spain's Kinepolis-Madrid Cuidad de la Imagen has a screening room that seats nearly 1,000), these eight screenings would provide access to a maximum of only 8,000 fans nationwide. Even assuming ticket prices double the $9 national average at this time (Kilday 2018), this is a maximum box office potential of $144,000. Real revenues would likely be much smaller than these generous estimates. Therefore, it again appears extremely doubtful that HBO's priorities centered on box office revenue alone.

Instead, what was offered to fans was not just an enlargement of the content they were able to see at home, but also an experiential form of engagement with the series that could only take place in shared, physical spaces. Replicas of the Iron Throne as well as the throne and map table of Dragonstone were to be put on display in each of these three venues to provide fans with an opportunity to enter not just a theatrical exhibition space, but also the space of the fantasy world itself. While the episode screening itself would last less than two hours, organizers promised that the event space would be opened a full three hours beforehand, "so that fans have time to work their way through the various photo opps onsite" (Prudom 2017). For exhibitors, this would increase the chance that loitering patrons might avail themselves of concessions, too.

Notably, this sense of the theatrical screening being only one part of a longer social experience echoes the industry rituals of the red-carpet events. While red-carpet celebrities may not have been present, the theatrical screening creates a pretense for gathering a community and building shared interest around a television series; in both cases, the same symbols and iconography—like the Iron Throne replica—work to mobilize these shared feelings of interest. This may not translate to direct revenue, but it can have value in promoting and generating visibility for the series (especially in a time of extended hiatus between seasons). Although the pool of fans who might have access to these screenings was extremely limited, coverage of them on Mashable and in other venues could indeed provide a vicarious distraction from clock-watching for a much larger group of viewers.

Lest it sound like HBO ignored financial concerns in favor of its viewers' affective desires, it should be added that this strategy carried a second dimension related to the home video release of Season Seven. These screenings were "only available to fans who bring their Season 7 DVD or Blu-Ray or proof of purchase with them" (Prudom 2017). In this way, theatrical exhibition offered a potential perk for those already investing a significant amount of money in the domestic consumption of *Game of Thrones*. With a manufacturer's list price of $59.99, the DVD adds a significant amount of per-consumer expenditure to the value proposition here: $144,000 in theatrical revenue turns into $624,000. That still may not seem like a consequential sum—especially when these revenues must be shared with theater partners selling tickets and retail partners selling discs. Yet the existence of these screenings and their visibility in the entertainment press now provides greater visibility as well for the home video product sold between seasons—even for those who can or would not attend the screenings, but might be reminded to pick up a Blu-ray.

Indeed, this connection to the home video market seems to have driven other televisual experimentations with limited theatrical exhibition. On April 25, 2013, for example, CBS Home Entertainment, in partnership with NCM Fathom Events, organized a special one-night screening of the two-part *Star Trek: The Next Generation* episode, "The Best of Both Worlds." These episodes had originally aired in 1990 as the third season finale and fourth season premiere of the series, but were slated to be released in new digitally remastered, high-definition home video formats. The third season Blu-ray was due to retailers five days after this theatrical screening on April 30, while the fourth season would follow on July 30 to resolve the famous season-ending cliffhanger in which Captain Picard is kidnapped and assimilated into the Borg collective, and a steely Commander Riker orders the *Enterprise* to fire a weapon expected to kill Picard along with the Borg. However, for fans eager to have both episodes in their collection, CBS Home Entertainment released simultaneously with the third season a single-disc Blu-ray (and Ultra-Violet) presentation featuring the complete two-part story. On the one hand, this was a cynical bit of repurposing in which CBS surely expected that many eager fans would buy the single-disc version in April to be able to see Part 2, and then purchase the fourth season Blu-ray two months later to get the episodes that followed (effectively buying the season premiere twice). On the other hand, the single-disc presentation of "Best of Both Worlds" offered something unique compared to the complete season packages. In addition to exclusive special features, the "Best of Both Worlds" disc presented the two-part episode as a single, uninterrupted presentation, excising the cliffhanger ending so that Riker's order to fire the weapon is immediately followed by its surprising failure. This unified presentation allows the viewer excited to follow the action to move seamlessly into the next story without having to change discs and sit through or skip over the "previously on *Star Trek: The Next Generation…*" segment that begins "The Best of Both Worlds, Part 2" in its complete fourth season Blu-ray presentation.

However, as Caetlin Benson-Allot (2021) argues, the re-editing of television content for presentation on home video can result in transformation and even a loss of televisuality. By doing so, CBS Home Entertainment could market this television program by promising a fundamental change in the nature of the fan favorite episode: this new version "transforms the beloved two-part TNG saga … into a reedited, 90-minute feature-length presentation" (*Star Trek* 2013). When Riker's line "Mr. Worf … fire!" is no longer followed by an ominous cut to black, a crescendoeing score, and the words "to be continued…" appearing on screen, the experience of watching this story is fundamentally changed. Whether experienced over the course of the summer of 1990, a change of Blu-ray discs in 2013, or the brief moment in which the "play next episode" interface appears on Netflix more recently—this cliffhanger break carries a particularly televisual quality in which one episode ending can sit heavy and viewers can breathe while anticipating the next installment. By contrast, this unified Blu-ray presentation imposes a different kind of narrative effect over these episodes, turning these moments of rupture and uncertainty into something more continuous. The transformation that CBS marketers promise is explicitly one of television becoming cinema, where the partitioned, episodic stories of the former are morphed into the unified feature format of the latter.

While this Blu-ray presentation reformats the television story to represent it as feature cinema, the subsequent theatrical exhibition of it equally transformed the experience of consuming that content. Like the *Game of Thrones* screenings that would follow later in the decade, this one-night, US-only screening on April 2013 was an extremely limited event, to be held "in select theaters around the country" (*Star Trek* 2013). In a blog post published on the official *Star Trek* website, fan Jordan Hoffman (2013) offers an account of the event that details the way in which the theatrical experience could alter the consumption of this familiar television content for many viewers. First and foremost, Hoffman presents the experience as an expanded one, in terms of both "seeing it big" on a larger screen and a greater scope of social experience where the episodes could be shared "with 200 of your new best friends." This latter quality defined the bulk of Hoffman's observation about the event, in that she reflects on the moments that everyone laughed at, spectators shouting at the screen, and rounds of applause when actors like Whoopi Goldberg appeared on screen. Nevertheless, Hoffman's commentary also makes significant claims about the cinematic nature of the big screen showing. She reflects on the way in which the eye rolls and sighs that communicate the conflict between Commander Riker and Borg expert Commander Shelby "play even bigger than they do on TV." The transformation of the two-part episode into a unified presentation also supports claims about its new cinematic quality: "This special 'feature-length' presentation of 'The Best of Both Worlds' plays through like a movie. As such, the gap we experienced in summer 1990 doesn't exist." Jordan is not necessarily celebratory of this change: she waxes nostalgic for the "freak-out moment" and swelling orchestral stings of the television cliffhanger now missing in the film presentation. But her acknowledgment of the episodes' claim to the cinema implies a necessary loss of the temporalities of television. "Eh, you can't have everything," she concludes. Her account ultimately reveals the theatrical exhibition of television as something felt to be transformative.

Returning our focus to *Game of Thrones*' experimentations with theatrical exhibition, then, we can consider such transformations not only as they impact the text and the experience of it, but also in terms of evolving industry strategies for distributing that content. Both HBO and CBS Home Entertainment have used limited theatrical runs as a means of supporting home video distribution businesses, where the aim of putting content in theaters is less to adopt the business strategies of the film industry and more to promote another television profit center. In that way, television's move into cinematic spaces of exhibition and retail has often aimed to reinforce television's status as a domestic medium and position home video (however successfully or unsuccessfully in an age of streaming subscriptions) for stronger revenues. Television enters public consumer space only on the way to moving through another distribution window in the private consumer sphere. At the same time that theatrical exhibition has been used to support a home video television industry, any experimentation along these lines has also had to be mindful of protecting other established windows of television distribution. Media industries cannot allow the transformation of television into cinema to cannibalize their existing markets. For example, HBO considered early on releasing the final season of *Game of Thrones* not via subscription cable and streaming service, but as a trilogy of three theatrically released films instead of six individual episodes (Hibberd 2018). The rationale for such a seismic shift held that only a wide blockbuster showing via theatrical exhibition could justify the outsized cinematic budget and ambition of that season. However, in 2017, HBO backed away from this possibility, realizing that such a release would put the cinematic experience of *Game of Thrones* in competition with the television experience that anchored its subscription model. "This is for subscribers," programming president Casey Bloys explained (Gennis 2017), making clear that whatever experiments might transform *Game of Thrones* into cinema, it could not be allowed to transform into something other than television. Bloys thus ruled out a model in which *Game of Thrones* could be film and television simultaneously—but he did allow for the possibility of the series transforming into theatrical product "after the series wraps up" (Gennis 2017). The transformation of television into theatrical content thus has to be carefully controlled, coordinated, and scheduled to maximize its profit potential in each perceived state of being. A more freeform state of media flux would disrupt the perceived boundaries and markets baked into media industry logics. Together, these cases show that while theatrical exhibition can alter the textuality, experience, and values surrounding television, this transformative potential is perhaps most disruptive to industrial structures that insist upon their differences.

A Particularly American Distinction?

If the theatrical exhibition of television points to the boundaries that media industries draw between themselves, it may be productive to consider how these circulation strategies play out on a global scale where the questions of borders and territories enable and constrain the shapes that media cultures can take (E. Elkins 2019). Television scholars have frequently discussed the ways in which television travels across international markets (Bielby and Harrington 2008; Havens 2006, 2013; Straubhaar 2007). Less explored, however, has been the way in which television has at times transformed into cinema in that process, and the role of theatrical exhibition in making it happen. By looking back to the broadcast era and considering the case of the original *Battlestar Galactica* television series, we can see how the circulation of "failed" television content as cinematic fare in international markets reveals contingent and culturally specific perceptions of these two media in the US context. Caetlin Benson-Allot (2021) has already made use of this television series as a way of revealing how "the commodity form—the commercial framing—of different video formats change consumers' perception of television's historical value." In her analysis, the multiple home video releases of *Battlestar Galactica* over several decades altered the interpretative and evaluative frameworks that could be brought to the series in its initial airing. International theatrical film release is an important part of Benson-Allot's account in that it generated new edits of *Battlestar Galactica* that could circulate in home video and (much as we saw with "The Best of Both Worlds," above) alter its televisual character. Yet while Benson-Allot is primarily concerned with the circulation of these home video commodities, the analysis here centers international theatrical exhibition to assess the way in which it, too, generates a significant commodity form and global reframing for television programming.

In the United States, *Battlestar Galactica* originally aired in the 1978–1979 television season as part of the ABC network's primetime line-up. Designed to tap into the hype surrounding *Star Wars* (1977) (and even employing some of that film's designers to do so), the series was at that time one of the most expensive television series ever made, incurring significant costs in its efforts to bring those big budget blockbuster movie appeals to television production. Each episode reportedly cost $1 million to produce, over double the average of $450,000 for scripted series in the United States at that time (Jay 2018; Shales 1978, B1). The series premiered on Sunday, September 17, 1978, with a special three-hour event episode called "Saga of a Star World"—which was extended to four following interruption that evening for breaking news coverage of the Camp David Peace Accords. Even with this interruption, the launch drew strong Nielsen ratings and proved to be the fifth-highest-performing program of the week (Jay 2018). Subsequent episodes would adopt a standard hour-long format, and by early October, *Battlestar Galactica* outperformed the competition from the other two US broadcast networks to win its Sunday time slot, as one of four new series on the ABC schedule that rated among the top-20 programs in the Nielsen ratings (Deeb 1978, A7). However, as television historian Robert Jay (2018) explains, this story of success would be short-lived, as the series soon faced stronger competition: CBS decided to move the hit sitcom *All in the Family* (1971–1979) to Sunday nights. Although *Battlestar Galactica* still showed "some ratings strength" against this new competition, the impaired ratings performance and the overall expense of the series raised questions at the network level about its sustainability (Jay 2018). ABC was not having a bad season, as many of its other new series were performing well, so the network questioned continued investment in this big budget sci-fi spectacle—particularly when its demanding production had led to delays. Ultimately, *Battlestar Galactica* was canceled at the end of the season. The next year, ABC would place an order for a revamped series that brought the space opera to more familiar settings on Earth (and thus potentially reduce costs). However, the new *Galactica 1980* (1980) would similarly be canceled by the end of the next season.

As an attempt to bring the cinematic spectacle of *Star Wars* to television, *Battlestar Galactica* proved to be a significant failure. However, at the level of exhibition, this failed television series would remain in circulation in theatrical settings, particularly outside of the United States. The special three-hour premiere of the series was cut into three parts for reruns in US syndication, removing the feature-length presentation of its original broadcast to transform it into something that could fit the temporal rhythms of everyday television scheduling (in some ways the opposite of the efforts to turn *Star Trek*'s "Best of Both Worlds" into a cinematic presentation 35 years later). Yet the feature-length "Saga of a Star World" persisted in other contexts—including, appropriately enough, in theatrical settings. So much money had been spent to produce what *Variety* called "a poor man's version of *Star Wars*" (Knight 1978) that Universal, the studio that produced the series, had sought to recoup some of those costs by releasing the feature-length debut episode theatrically (Jay 2018). Notably, this was not an afterthought or an attempt to repurpose the series following its failure in US network broadcasting, but part of an initial release strategy. Although the television series premiered in the United States in September 1978, a theatrical version had previously been released in April 1978 for the United Kingdom and in July 1978 for Canada, Australia, and other territories in Europe. This international theatrical release was not identical to the version that would air a few months later on US television: in addition to commercial interruptions, the US television version presented a somewhat different narrative outcome. While the villain Baltar was beheaded in the international release, he survived the US television version of "Saga of a Star World" in order to continue menacing the protagonists in series production. Nevertheless, it would be in the international cinema that the *Battlestar Galactica* narrative would first be seen, and with those immediate box office revenues, Universal began to make back its investment in the series before it ever aired on television (much less before the syndication revenues that would follow years later).

This international release raises important considerations about the mutability of film and television at the level of exhibition. When traveling across international boundaries, content that could function as cinema in one country or region could serve equally as television in another. Translation across cultures could also involve fundamental transformations in media form—or, perhaps, problematize the distinctions between those media forms. Although it circulated before media industries framed entertainment in the explicit terms of franchised intellectual properties, *Battlestar Galactica* seemed to function as content equally viable as film or as television in a global marketplace. Yet this content did not function equally in all places; *Battlestar Galactica* was held back from initial theatrical distribution in the United States, designed (and reedited) to fulfill a different, televisual function than in cinematic function in international markets. What could be cinema and what could be television had been strategized and territorialized across these global boundaries. Although the practices and technologies of geo-blocking have more recently worked to impede the free flow of content across international borders (E. Elkins 2019), the 1978 release of *Battlestar Galactica* represented an attempt to regulate what would and would not flow across the borders of different media platforms as they moved between territories. This industrially coordinated move from Europe to the United States was one of geography and of media system. As a result, *Battlestar Galactica* offers a point of comparative analysis not just between cinema and television, but between content constructed alternately as international cinema and US television. In that move, we can see that distinctions between television and film can be nationally and culturally specific, in that the content that functions as television and distinctly *not* cinema in one national context can nonetheless serve as cinema when exhibited in another.

This distinction takes on ideological valences, too: in the United States, the claim that *Battlestar Galactica* was, when reviewed as a cinema presentation, a "poor man's *Star Wars*" cemented its better suitability for television, even as the theatrical release proved successful elsewhere in the globe. The denial of cinematic status in its US circulation implicitly frames international film cultures as an inferior, third world, "poor man's" cinema.

Although the international release of "Saga of a Star World" was thus not a dumping of failed television product on the global market but a simultaneous and parallel manifestation as cinema, the failure of the US television series did trigger more action in these theatrical venues. For theatrical release in Europe, Mexico, South America, Japan, the United Kingdom, and Australia, Universal cut together the episodes "The Living Legend" and "Fire in Space" as a single presentation renamed *Mission Galactica: The Cylon Attack* (Greenwood 2017). As the tenth, eleventh, and twelfth episodes aired in the United States, these episodes had already been aired on television in November and December 1978 before the first international theatrical run in West Germany on August 9, 1979. *Mission Galactica* then ran intermittently in different international markets for the next several years—beginning runs as late as June 1981 in Japan and December 1983 in Finland (IMDB, "Mission" n.d.). Following the failure of the *Galactica 1980* television revamp, Universal would once again employ this successful theatrical release strategy, offering the episodes "Galactica Discovers Earth" and "The Night the Cylons Landed" as a single, feature presentation for international markets beginning in May. Although the episodes may have been "mashed together" (Greenwood 2017), they represented the persistent ability of US television to function as cinema beyond its national boundaries.

This strategy did not go unnoticed by Universal distributors responsible for the US territory. As *Variety* suggested, the prior theatrical release of "Saga of a Star World" in European and Canadian cinema was sufficiently successful—"enough to encourage a domestic release" (Knight 1978). This led to a US release as well, where *Saga of a Star World* was one of four films Universal released with a Sensurround sound mix (Greenwood 2017). Thus, the transformation of this television production into a theatrical presentation was not unique to the international market, even if initially driven by that market and sustained much longer in it. This development demonstrated that while *Battlestar* may have been a "poor man's Star Wars," it did, in that reputation, still have the capacity to share the same spaces of exhibition as *Star Wars*. Failed television, in this instance, could still function as cinema in the United States, even if marked as inadequate to that task.

Battlestar Galactica is certainly not the only television property to be reconfigured as cinema in international distribution. Made-for-television movies, in particular, have held significant potential for international cinema sales. For example, the Cold War drama *The Day After*, one of the most notable TV movie events of its time, was released into the international theatrical market following its November 1983 US debut—only a week later in the case of its run in Denmark. Many more examples could be traced. This is not to say that all television has been able to make this transformation into theatrical exhibition by tapping into an international distribution culture that troubles these media-based distinctions. Focused on the Black experience in America from the 18th to 20th century across eight episodes and over nine hours of programming, the immensely successful 1977 television mini-series *Roots* might have presented a greater challenge than other television properties for distributors envisioning theatrical strategies, given its length alone. Thus, in international distribution to territories including France, West Germany, Italy, Spain, Hungary, Sweden, and more, *Roots* remained a television product as it traveled the world from 1977 to 1980 (IMDB, "Roots" n.d.). However, as Tim Havens (2006, 2013) points out, distributors have also discounted the appeal of African American stories, stars, and reputations in the global market. So while the event status of the original *Roots* mini-series gave it a visibility that drove international sales, its subsequent sequels and spin-offs proved less mobile, both across borders and across media. The 1988 TV movie *Roots: The Gift* saw international television distribution in Finland alone (IMDB, "Roots: The Gift" n.d.). With a runtime of one hour and forty minutes, this television movie would have been well suited to theatrical exhibition. Yet its mobility in this intersection of television and film distribution appeared considerably less than an imitation of *Star Wars*. Havens' claims might then have relevance not just for understanding whose television *travels*, but also whose television is allowed to *transform* when it crosses global boundaries. Some creators, genres, stories, and representations have the privilege to escape the contingent and constructed boundaries drawn between film and television, while those more marginalized may not.

In fact, while this chapter considers exhibition plans and strategies, its interest in the intersection of television and film globally demands recognition of the ways in which American or Western perceptions of these media and these essential qualities do not enjoy universal status around the world. Instead, exhibition spaces throughout the world challenge these distinctions considerably. As Jonathan found in his ethnographic work in Malawi in 2008 and 2010 (see Gray 2011), for instance, the theatrical spaces available for public exhibition of films consisted only of an 80-person capacity room in each of the two largest cities, Blantyre and Lilongwe—with the former having reportedly been closed. This changes the very terms of filmgoing, where the primary means of watching film was either to do so at one's own home, or else to attend a video show in which paying patrons sat on planks of wood set over plastic cartons to watch films in a shared space. In both settings, film would be watched on a television set, usually a small tube device. Video shows, moreover, would run content back to back, with no distinct start or finish times; though film content predominated, it would frequently be mixed with content originally produced for television distribution. At the marketplaces, meanwhile, pirate stalls did not distinguish between film and television in the organization and presentation of their offerings. Not surprisingly, then, when asked about their interest in American "movies," retailers' answers could often turn to *Lost* (2004–2010), *Prison Break* (2005–2017), *CSI: Miami* (2002–2012), or other locally popular television series. Malawi is a country too poor to factor into transnational media companies' release and exhibition strategies, but in this respect, it is representative of much of the Global South. Thus, if this section has illustrated how the distinctions between film and television can break down in studio release and exhibition strategies the second we look outside the United States, it ends with acknowledgment that those distinctions further crumble when we look beyond those industry strategies at the level of everyday screening realities for much of the world.

When the Theater Shuts Down

While both the broadcast and digital eras have clearly afforded opportunities for television to double as cinema through theatrical exhibition, film too has frequently transformed into television in sites of domestic consumption. The film libraries controlled by studios have been sold into television distribution from the earliest days of the electronic medium (Kompare 2005), and on platforms like Netflix and Hulu, that content now streams into our homes on smart television sets, cell phones, tablets, and other mobile devices. Furthermore, in this intersection between television and the cinema, the domestic space has often been transformed into a theatrical one. Consumers have invested in complex home theater systems meant to remediate the filmgoing experience in the living room. As Barbara Klinger (2006) writes, these post-theatrical exhibition cultures have not just created a new domestic space in which films can be shown, but have also transformed cinema in the process. Film cultures have been reshaped by their encounters with the domestic exhibition technologies of television.

However, as with all the potential convergences of film and television exhibition in this chapter, these encounters are not even or essential, but instead determined by the social and industrial contexts that impose boundaries and hierarchies on these distinct media. Perhaps most exemplary of the persistent imposition of difference between film and television is the US industry response to the COVID-19 pandemic, in which the 2020 closure of theatrical venues due to social distancing policies prompted a reinvestment in television technologies as a means of distributing cinema product. At the same time, however, ingrained industry assumptions about the value of theatrical exhibition have limited the potential of film products to be rerouted to television markets that remain more viable.

In early 2020, the spread of COVID-19 across the globe required nearly every industry to reorganize and rethink to adapt to a changed set of socio-economic conditions. Throughout much of the world, consumers' abilities to leave their homes were curtailed due to government policies that restricted the opening of businesses and limited the size of social gatherings; "stay-at-home" orders required all but "essential" workers to shelter in place. Meanwhile, with many businesses forced to close (whether temporarily or permanently), many individuals found themselves out of work, drastically reducing the consumer spending power upon which global capitalism depended. In April 2020, unemployment in the United States rose to 15% according to the Bureau of Labor Statistics—an increase of over 10% from the beginning of the year before the impact of the pandemic began to be felt (*Bureau of Labor Statistics* 2020). Overall, the US economy suffered the largest quarterly decline ever recorded, shrinking by almost a third at 32.9%. Previously, the largest quarterly drop in gross domestic product had been a 10% drop in 1958 (Ivanova 2020). For many industries in the United States—and elsewhere throughout the globe—these conditions imposed new challenges and even existential crises.

For the Hollywood film industry, the pandemic disrupted its supply chain from production to exhibition. The production of film content—an intensively collaborative, close-quarters enterprise often involving hundreds of on-set crew people—was not compatible with new social distancing measures. Studios thus found themselves forced to engage in a production shutdown, cutting off their supply of new content. Some projects in post-production could still be completed by editors and effects artists working remotely from home, but within months there would be little to prep for release. However, distributors also found themselves sitting on a supply of finished product that they could not release theatrically. Because consumers were unable to gather in the public spaces of movie theaters, there was effectively no market for films released theatrically, and major Hollywood releases like *Mulan* (2020), *Wonder Woman 1984* (2020), *Black Widow* (forthcoming), *Top Gun* (forthcoming), and more were delayed—often multiple times, and sometimes pulled from the schedule indefinitely (Zeitchik, "Mulan" 2020). By late 2020, distributors increasingly battled over crowded release dates in 2021 and beyond as so many films were repeatedly delayed into the future; as one executive put it, the typically considerable challenge of scheduling releases now heightened to the point of "playing four-dimensional chess on acid" (McClintock 2020). Even when local governments began to allow the limited reopening of movie theaters, distributors appeared reluctant to start the flow of content again, knowing that a depressed audience turnout would limit the revenues for blockbuster films in which hundreds of millions of dollars had been invested on the promise of pre-pandemic returns. For all intents and purposes, the flow of new Hollywood films from producer to theater-going consumer stalled.

In this environment, the ability of theatrical exhibitors to survive appeared dubious. As reported in *The Los Angeles Times*, movie theaters faced "an existential threat" (Faughnder 2020). Although some 293 drive-in theaters were doing brisk business (mostly showing library fare as studios continued to hold back major new releases like *Black Widow*), the one thousand indoor movie theaters in the United States remained closed by July 2020. With summer blockbusters typically accounting for 40% of theater revenues, this continued closure meant a significant loss, with Wedbush Securities estimating that the 2020 North American box office total would drop 61% from the previous year due to the impact of the pandemic (Faughnder 2020). Many theater operators elected to remain closed due to doubts about audience readiness to come back to the public space of the theaters, while those that did contemplate reopening imagined a changed experience with mandatory masks, hand sanitizer, and temperature checks coming to be more important than the high-end amenities that had previously defined the 21st-century theater experience (Molnar 2020; Truitt 2020). In this environment, the largest theatrical chain in the world, AMC, anticipated near-term bankruptcy before striking a deal with private equity firm Silver Lake Group for an injection of cash needed in the efforts to reopen its theaters. This deal, however, did not eliminate bankruptcy fears, as it was somewhat pessimistically seen as a means to improve the outcome for investors "if AMC does end up filing for chapter 11 protection" (*Fox Business* 2020). All in all, the COVID-19 crisis did nothing less than decimate the business of theatrical exhibition.

Undoubtedly, this crisis had similarly negative impacts on the television industries. The shutdown that put film production on hiatus equally curtailed the creation of television content. Prior to the pandemic, analysts spoke of an era of "peak TV" in which the demand for original content across so many competing channels and subscription services had led to a boom in the sheer number of scripted series being produced. The shutdown, however, triggered declarations that peak TV was over, as the supply of new television programming appeared sure to run out in a matter of months (Baysinger 2020; Guyette 2020). Yet while the production of television faced a similar threat, the domestic exhibition context of television afforded potential opportunity. For some sectors of the television industries, the pandemic proved to be a boon. With consumers trapped at home, television viewing increased. Research by Comscore revealed that in the broadcast arena, viewership for the four major US television networks had increased by 19% in March 2020 compared to a year prior (with children's television programming increasing by an even larger 31% as younger viewers looked to television during school closures) (Sullivan 2020). Other research confirmed that the bulk of this increase appeared in daytime television when many viewers had previously been out of the home (Watson 2020). While traditional television outlets gained additional viewership, new online competitors also saw surges in consumer interest too, estimated at a 34% spike in March (Epstein 2020). Netflix reported a gain of 16 million new subscribers in the first three months of the year (doubling those who had signed up in the previous three months), attributing that interest to the increased demand for the entertainment it could offer (Thomas 2020). Similarly, although the Walt Disney Company faced significant losses due to its disrupted film investments, its Disney+ streaming service offered a singular ray of hope. In February, the service had attracted 29 million subscribers after three months of operation. By April, that subscriber base had grown to 50 million, a sustained growth credited to the "global health crisis forcing hundreds of millions of people to stay home" (Epstein 2020). These positive indicators did not come without some caution—the surges in viewership and subscription in March, for example, fell off as the pandemic wore on (Lane 2020). The sustainability of growth was further put into question by the coming content drought that the production shutdown would bring (Albasi 2020). Nonetheless, the domestic settings in which these television services could be consumed gave them a significant advantage over the exhibition models of theatrical film.

Given these conditions, it might seem logical for the film and television industries to consolidate their exhibition efforts. History has shown the ability of film and television content to be repurposed across exhibition contexts. Television had a secure pipeline to the consumer still in place, whereas the cinema had a glut of unreleased content that could make use of that pipeline while helping to put off a television drought. And in some cases, Hollywood did indeed look to home entertainment as an alternative means of distributing the content that it could not release due to the pandemic. The animated film *Trolls World Tour* (2020), for example, was originally slated to be released theatrically on April 10, and instead of delaying that opening, distributor Universal decided to make the film available for digital rental on platforms including Apple TV. In the first three weeks of release, the film earned $77 million through these rentals—exceeding what the original 2016 *Trolls* film made in five months of theatrical exhibition (Schwartzel 2020). This rental model represented a commitment to continuity with theatrical business models—$19.99 bought the consumer a window of access to the film at a price point far more comparable to a family night at the movies than a monthly subscription fee that provides longer-term access to a whole library of content. While piggybacked on platforms like Apple TV, this was only a limited experiment in redirecting film content to the television industries. Nevertheless, it seized on the potential to embrace the domestic context of television consumption as an alternative to the theatrical model.

Although Disney was slower to embrace streaming as an alternative to theatrical release, analysts and fans alike wondered if long-delayed films like *Mulan* might ultimately debut on Disney+ (Pallotta, "Here's Why" 2020). As the pandemic wore on, though, Disney became more open to the possibilities. The company's first move in the United States was to release a film version of the stage hip-hop musical *Hamilton*, originally scheduled for release in October 2021, on the Disney+ streaming platform in July 2020. It may seem surprising that Disney would choose to release this film well over a year early with so many other films already delayed by that point. Yet compared to big-budget blockbuster spectacles in which Disney had invested hundreds of millions of dollars, less was at stake in this experiment—the relatively small $75 million spent to acquire the rights to a filmed version of the stage show (Lindahl 2020). Given the visibility of Black Lives Matter protests and anti-racist activism in summer 2020, this early release also communicated a timely corporate commitment to Black consumers and experiences. By contrast, Disney was far more reluctant to consign to Disney+ big-budget productions like *Black Widow* and *Mulan* intended for theatrical release. The former was ultimately moved to 2021; but in the case of the latter, Disney finally relented and planned a streaming video-on-demand release similar to *Trolls World Tour*. However, to access *Mulan* upon its September 4 release, consumers had to have a base Disney+ account and pay an addition $30 for "Premier Access" to the film, which would persist as long as the account remained active. For many, this seemed a fairly hefty price for home video; for others, it posed a bargain compared to a night at the movies that might cost a family far more than that after accounting for concessions. Assessing the success of this strategy remains difficult, however, as there are few benchmarks for video-on-demand releases, and analysts are at the mercy of the information Disney wishes to provide (Brueggemann 2020). Moreover, Disney's decision to release *Mulan* in this form in the United States did not preclude different release strategies elsewhere in the world (especially where Disney+ does not operate) or subsequent theatrical releases in the future. A week later, *Mulan* did open theatrically in China; but it debuted to only $23 million in box office revenues in the largest market in the world, hamstrung less by the pandemic and more by a government-imposed media blackout as the film had become a lightning rod for criticizing human rights abuses in the region in which it was filmed (Davis 2020). *Mulan* therefore remains an early proof of concept rather than commitment to streaming release strategies.

Yet while experiments like *Trolls World Tour, Hamilton,* and *Mulan* hinted at new distributional possibilities that could transform filmgoing into something experienced through streaming services, established industry norms and hierarchies of value reasserted the necessity of boundaries around theatrically exhibited cinema. Beyond the threat to the economic survival of these industries, the disruption of exhibition boundaries threatened to destabilize some of the fundamental assumptions about what makes a film different from television and how that distinction can serve as a means of aesthetic evaluation. Recall that HBO considered releasing the final season of *Game of Thrones* theatrically: such a move would challenge fundamental ontologies of the cinema as constructed in professional and consumer cultures. While such a theatrical release could be profitable, it would also raise questions about what counts as cinema.

Even those who advocated for the theatrical exhibition of cinematic television content recognized that the strategy would cause confusion. If a television series like *Game of Thrones* were to have been released theatrically, would this have qualified it as a film eligible for Academy Awards (Kohn 2019)? However, only a year after the series' conclusion on television, such questions would be largely moot amid the pandemic-driven collapse of film exhibition. Indeed, at that point the Academy of Motion Picture Arts and Sciences had to revise its longstanding policy that only films released theatrically could qualify for its awards—lest the 2021 ceremony be forced to focus on the much smaller pool of films that had seen theatrical release. Thus, the Academy rewrote the rules of eligibility to make an exception, allowing that "Until further notice and for the 93rd Awards year only, films that had a previously planned theatrical release but are initially made available through commercial streaming, VOD service or other broadcast may qualify for awards consideration" (Academy of Motion Picture Arts and Sciences 2020).

As much as this exception shows flexibility, it also reveals a refusal to dissolve the boundaries between film and television cultures; a "planned theatrical release," even if it never came to fruition, remains the marker of eligibility, even if a film is eventually forced to release through other means. Despite the disruption of the pandemic, theatrical exhibition remains the defining characteristic of film for organizations like the Academy. Ironically, a Netflix film like *The Old Guard* (2020) starring major Hollywood talent like Charlize Theron and Chiwetel Ejiofor and featuring the same slick action scenes as a summer blockbuster still would not be eligible for an Oscar, despite these changes, while *Mulan* will—even though both seem to share the same aesthetics, production values, and release platforms. This insistence on the symbolic importance of theatrical release, while highlighted in the pandemic, also has a long tradition in genres such as documentary, which can similarly confuse the boundaries of film and television. Feature documentaries regularly make their money from television release, but moments of exhibition at Sundance and other prestige venues—however more fleeting—matter for attracting Oscar nominations and other marketable markers of prestige that can help drive success on Netflix, HBO, or Amazon Prime Video (Stone 2018). The theatrical appearance marks as non-televisual that which depends on television.

As media analyst Paul Degarabedian explains, there are "both financial and symbolic" reasons for Hollywood to defend its investment in and insistence on theatrical exhibition as the essential component of film cultures (Pallotta, "Here's Why" 2020). These financial reasons are considerable: a film like *Mulan* costs hundreds of millions of dollars and depends on the direct revenues of ticket sales (domestic and global) to generate a definite return on investment. Studios must also consider their relationships with exhibitors to whom they have promised these releases; for example, the release of *Trolls World Tour* via digital home entertainment prompted the AMC theater chain to ban Universal films from its screens (Pallotta, "AMC" 2020). Pursuit of a new set of financial transactions could come at the expense of the old. Yet the symbolic proves equally important, as Hollywood attempts to protect the "event-like feel of going to the movies" and the rituals that come along with it (Pallotta, "Here's Why" 2020). Once studios start releasing films directly to home entertainment platforms, they risk evaporating that cinematic prestige and giving audiences the chance to decide they can live without the practices of filmgoing, concession buying, and more. If audiences begin to feel like the theatrical experience doesn't matter, efforts to resecure that revenue stream might be doomed even if the public health crisis came to a quick end.

The symbolic value of theatrical release as a means of legitimating cinematic work also underpins Hollywood's cultures of production. *The New Mutants*, a 20th Century Fox superhero horror film directed by Josh Boone, had been scheduled for theatrical release as early as 2018, but due to production delays, reshoots, and strategic reorganization following the studio's acquisition by Disney, it was delayed until August 28, 2020. The pandemic, of course, threatened to impose further delay, compounding the frustration of anyone anticipating the long-awaited film. Yet as the director explains, alternative forms of release are simply not possible to contemplate without disrupting both the expectations of creative professionals and the legal practices designed to manage those expectations in their relationships with employers. For filmmakers like Boone, signing a contract to direct a film means signing a contract to direct something that will be released theatrically. "With most movies, you sign contracts that guarantee a theatrical release, so it needs to open to ever go digital in the first place," he explains. "We just, too, would like to see people to see it in the theater. But it needs to obviously be at the right time when it's safe to go back" (Gemmill 2020). Boone essentially communicates to those impatient for film releases that they should buckle in for a long wait because studios had effectively promised their filmmakers that their work will debut theatrically. Without renegotiation of those contracts—and a transformation of the creative norms by which film directors expect theatrical release to be commensurate with that role—the potential for film work to release on television platforms remains limited.

What Hollywood's response to the COVID-19 pandemic as the writing of this book reveals, then, is that despite the potential for the film industry to look to domestic television release as an alternative to public exhibition spaces decimated by public health crisis, such a transformation was shaped by both economic and cultural frameworks that insisted on limiting that transformation or reimposing fundamental distinctions. Film content could easily run on television exhibition platforms—but doing so threatened the cultures of exhibition around which film consumption and creation had been defined. Indeed, it was the sense of greater value and prestige in theatrical exhibition that industry strategies deemed essential to preserve, and that circulation in the domestic spaces of television might have cheapened. Hollywood was willing to risk losing money by keeping films off television in order to maintain its investment in the value and prestige of this distinction. The story of the pandemic is one of television and film's potential convergence as well as the efforts made to reassert exhibition as the site of their distinction.

Conclusion

The boundaries between media such as film and television are mutable at the level of exhibition—but that mutability is limited by social and industrial factors. When prestige television programs in the contemporary era like *Game of Thrones* have been released as part of limited, special engagement theatrical events, these screenings have significantly transformed the televisual experience into something larger, of course, but also something public-facing. At the same time, however, such screenings have remained limited because of industry strategies that depend on the maintenance of boundaries around television markets. Similarly, the release of broadcast-era television programs like *Battlestar Galactica* as theatrical films on the international stage reveals the potential for television to cross the boundaries between media in the course of traveling across geographic territories. Yet there, too, the unevenness of these boundary crossings demonstrates the continued investment in constructing and maintaining a sense of difference and hierarchy between different global cultures and media both. Finally, as much as film libraries have enjoyed a long history of exhibition in the domestic space of television after their theatrical release, the potential of cinematic works to make their debut on television remains technologically and strategically possible while also economically and socially dubious. The COVID-19 crisis dismantled the business and culture of theatrical film-going, leaving television release as a potential alternative. Yet Hollywood's investment in the theatrical experience as a symbol of value in cultures of consumption and production alike has, at least as of Fall 2020, limited the capacity for convergence and transformation across these media.

With all this in mind, it is possible to conclude that there is no fundamental difference between film and television that cannot be transmuted or adapted. And yet, the place in which we experience these media still seems to matter a great deal—to consumers, to industries, and to the systems of value by which media entertainment is made meaningful and valuable. As much as we have to recognize these different cultures of exhibition, we must also stop to interrogate them, and in doing so better understand how and why these boundaries are constructed and who they might serve.

2

TELEVISION'S DETRACTORS GO TO THE MOVIES

Cinematic Representations of Television

While Chapter 1 examined how television *shows* are exhibited at movie theaters, television *as a medium* is also regularly exhibited at the movies, through being the subject of many films. Hollywood has long loved making films about films and filmmaking, and though films about television and the making of television are less numerous, television still appears as star or (as we'll see) villain, and as topic of analysis, critique, and consternation in multiple films. Each of these films about television could individually warrant attention, to see what they're saying about the medium, and what discursive work they're doing to distinguish television from movies. But rather than turn to one or two sustained examples at the risk of probing only them, this chapter examines a swathe of such films, looking for patterns, echoes, and repeated statements or suggestions across them. Rather than ask simply what does this or that film and its creative team think about television, therefore, our interest is in what discursive work film does in general to frame what television is or isn't. What do we learn about television from cinematic representations of the medium?

An inspiration for this chapter comes from Lynn Spigel's superb examination of how television was marketed and domesticated in its early years, *Make Room for TV: Television and the Family Ideal in Postwar America*. Spigel examines ads and articles in women's magazines between 1948 and 1955 to document their "installation into domestic space" (1992, 1) of television. What, she asks, did people expect of television in its early years in the United States, and from where might some of these expectations have come? Using women's magazines of the era, she notes a determined, repeated attempt to situate the television set as a central new member of the family, through pictorial representation of families happily congregating in front of the television, and through articles that reported on research into television's new roles in the family circle.

She illustrates, too, that these efforts to place television pitched heavily to women, addressing them as housewives, and nominating their special role in integrating television into their domestic labor routines and their families' lives. If television came to exist in many people's imaginaries as a medium of and for housewives, in short, Spigel shows how these imaginaries didn't simply develop naturally—they were very purposefully constructed by women's magazines and their advertisers.

If advertisers can play the game of discursively constructing television, though, so too can other prominent speakers. With direct relevance to our interests here, in his book *The Cinema Dreams Its Rivals: Media Fantasy Films from Radio to the Internet* (2006), Paul Young studies how film discussed, framed, and "fantasized" various media that were innovated following its own arrival on the popular cultural scene. In a chapter on films fantasizing television, he considers numerous films—including *Murder by Television* (1935), *Double Indemnity* (1944), *White Heat* (1949), *In a Lonely Place* (1950), *Sunset Boulevard* (1950), *The Glass Web* (1953), and *A Face in the Crowd* (1957)—and their variously overt and metaphorical envisionings of and commentary upon television. While recognizing the peculiar threat television may have posed to some degree to film, being not only another audio-visual medium, but one that broadcast to the home for free, Young ultimately sees film's fantasies invested less in rivalry and more in policing a very specific notion of classical film style and address. As Spigel notes of the ads that encircled television's early days, Young also sees the films as "constructing television as a technological-institutional nexus of domesticity" (2006, 140) while fantasizing film as a bolder, grander form of public address. To do so, though, involved "constantly" exuding suspicion about television and its audiences (xviii).

Jon Nelson Wagner and Tracey Biga MacLean then update the story of film's treatment of television as subject in *Television at the Movies* (2008). From the 1970s' *The Last Picture Show* (1971)—which they write of as an elegy to cinema which "ultimately sees, as high cinema often does, the arrival of television and the usurpation of film as the end of the world" (23)—to the 1990s' *The Cable Guy* (1996)—which focuses, they suggest, on a titular character whose masculinity has been "deranged" by television (106)—they also offer longer analyses of *Videodrome* (1983), *Being There* (1979), *Max Headroom* (1985), *My Favorite Year* (1982), *Tootsie* (1982), *Network* (1976), *Bulworth* (1998), *Henry, Portrait of a Serial Killer* (1990), and *The King of Comedy* (1982), while discussing many more films in passing. Asking what cinema says about television, they argue at the outset, is made permissible by how often cinema treats television as a "monolithic presence" (1). And that presence, they document, is inevitably threatening in one way or another: "To say that cinema often presents a contemptuous view of television doesn't begin to capture the extremity of that representation" (25). All frame television as "bad," where what is meant by bad "is multiple, shifting, and unspecific" (14). As "a carrier of pathology, brainwashing behavior, or creative enervation" (11) to some, forever tinged by a "sense of pollution" (25), television on film continually upsets societal institutions and comforts in worrying ways, charged with being commodified, commercialized, and capitalist to a tee, of pitching to audiences' basest desires in ways that drag those desires ever lower, of attracting the worst, most self-centered and unhinged talent, and of being a feminizing influence, where feminizing is regarded pejoratively and dangerously.

In this chapter, we cover the next two decades of this story, asking about television on film in the 2000s and 2010s. This was a time, we repeat from our Introduction, when every major studio shared a corporate umbrella with a major producer and distributor of television, when transmedia franchising provided ample reasons to work together, when long-held criticisms of television's relative weakness as narrative form were regularly being challenged by successive waves of programming that commanded critical adoration, and when creative personnel were moving between media as rarely before. Thus one might expect a détente and a thawing of the relations somewhat. Of course, just as Spigel never suggested that *only* women's magazines and their advertisers constructed television's early character in the United States, or just as Young never suggests that *only* film fantasizes television, in turning to film we similarly don't mean to suggest it is the first or only speaker. Others might also ask how politicians and their speeches frame any medium and its possibilities, how any given medium frames itself, how religious, educational, or other institutions ask for us to engage (or not) with a medium. Film by no means has the first or last word. But what do films of the post-merger 2000s and 2010s say about television, and what is film's current framing of television?

To answer these questions, we watched films about television released since 2000, although when some films released earlier than 2000 have enjoyed continued popularity and notoriety into the 2000s, we considered them too. We scoured lists on the Internet, from Wikipedia to fan-made lists on IMDb and other film list sites, to create a master list of films about television (or in which television features prominently), and then started watching many of them. We limited ourselves to English-language and mostly American films, and thus our results may say little about television's framing outside of the United States, even though the international distribution of many of these films likely ensured a fair degree of global travel. That list included:

---

15 Minutes (2001)
Anchorman: The Legend of Ron Burgundy (2004)
Anchorman 2: The Legend Continues (2013)
Bewitched (2005)
Broadcast News (1987)
The Cable Guy (1996)
Cinema Verite (2011)

Network (1976)
Nightcrawler (2014)
Pleasantville (1998)
Poltergeist (1982)
Quiz Show (1994)
The Ring (2002)
The Show (2017)

Confessions of a Dangerous Mind (2002)

Death to Smoochy (2002)

Dickie Roberts: Former Child Star (2003)

EdTV (1999)

Good Night, and Good Luck (2005)

The Hunger Games (2012)

The Insider (1999)

Jingles the Clown (2009)

Little Black Book (2004)

Morning Glory (2010)

Showtime (2002)

Slumdog Millionaire (2008)

Terror Toons (2002)

The Truman Show (1998)

Truth (2015)

The TV Set (2006)

Twilight Zone: The Movie (1983)

Videodrome (1983)

Wag the Dog (1997)

Welcome to Me (2014)

Originally, we had intended to write about the other direction of messaging and boundary maintenance too, asking what television says about movies. However, we soon noted a significant relative dearth of material to study. Numerous television shows have sought to satirize or play around with Hollywood more generally, whether in the forefront or background—including *Barry* (2018–), *Better Things* (2016–), *BoJack Horseman* (2014–2020), *Californication* (2008–2014), *Curb Your Enthusiasm* (2000–2020), *Entourage* (2004–2011), *Episodes* (2011–2017), and *Extras* (2005–2007)—and we watched many of these (and others) too. But we were struck by how often television treats "the industry" as one involving the integration of film and television (and sometimes theater). The actors, directors, writers, and executives we meet in such shows may be working on a television show at this point, a film at that point, and while they are engaged in that project the text's commentary may seem to be directed at that medium, but that commentary soon repeats itself in relation to work in the other medium, such that the object of commentary (and often scorn) is "show business" writ large, not a specific medium. *BoJack Horseman*, for instance, hardly reserves particular satire for movies alone. Some other shows are more specifically about television (such as *30 Rock* [2006–2013], *Studio 60 on the Sunset Strip* [2006–2007], *The Larry Sanders Show* [1992–1998], or *UnREAL* [2015–2018]), but television shows about films have nearly always been about television too. This in itself works in stark contrast to many of the films that quite carefully direct their commentary toward film or television specifically. Even when "Hollywood" is invoked in film, it is far more often the movie industry, with television perhaps positioned to pick up the leftovers from failed careers, (framed-as) awful remakes or transmedia continuations, and greedy producers, but with little sense that the industries are one. By contrast, scant few television shows have distinct commentary on the movie industry, certainly not enough to justify any extended examination of "patterns."

Nevertheless, we not only watched significant portions of the above-listed shows, but we also sought a "control group" of sorts, and thus watched numerous movies about movies. Even if, as noted above, films about television are notable in comparison to television shows about film and television inasmuch as the former envision two separate entities while the latter tend to envision a single industry, we wanted to see if films about films echoed similar critiques, or whether, in total, they suggested a different character to television as medium and industry. As we'll discuss, we very much saw the latter, as films about films may run the gamut from biting critique to loving embrace, but what they see as variously heinous or lovable differs significantly from what films about television tell us about television. Movie-makers have long adored looking in the mirror and making films about films, so we could not feasibly watch all such films. However, for a recent sample, we again worked off numerous lists to watch the following, with acknowledgment this is an incomplete list, intended more to sample than to audit:

Argo (2012)	*Knight of Cups* (2015)
The Aviator (2004)	*The Life and Death of Peter Sellers* (2004)
Be Kind, Rewind (2008)	*My Week with Marilyn* (2011)
Boogie Nights (1997)	*The Player* (1992)
A Cock and Bull Story (2005)	*The Road to Nowhere* (2010)
The Deal (2008)	*Rules Don't Apply* (2016)
Hitchcock (2012)	*Saving Mr. Banks* (2013)
Hollywood Ending (2002)	*State and Main* (2000)
Hugo (2011)	*Super 8* (2011)
The Independent (2000)	*Tim and Eric's Billion Dollar Movie* (2012)
Judas Kiss (2011)	*Tropic Thunder* (2008)
The Kid and I (2005)	*Walt Before Mickey* (2015)

The watching and interpreting "we" in this chapter includes Jennifer Smith, who worked as a research assistant for this part of the project across two years. Derek and Jonathan had seen a healthy handful of the films listed, and especially much of the television noted above, but Jennifer cast a much wider net, returning from bouts of watching with superb notes and observations that guided much of our analysis.

The Material Presence of Television

Even looking across numerous films, and even when we focus on patterns instead of singular scenes of texts, a significant risk exists that we might "overdo" a reading of these films. Just as movies about, say, architects are not necessarily about architecture, a story about a person working in television might "just" be a story about an individual. When is it a story about television? We admit to approaching the texts with apprehension caused by this key question. Yet many of the films quickly allayed our fears, as the materiality of television features so prominently in many of them. Many of the films, in short, make it clear that they are not just about individuals, as endless shots of television sets can be found interwoven amidst the plot, often appearing at key moments no less, to visually demand that viewers consider television a star.

This materiality is especially notable in many horror films about television. *Poltergeist* deserves special mention here, as the image of young Carol Anne (Heather O'Rourke) sitting in front of a television set filled with static, seemingly entranced, is easily the film's most iconic image, and served as its poster, too. In the film, a family moves into a haunted house, and it is their young daughter who first communes with the poltergeist, through the television set that she watches alone at night. The television serves as a portal, in short, from the world of the evil and the dead to the world of the living—or, as Young notes, "a conduit between the suburbs and the world of the angry dead" (2006, 189)—and its grip over unsupervised children is rendered as actively dangerous, such that most shots of the television come to be ominous.

Twilight Zone: The Movie, too, offers a story "It's a Good Life," in which a woman returns a young boy to his home and stays for dinner, only to find he has supernatural powers, which he uses to terrorize his family. The story adapts a classic *Twilight Zone* (1959–1964) episode of the same title, but now Anthony's impetuous, spoiled nature is linked directly to his love of video games and of television, as are his tortures: he traps his sister in the set, for instance, leaving her to be pursued and ultimately devoured by a cartoon monster. Whereas the original *Twilight Zone*'s Anthony had wished away electricity from his town, offering only one night of "television" (of model dinosaurs fighting each other) each week, in the remake television becomes every bit as monstrous and as active a culprit as Anthony. As in *Poltergeist*, the television is shot ominously, as a monster and a conspirator in Anthony's reign of terror, its horrible blue glow enveloping the family.

More recently, *The Ring* (based on the Japanese film of the same translated name) is about a video tape whose viewers are doomed to die within a week of watching it, the "weeklong delay acknowledg[ing] television's most fundamental unit of programming time" (Wagner and MacLean 2008, 56). Caetlin Benson-Allott (2013) offers a compelling reading of *The Ring* as more about VHS tapes and—metonymically and by extension—DVDs than about television per se. This reading in turn offers a firm reason for why *The Ring* attacks television, for Benson Allott suggests it is a horror well timed for a moment when Hollywood and the MPAA were fighting global piracy, and hence when they would be well served by stoking anxieties about the provenance of strange video tapes or DVDs. We certainly see the strength of this interpretation, but even if television is only guilty by association, television sets and screens loom more forebodingly than VCRs throughout the film. Even the opening takes a quick, establishing swipe at television, not VCRs, as two teenagers discuss television as they watch it, one noting that it gives her headaches and that its "microwaves" destroy brain cells. Right from the outset, then, media panic about television frames the narrative.

Throughout the movie, televisions serve not simply as medium for the video, but as co-villain: characters struggle to turn them off, can't find the remotes, need to unplug them, and yet sometimes the television lives on. Television enshrouds the narrative and the visual staging—at one point, for instance, a young child wanders into a room and stares at the (switched-off) television, silently transfixed. One of the teenagers who open the film ends up in a hospital for the mentally ill after the other dies, and she experiences intense distress when she sees others watching television, but the film of course asks us to side with her—she is right to worry. Shots of different types of televisions abound, from closed-circuit TV to multiple screens in a studio. One character kills himself by plugging in all his TV equipment and taking it into the bath with him. His daughter is said to have been locked up in a room "alone," until the speaker is corrected that she was "not alone" with a gesture to the television as threatening co-presence. Thus, although nominally it is a mysterious figure *on* the television and the video cassette linked *to* the television that are responsible for the film's deaths, the plot and filming work together to make television itself an evil aide.

Outside the horror films, television sets and other apparatus still loom large. *Welcome to Me*, for instance, is a comedy-drama about television-obsessed Alice (Kristen Wiig) who wins $86 million in the lottery, which she puts into buying herself an autobiographical television show. To situate her as unhealthily attached to her television, the opening shot is of a commercial, which we soon see as playing while she sleeps. As the camera continues to pan through her apartment, we see shelves overflowing with recorded VHS tapes. Later in the film, someone drives Alice home, tells her she left the television on, and Alice responds that it's been on for eight years, before she hugs the set. *The Cable Guy*, too, introduces us to an unhinged cable delivery man (Jim Carrey) who won't leave one customer alone. Like Alice, Chip has been "raised" by television due to his single mother's absence, and, like Alice, his television obsession is linked to and framed as generative of his pathology. Far from simply giving us characters who are obsessed with television, then, both films enact and document the dangers of television visually, offering us images of Alice and Chip engaging with the medium improperly, and of it commanding their lives.

Thriller *Nightcrawler* examines a seedy underbelly of independent journalists filming violent events to sell to tabloid television news programs. Early on, the materiality of television once again looms, though, as following the opening scenes' focus on the filming of a car accident, the sun rises and the camera offers us shots of satellite dishes, broadcast towers, cables, power wires, and other TV apparatus, thus once again underlining that this is a story about television through focusing on its materiality. Or buddy cop action comedy *Showtime* similarly situates its tale about two LAPD officers starring in a reality police show with numerous material reminders of television's presence as medium, force, and power, such as when Mitch (Robert DeNiro) runs a sting on a drug dealer in a room full, floor to ceiling, with televisions, some off, some staticky, some tuned into a boxing match. Mitch quips that the dealer should "throw in a free set," and in an ensuing shootout, the camera is careful to focus on some of the televisions being shattered. And black comedy crime film *Death to Smoochy* opens with a character skipping through the set of a children's show, yet the control panels, light rigging, and other technological indicators of a set are carefully included in most shots, visually insisting the movie will be as much about television as about any specific characters.

Many of the other films contain similar such moments, where audiences are reminded—or nagged even—to see the commentary as far more than individual, as about television. The remainder of this chapter focuses on the other meanings attributed to television, but as the above should indicate, few are flattering, most critical. Films about films, by contrast, regularly relish in the materiality of specific movie theaters that may perhaps be crowded, smoky, and/or hot but that exude romanticism. Indeed, even in *EdTV*, a film about a television show focused on one man's evolving life, when Ed (Matthew McConaughey) needs to escape the TV cameras that won't allow him a moment of solace, he retreats into a movie theater. Movie theaters are painted lovingly on celluloid by films ranging from *Hugo* to *Cinema Paradiso* (1988) to *The Purple Rose of Cairo* (1985). Television is no less materially present in films about television, but those material representations regularly serve to paint it as a looming, ominous presence, and/or to gesture to the conspicuous, troubling absence of other humans (mothers, boyfriends, friends).

The Good News

The representation of television on film is not all a cavalcade of misery, however, as a strong vein running through several of these films is a love of television news at its best. Admittedly, television news "at its best" is more often depicted through threat, by showing us those who are failing at it, and/or by documenting real stories of journalistic struggle and eventual triumph. Good journalism is often presented as by default incompatible with television's commercialism. But behind all such depictions is at least the promise and possibility of television news serving an important role in society at the rare moments when heroic journalists break through the system.

Hollywood has been fond of heroic journalist stories in general (see McNair 2010). Classics such as *All the President's Men* (1976), with its account of Bob Woodward, Carl Bernstein, and *The Washington Post*'s revelation of Nixon's abuses of power, or *The Killing Fields*' (1984) focus on Sydney Schanberg and Dith Pran's reporting on Khmer Rouge atrocities, meet more recent offerings such as *Spotlight* (2015), an account of *The Boston Globe*'s investigation into sexual abuse in the Catholic Church, or *The Post*'s (2017) recounting of reporting on the Pentagon Papers. Many look at newsprint journalism. But television journalism has received a few paeans, too, in the form of *The China Syndrome* (1979), *The Insider, Good Night, and Good Luck, Frost/Nixon* (2008), and *Truth*.

The heroic journalist genre regularly pits inexhaustible journalists against a system determined to thwart them. That system involves editors, owners, and other executives at their own paper or station, but our heroic journalists' determination to find the truth and tell the public drives them onward, often picking up respect from some of their antagonists along the way. The genre prefers true stories, to ratchet up the stakes and showcase moments in which journalists have served the nation well. *The Insider*, for instance, tells the story of tobacco industry whistleblower Jeffrey Wigand, whose information on the tobacco industry risked going unreported when CBS tried to kill *60 Minutes* producer Lowell Bergman's segment on Wigand out of fear of a reprisal lawsuit. Al Pacino plays the unstoppable Bergman, itself an act of imperious casting that lends Bergman all of Pacino's significant gravitas. CBS, meanwhile, is depicted as skittish amidst a takeover bid of the company. CBS is once again depicted unflatteringly in *Truth*, a film about the Killian documents controversy that similarly uses imperious casting to offer Robert Redford as Dan Rather and Cate Blanchett as Mary Mapes. A story of journalistic failure in many ways, it nevertheless holds up the integrity of Rather and Mapes working against a capricious system. *Good Night, and Good Luck*, meanwhile, sees David Strathearn's Edward R. Murrow going up against Senator Joseph McCarthy. Filmed in black and white, the camera oozes love for Murrow (and his cigarettes), taking great care to frame and situate him as lovingly and heroically as does the script.

These films hold up their reporters as tireless defenders of American democracy. In doing so, they situate the dangers of television news—the system that works against our heroes could obviously swallow up lesser individuals, they warn—and hardly depict television news as always on the side of the angels. But they also focus on great journalists who in mastering their form serve the American population nobly and invaluably, celebrating such moments as television at its best and calling for more of this in the future. *Good Night, and Good Luck* even ends with a speech given by Murrow to the Radio and Television News Directors Association, in which he lays out a goal for the medium writ large:

> The instrument can teach, it can illuminate, yes, and even it can inspire. But it can do so only to the extent that humans are determined to use it to those ends. Otherwise, it's nothing but wires and lights in a box. There is a great and perhaps decisive battle to be fought against ignorance, intolerance, and indifference. This weapon of television could be useful.

The heroic journalist narratives offered in *The Insider, Truth, Frost/Nixon*, and *The China Syndrome* similarly laud television's rare journalistic powers, and call for more of this, less of the rest, from the medium.

Beyond the hero narratives, though, numerous films have focused on television news in a state of disrepair. *Network* and *Broadcast News*, for example, both offer classic satirical accounts of television news as regularly guided by ratings, venial priorities, corporate interference, sexual politics, and plastic gloss. *Wag the Dog* focuses more on the political system than on news per se, posing a world in which the president's sexual indiscretions result in a PR team "directing" a fictional war with Albania to distract Americans from the real news for just a few days until the election. Implicated throughout the movie, though, is the US press corps (represented most commonly in the film through television news specifically) for believing and accepting uncritically the PR footage given to it about this supposed war. *Anchorman* and *Anchorman 2*, while both light and silly, take the infinite fecklessness of local and cable news respectively, and of their journalists, as baseline for much of their humor. Will Ferrell's Ron Burgundy has "the voice" but little else, a man of stunning ignorance who will read whatever is put on the teleprompter, whose ego and sexism are toxic, and whose station has no notion of news priorities. The "big story" of the summer for *Anchorman*, for instance, is a pregnant panda.

Tabloid or "light" news features more prominently in *15 Minutes, Little Black Book, Morning Glory,* and *Nightcrawler*. *Little Black Book*'s protagonist Stacey (Brittany Murphy) idolizes Diane Sawyer, wishing to be a "real" journalist, and soon after joining a daytime talk show, pitches an idea of looking at underfunded inner-city schools, only for everyone in the room to laugh, assuming she's joking. *Nightcrawler*'s ambulance-chasing freelance crews film violent and disturbing scenes, yet we're told they will sell to whichever station pays the most, suggesting a heated competition and a race to the moral bottom. Lewis (Jake Gyllenhaal), our key stringer, delivers a speech on how he "loves" TV news, but we then cut to a montage of him filming multiple tragedies, making it clear this is the news he loves. *15 Minutes* similarly depicts a TV news guided by a lust for blood: the crime action thriller centers on a spate of murders that are videotaped and then released to a local tabloid television news program that shows no ethical quandary in choosing not just to play the videos but to pay large amounts for them. And *Morning Glory* sees Rachel McAdams' Becky Fuller hired as an executive at a morning news show that runs frivolous stories. Harrison Ford's Mike Pomeroy is introduced as a veteran "serious" news journalist who balks at the news he's now asked to read, and we're now far from Bergman, Rather, and Murrow, even if Pomeroy is there to invoke their likely disapproval.

Across these various films about television journalism, then, we hear a familiar refrain, that "real," serious, hard-hitting journalism matters; it is television's ultimate calling, one that occasionally heroic journalists live up to, but that more often is ignored outright in favor of exploitative, spectacularizing fluff, and/or because of commercial pressures. Television could be so much more, in short, but most of the time it is not.

The Artless Industry

Corporate squeamishness in the face of "real news" from Lowell Bergman, or directives to follow the ratings, though, don't just abound in narratives about news. Rather, if one message resounded across every film we watched about television, it is that television is first, foremost, and often only a business, and an utterly artless one at that.

We see this first in the starring role that "the ratings" and other metrics play in most films about television. Repeatedly, the ratings work as a primary plot motor. *EdTV*'s various plot turns, for instance, are mostly set into motion by dipping or soaring ratings, leading up to Ed's criticism near the end that "ratings are most important." *Morning Glory* moves as its ratings (or as YouTube viewer numbers) move. "Whatever it takes," an executive offers as something of a motto, "just get the ratings up." *Death to Smoochy*'s characters lurch where the ratings go, and *Showtime*'s premise—a buddy cop reality show—also relies on a plan to raise the network's ratings. *Nightcrawler*'s protagonist tries to blackmail a woman into dating him because, he claims, he's raised her show's ratings. *The TV Set*'s network exec Lenny (Sigourney Weaver) describes a harrowing near-death experience that led her to believe she had to live life to the fullest … by fighting to win the ratings war on Thursday nights. *Bewitched*'s romantic comedy, meanwhile, hits its crisis point when Will Ferrell's Jack Wyatt discovers not only that his test scores are horrible but that those for Nicole Kidman's Isabel are sublime. The scene in which Jack explodes in rage and jealousy is notable, too, for echoing a similar jealous explosion from Will Ferrell in the previous year's *Anchorman*. Veronica's (Christina Applegate) first show as anchor brings in a two-point ratings boost, she is made permanent co-anchor, and Ferrell's Ron—like his fellow narcissist Jack—cannot take the humiliation. Once again, then, a lower rating is seen as a challenge to a narcissist's pathetic sense of manhood, and once again it becomes the crisis point in a romance. Then *Anchorman 2* includes bets over ratings success, character hirings and firings due to ratings, and ultimately Ron and Veronica's triumphant ending is marked by them receiving the channel's highest ever ratings. Or in *Dickie Roberts: Former Child Star*, ratings are invoked to signal both a moment of unravelling for its titular character, and his triumphant "comeback." In a dream sequence, Dickie tells some children a "horror story" of what he calls "The Day the Sitcom Got Cancelled," noting that since "the ratings [were] at a six-year low," his show was canceled, and his life was turned upside down. At the film's conclusion, though, Dickie's new sitcom gets amazing ratings, signaling his return and recovery. Across the films we saw, many other premises, crises, plot turns, and triumphs follow ratings.

Yet the ratings are never the only vestiges of an industry. Pitch meetings are also common, especially since several of these films revolve around the bizarre premise of their diegetic shows, and thus especially since the pitch meeting serves as a convenient plot device to explain that premise to audiences. Whether it's *Welcome to Me*'s autobiographical talk show, *Showtime*'s reality buddy cop drama, *EdTV*'s reality show following one man, *Confessions of a Dangerous Mind*'s interest in *The Dating Game* (1965–1973), *Cinema Verite*'s fictionalized account of *An American Family* (1973), *Bewitched*'s reboot of *Bewitched* (1964–1972) with Darren at the center, *Little Black Book*'s talk show focus on all of a character's exes, or *The Show*'s reality show about people committing suicide, pitches feature prominently. *The TV Set* adds primers on multiple other aspects of the television industry, including testing, the upfronts and ad buying, and it even opens with an animated sequence that explains pilot season.

More generally, many of these films exist precisely to mock the industry. *Broadcast News* and *Network* most famously lampoon the excesses of television news, and while neither *The Insider* nor *Anchorman* or *Anchorman 2* is satire (the former a gritty drama, the latter two silly comedies), all three take aim at the television news industry at regular points, as does *Morning Glory* as light satire and as do *15 Minutes*' and *Nightcrawler*'s attacks on tabloid news. *Little Black Book* and *Welcome to Me* both charge talk shows with being exploitative genres that profit off their participants' (or, in the case of the latter, host's) misery. Game shows are criticized in *Confessions of a Dangerous Mind*, *Quiz Show*, *Slumdog Millionaire*, *The Running Man* (1987), and *Deathrow Gameshow* (1987). *Bewitched* and *The TV Set* mock the process of sitcom production. And reality television in its various forms is subject to heavy attack—as will be discussed more later— by *EdTV*, *The Truman Show*, *The Show*, and *Showtime*. Central to the attack or critique of all the above-listed films is that the shows allow business "needs" and desires to trump ethics, humanity, or a sense of caring about people. Even if some of these films have "good people" in them, who fight for a better way and see the ills of the business, the system itself is clearly one of cold, profit-centered, dehumanizing apathy.

Take *The Truman Show*, for example. Truman (Jim Carrey), we learn, was quite literally born into a reality show, his birth broadcast and a manufactured environment set up around him thereafter. Everyone around him is an actor; everything is part of a set. He lives in a dome, where the sun can be switched on or off, storms started at the flip of a switch. None of his relationships are real, inasmuch as everyone is hired, scripted, and can be removed at speed if need be. The movie follows his burgeoning realization that the life around him is fake, and his attempt to escape, but the force he must fight is the business interest of The Truman Channel in keeping him. Or, *The Show* offers another dystopian vision of the television industry eschewing ethics and decency simply to get viewers and make money. A dating reality show turns especially dark when, on camera, one contestant shoots the man who rejected her, then tries to kill the woman he chose, only for the host (Josh Duhamel) to jump in the way of the bullet and for her to take her own life. Excited, not appalled, by the buzz created by this event, the producers hire the now-hero host to lead a new show in which people commit suicide on live television. Although the host agrees to the job with visions of handling the suicides respectfully, he soon loses his way, at one point encouraging someone who was reconsidering their decision to indeed go ahead with it. Or, losing any subtlety is *The Running Man*, with its vision of a futuristic game show in which characters race through a variety of challenges, killing each other along the way, a premise off which *The Hunger Games* later more famously riffed.

And yet if the pursuit of ratings at any ethical cost is one charge laid against television, a persistent hucksterism in filling its shows with ads is another. *The Truman Show* often depicts Truman's wife delivering product pitches to the camera, or plays with characters gently moving a conversation so that it can take place in front of an ad. In the similar *EdTV*, ads instead run along the bottom chyron of the show. *Welcome to Me* opens with an ad playing on television. The annoying centrality of ads to television produces many acerbic jokes across the other films too. Harrison Ford's journalist Mike Pomeroy, for instance, complains to executives in *Morning Glory* that "You want me to pander so you can sell erectile dysfunction medication." On *Little Black Book*, where workers at the Kippie Kann Show brand many things with alliterative k's, they jokingly note a need to be aware of "kommercial koncerns." And a character on *Death to Smoochy* offers the instruction that "This is network television, not a sprout farm. You're here to sell sugar and plastic," as the show is framed as existing solely to sell its own merchandise.

Other costs and budgetary restrictions are featured across the films too. *Cinema Verite*'s executives are shown to be remarkably concerned about "burning through film" by filming a family's everyday lives. *Welcome to Me* sees Alice complain about the low quality of her show, leading to a brief lesson on how expensive television is to produce, and thus a call for her to kick in even more to her self-funded show. In *EdTV*, in response to a character's question whether the station did any research on Ed prior to placing him on television, another responds, "Research? We don't have money for coffee filters." Or *The Insider*, as noted above, centers on the real-life case of *60 Minutes'* reporting on tobacco whistleblower Jeffrey Wigand. The item is cut because CBS fears legal reprisal from tobacco giant Brown and Williamson, at a point in time when Westinghouse is about to purchase CBS, and hence when an expensive lawsuit could jeopardize the sale. And for all its comedy and espionage, *Confessions of a Dangerous Mind*'s tale of game show host Chuck Barris (Sam Rockwell) working for the CIA similarly seeds a lot of information and commentary about the business and finances of television production. One can, indeed, learn quite a lot about the television industry as an industry, and about its various pressures, from watching these films.

Admittedly, these films are not alone, as television regularly echoes the same criticisms. *Studio 60 on the Sunset Strip*, *30 Rock*, *UnREAL*, and a slate of other shows about television have satirized television's financial imperatives. What we see as salient, though, is not so much that these films attack along these lines, but rather that they only attack. Missing from almost all of these films is anyone who considers their job an art. A rare exception, *The Truman Show*'s diegetic creator Christof (Ed Harris) may be dressed in all black, wearing a beret, and affecting a stereotypical artist style, with the name to boot, but the joke is that his "art" is someone's life. Wide-eyed optimism and belief in a better way are allowed in films about journalism, but those films focusing on entertainment staunchly refuse to see that entertainment as art—it is simply a business of giving audiences what they want, keeping advertisers happy, staying within budget.

Another exception is to be found in *The TV Set*'s protagonist Mike Klein (David Duchovny), yet his journey is one of capitulation to the industry's artless and crass desires. Klein is writing a more soulful sitcom about a character whose brother committed suicide. Network exec Lenny worries constantly that this will be too depressing for audiences, and she and others force him to make compromise after compromise. Lenny spits out scornfully that Mike's show is "just so fucking artsy and smart" and announces "original scares me a little. You don't wanna be too original." Mike's legitimacy as artist, by contrast, is signaled by and tied to his love of film, as a key point of contention in the plot is that his manager hasn't seen *Taxi Driver* (or "*The Taxi Driver*" as she calls it). Despite his desire not to "pump shit into people's living rooms," since his family needs the money he nevertheless allows his show to be transformed, even becoming the agent of transformation at one point by challenging his director's choice to focus the camera on a homeless man passing by during one scene of dialogue—a choice that is described as filmic and artistic, and hence one that has no room on television, Mike intuits. By the film's end, Mike rationalizes that the history of television (not, we note, of Hollywood more broadly) is full of "thousands" of examples of others similarly sacrificing their visions in order to produce a successful show. His cerebral dramatic sitcom *Wexler Chronicles* thus ends up the broad comedy *Call Me Crazy!*

Especially notable across the 34 films in our sample is that none focus on scripted drama production or producers—instead we see news programs, reality shows, game shows, talk shows, kids shows, morning shows, and the rare sitcom. *The TV Set* comes closest with a dramatic sitcom, but even that is killed at speed. We share others' critique of a vision of television that sees art *only* in "quality drama" (see, for instance, Newman and Levine 2011). But given how widely quality drama is talked of as the most artistic genre in television, and given that most insistences of how "TV is now better than film" reel off a long list of dramas or high-concept sitcoms, we find it telling that the drama, its writers, and its producers are wholly absent from the cinematic portrayal of television. Perhaps the increasing traffic of writers moving between film and scripted drama television left these individuals less keen to satirize their own field, to bite a hand that feeds them, but this increasing traffic should also allow such writers plenty of material and familiarity.

Here, we must then contrast films about television to films about film. Numerous films about film, admittedly, have been eager to satirize the movie industry, meaning there is no contrasting lack of focus on film as also being beholden to metrics, presumed-to-be base desires from audiences, witless producers and "suits" who get in the way, and other trappings of an industry. However, alongside these films are many that focus either completely on film as an art, or that seed these stories about The Industry with artists seeking a better way. Film is full of love letters to film, in short. Movies about movies specialize in offering us struggling, presumed-to-be brilliant artists, and often celebrate the act of picking up a camera. Witness, for instance, *Super 8*'s romantic embrace of filmmaking. Even genres of film that are regularly derided, that could lay themselves open to brutal satire, are often depicted with a great deal of love, as in *Boogie Nights*' depiction of the 1970s porn industry, *Be Kind Rewind*'s focus on fan film, or *Argo*'s depiction of the making of a low-budget science fiction film designed simply to allow spies access to Iran. We also see no shortage of biopics about filmmakers and actors—see for example *The Aviator*, *Hitchcock*, *The Life and Death of Peter Sellers*, *My Week with Marilyn*, *Saving Mr. Banks*, or *Walt Before Mickey*. And even two of the more prominent satires of filmmaking, *The Player* and *Hollywood Ending*, are so filled with stars, nudges, and winks that they are as much celebrations and loving embraces of filmmaking as they are criticisms of it.

Granted, we should expect to see filmmakers write valentines to their craft, so the plethora of such films does not surprise us. However, we first note the contrast that whereas television scripts regularly see "the craft" or "the industry" as a merged Hollywood containing film and television, film valentines are to filmmaking alone. Second, we note a stark contrast between film's apparent inability to show respect or love for television (outside its journalists) and television's own willingness to shower film with love. To draw but two of many examples, both *Watchmen* (2019) and *Stranger Things 3* (2019) open with characters excited to go to and to be in a cinema, the latter incorporating the experience of attending a cinema with one's adolescent friends into its general nostalgic embrace of 1980s media culture. Both scenes sour as threats interrupt the respective films, but in doing so they rely on and recirculate a notion that a movie theater should be a safe space, a glorious escape from the harsh realities of the world outside. To boot, the titles that identify *Stranger Things 3* as such (rather than *Stranger Things*, Season 3) exude a nostalgia for the excesses of film sequelization. Instead of a critique of the film industry's willingness to squeeze good ideas dry, the film sequel is invoked as something beloved to be emulated by television. Third, regardless of whether it is fair or not to ask for film to depict television as an art, we are left with an abundance of valentines to film across both media, yet a dearth of respect for television artistry on film, producing a lop-sided discursive record.

Television on film is only an industry. All the artists, we are led to believe, are on sound stages elsewhere in Hollywood working on films, or sitting on a friend's futon writing the next great film. Television has a few noble *journalists*, but no artists. The lone biopic in our sample is a fictionalized account of Chuck Barris, who is framed as an oddity (creator of *The Dating Game* and rumored to be a spy) rather than as a master of the form. Television's fiction, moreover, is largely seen to exist in manipulation—on quiz shows that are staged (such as *Quiz Show*), or on reality shows that don't show us all the reality (such as *The Show*)—rather than in scripted dramas. Even scripted sitcoms hardly exist in this filmic world, limited to *Bewitched*, *Dickie Roberts: Former Child Star*, *The TV Set*, and *Pleasantville* (none of which see much artistry in the genre, no less). Television documentary is also entirely missing, as are made-for-TV movies. Film's version of television allows for journalism, reality shows, game shows, talk shows, kids shows, and morning shows, but is conspicuously selective in a way that opens the door wide for industrial and ethical critique, while shutting the door to the possibility of art, creativity, and beauty. When television is "good," therefore, it is journalism, since nothing like *Watchmen*, *When They See Us* (2019), *Pose* (2018–), *Unbelievable* (2019), or other narratives that ask audiences to engage thoughtfully with social injustice are anywhere to be seen in the celluloid version of television.

Tawdry, Cheap, Exploitative, and Mind-Deadening

Television is frequently portrayed as tawdry, cheap, exploitative, and mind-deadening. Comments on or about the depicted shows' complete lack of morality, taste, and decency abound. *The TV Set* offers numerous examples, as every note given to its struggling writer and the changes forced upon his show combine to offer a profile of a debased medium. Early on, for instance, network exec Lenny interrupts a more thoughtful discussion of the relative merits of two actresses vying for a role by declaring

> they're both attractive, but Laurel is also really cute and I think that's a good thing. She doesn't let her cuteness get in the way of her hotness and that's really special. To me. Also, I think that Jesse has fake breasts and I believe that over the life of a series the audience can feel that.

Thus, Laurel (Lindsay Sloane) books the role entirely because of her cuteness/hotness. Then, at the end of the film and of the diegetic sitcom's devolution, a clip reel spuriously adds a whiplash sound effect to a brief clip of Laurel's behind, and a fart to an otherwise serious scene. And while *Call Me Crazy!* ends up a mess, all mentions of other shows in the diegetic programming of the film similarly announce their tawdriness—*Slut Wars* and *Infidelity 101*, for example, are both heralded as ratings giants.

A particularly common theme across these films, meanwhile, is about lives chewed up and spit out by a machine that doesn't care about the people in it.

The TV Set's "brilliant," cerebral British import executive Richard McAllister (Ioan Gruffudd) loses his wife and child due to his dedication to the industry, and Lenny consoles him that "spouses are not necessarily a fixture of the schedule," before telling him to get out there and sell some ads. *The Truman Show* and *EdTV* both focus on the damage done to Truman and Ed respectively by shows that never leave them alone. When Truman's "wife" (Laura Linney) decides she must leave the show, producers excitedly pitch another love interest and the possibility of television's first ever on-air conception. *Cinema Verite*'s fictionalization of the real story of *An American Family* likewise shows a family falling apart as the cameras track their every move. All three films contain voices of concern for the reality stars, but those voices notably come not from the executives behind the shows, who express only breathless excitement and overwrought rhetoric for the supposed greatness of what they're doing.

Little Black Book sees Stacey convinced into focusing a series of talk show segments on her boyfriend's exes, tricking each to appear on the show for ulterior motives, but later in the film, Stacey realizes she too is part of the experiment, and that her colleagues put her up to it in order to make her the central, ultimate focus of the segments. *Welcome to Me* offers the distinctly uncomfortable experience of watching a woman exploit herself, by turning her damaged mental health into fodder for a television show, even as the producers keep apathetically cashing their paychecks. The film echoes *The King of Comedy*, another film in which, as Wagner and MacLean argue, "the desire to display the self on television is both self-affirming and a manifestation of insanity" (2008, 164). Even the heroic hero journalist narrative of *The Insider* focuses in large part on the personal costs to Jeffrey Wigand (Russell Crowe) of coming forward as a whistleblower, and on the injustice that it may all have been for nothing, until the interview is finally aired. *Dickie Roberts: Former Child Star* takes the premise that television uses then discards its child stars. *The Show*, meanwhile, and as already noted, follows a host of a reality show that at first features people committing suicide, before actively encouraging them to do so; here, it echoes a suggestion from Chuck Barris at the conclusion of *Confessions of a Dangerous Mind* for a show in which old people would discuss their lives and decide whether or not to commit suicide. And *Slumdog Millionaire* shows a quiz show's zeal for featuring a poor, "slumdog" competitor, until he does well, at which point he is victimized and tortured.

Indeed, the exploitation often becomes actively dangerous. Joining *The Show*'s deaths by exploitation, and *Slumdog Millionaire*'s torture scene, are other films in which characters are killed for sport. In *Deathrow Gameshow*, a television channel allows death-row inmates to participate in demeaning, deadly games on a gameshow. *Hunger Games* and *The Running Man* require contestants to fight to the death for the pleasure of viewers at home. *Network* begins with Harold Beale promising to kill himself, and rather than find him help, the network decides to ride his ratings success to see what happens. Both

Nightcrawler and *15 Minutes* involve tabloid news programs paying large sums for footage of people being killed. A news producer in the former offers, "Think of our news show as a woman running down the street with her throat cut." And *Videodrome* focuses on a television program in which people are tortured and killed. As we have already noted, television is actively dangerous in many of these films, ruining lives in some, actually ending them in others. If horror films such as *The Ring, Poltergeist, Twilight Zone: The Movie, Jingles the Clown, Terror Toons*, and *Videodrome* literalize television as horror villain—*Terror Toons*, for instance, includes a DVD created by Satan himself—films ranging across various other genres still share a general concern for the danger of the medium.

Television *audiences* are dangerous too, though, or so suggest many films. Ratings, after all, are measures of who watches and who doesn't, so in every film in which ratings are bemoaned, audiences and their artless, exploitative, and/or venial desires are similarly suspect. *The Truman Show* notes an activist resistance to the show, but also gives us many images of beguiled and entranced audiences watching Truman's every move. *EdTV* shows Michael Moore (as himself) calling the show a "new low point," while another commentator calls it "a celebration of boobery," but this scene follows one in which we see many audiences compelled by the show, unable or unwilling to turn away. Ron Burgundy's audience turns on him when he reads off a teleprompter, "Go fuck yourselves, San Diego!" but the suggestion is that prior to this he and his equally hapless news team were beloved. The opening monologue to the film even establishes the time period as one in which "people believed everything they heard on TV." Every damning minute of television we see in these films is a minute that is framed as being watched eagerly by millions.

The TV Set throws particular scorn at television audiences. The diegetic success of *Slut Wars* and *Infidelity 101* mocks audiences' base desires. The above-noted whiplash and fart sound effects added spuriously to a clip reel elicit the most approving reactions from a room full of television execs and ad buyers watching the reel. And whenever we see actual audiences, they are denigrated, as when the testing audience is full of slovenly dressed, dead-eyed viewers, a granny who can't work the dial, and a young man who excitedly announces that the dial is "like a volume knob, yo!" Later, when we're told the network is testing other titles, we cut to a scene in which a woman asks a man in a shopping mall about *The Wexler Chronicles, Rhyme or Reason, What Next?*, or *Call Me Crazy!* as potential names, and he guffaws at the latter, saying he likes it because it means the lead is crazy. Buffoons like him, the granny who can't work a dial, and the room who adore fart jokes are posed to be the television audience.

Audience passivity and fandom are also attacked. *Poltergeist* and *Twilight Zone: The Movie* feature children who can't turn away from the box. *Welcome to Me* and *The Cable Guy* present characters whose dysfunctions are framed as related to their obsessive fandom, joining the more famed Rupert Pupkin from *The King of Comedy*—and, more recently, his analogue in *Joker* (2019).

Pleasantville offers protagonist David (Tobey Maguire) the chance to enter his favorite object of obsession, sitcom *Pleasantville*, only for him to find that its "pleasant" world is based on fascist conservatism, and thus to realize that his devotion to the show was misguided. And *Death to Smoochy* posits children as mindless followers of whatever children's shows will put on, ripe for exploitation, "wallets with pigtails" as one character memorably dubs them.

Willy Wonka's Oompa Loompas sum up the dangers of television across *Charlie and the Chocolate Factory*'s adaptations. First in Roald Dahl's 1964 book, Mike Teavee shrinks himself with Wonkavision, leading the Oompa Loompas to sing with moral censure about letting children near "the idiotic thing," television. "We've watched them gaping at the screen," they sing, "They loll and slop and lounge about, / And stare until their eyes pop out," and they decry "they're absolutely drunk / With all the shocking ghastly junk" (Dahl 2016, 161). The 1971 *Willy Wonka and the Chocolate Factory* then offered new lyrics that similarly warn of children losing intelligence by watching instead of reading a book, albeit now milder and significantly shorter. Despite taking numerous liberties with the plot in an effort to update the characters and recode Mike's deadly sin to include video game play, the 2005 *Charlie and the Chocolate Factory* returns to Dahl's original, television-focused invectives. The original song was 98 lines long, but Tim Burton and Danny Elfman truncate the 98-long original version significantly, cutting over two thirds but retaining and revisiting Dahl's most emphatic, television-despising lyrics (capitalized in the original):

> *IT ROTS THE SENSES IN THE HEAD!*
> *IT KILLS IMAGINATION DEAD!*
> *IT CLOGS AND CLUTTERS UP THE MIND!*
> *IT MAKES A CHILD SO DULL AND BLIND*
> *HE CAN NO LONGER UNDERSTAND*
> *A FANTASY, A FAIRYLAND!*
> *HIS BRAIN BECOMES AS SOFT AS CHEESE!*
> *HIS POWERS OF THINKING RUST AND FREEZE!*
> *HE CANNOT THINK – HE ONLY SEES!*

(Dahl 2016, 162)

Heavy television viewers fare poorly across various media, admittedly: Oompa Loompas on the page judge the Mike Teavees of the world as much as their cinematic counterparts. And fans in general are regularly derided across media, as *The Simpsons*' (1989–) Comic Book Guy, *Buffy the Vampire Slayer*'s (1997–2003) geek bad guys, obsessed fan Annie Wilkes in Stephen King's *Misery*, and multiple others serve as lightning rods for media producers' criticisms of engaged fans (see Bennett and Booth 2016). Film is not alone in looking askance at fans, therefore. However, just as film contains many love letters to film, it contains many love letters to cinephilia. Films as varied in genre and source as *Cinema*

Paradiso, Clerks (1994), *Be Kind Rewind, After Life* (1998), *Me and Earl and the Dying Girl* (2015), *Hugo,* and *The Purple Rose of Cairo* see beauty, humor, and charm in cinephilia. But since television is depicted as an artless medium, its audience is prone to be attacked as an artless lot, passively or actively encouraging the medium's worst excesses.

Across film's unflattering portrayals of television audiences we see significant anxiety about television's publicness. As was noted in our Introduction, many of the trade journal or blog pieces that aim to compare film and television, and to protect film against the charges of having lost its little league game with television, exhibit particular concern and disdain for television's popularity. Many of those pieces begin with the "problem" of television being talked about more than film only to then problematize a medium that is talked about so much, regularly insinuating obsession and exploitation. In this regard, therefore, they are bolstering an attack in which films about television are themselves engaged, as both propose an unhealthy relationship between medium and audience that stands in stark contrast to images of cineastes as aesthetically minded, soulful, and contemplative.

Beyond the exploitation and the audience that allow it, though, television is quite simply often portrayed as tawdry and cheap. *EdTV*'s producers note they need more sex in the show. *Morning Glory*'s *DayBreak* includes a story about a Playboy bunny biting a dog. *Anchorman*'s Veronica asks to get more serious work than covering a cat fashion show, and is given an assignment to interview an old woman about her meatloaf recipe. *Welcome to Me*'s Alice likes to talk about masturbation on her show, and at one point neuters a dog on the show. A producer's job in *Nightcrawler* is described as involving little more than telling a woman weather reporter to "turn sideways." And though the officiant at Chuck Barris' wedding in *Confessions of a Dangerous Mind* lists Barris' achievements and television properties, saying they "stimulate and educate and keep us on the edge of our seats," the statement is played for laughs. An odd hypocrisy exists, wherein the films that are charging television with tawdriness, sexism, and exploitation are often including extraneous sex scenes, employing the male gaze in their filming, and the starker, more violent storylines all come in films that could themselves be charged with exploitation for relishing in some of the scenes of violence. Hypocritical or not, though, film's overall framing of television is regularly as tawdry, cheap, and exploitative.

Melodramatic, Familial, and Feminine

Considering films about television mostly from the 1970s through the 1990s, Wagner and MacLean declare that "A dangerous association with femininity is implied in most films about television" (2008, 103). Of *Network*, for instance, they write that "Diana (Faye Dunaway) *is* television" (105), noting the traditional role of femme fatale she plays in threatening Max (William Holden), who in turn "represents imperiled male dominance, equated with reality, love, identity, and nobility—all threatened by television" (107). Studying films predominantly from the 2000s and 2010s, though, we see little change, as television's sins and indiscretions are still regularly framed in feminizing terms. Operating behind many of these films, in particular, is an obvious—if tired— division of the world into the public sphere of interesting and important things, and the domestic sphere of banal and private things, with approbation shown toward television for focusing on the latter instead of the former. The public sphere is envisioned to be one of action, the latter one of melodrama. And though this distinction was by no means created by these films, and has been well documented elsewhere (Fraser 1992; Hartley 1996), television is thus both associated with a feminine realm of melodrama, discussions about emotions and relationships, and domestic interests, and framed pejoratively because of this association.

The stark disparity of televisual genres on show should already indicate to us that a very specific notion of television is on offer. In particular, most of the television genres under analysis are those that are regularly associated with women: talk shows, reality television, game shows, romantic and/or family sitcoms, and morning news shows. Our only exceptions are *Showtime* (about a buddy cop reality show), the few movies about kids shows (a genre that, in fairness, is often feminized too), and the films about evening journalism (some of which, as already noted, offer the few laudatory depictions of television and its potential). Actual television includes many shows about policing, the criminal court system, espionage, clashing clans, epic quests, serial killers, dark forces, friend groups walking around cities, superheroes saving those same cities, the undead, political machinations, and more, regularly voyaging into the public sphere in one form or another, yet none of these forays register in the cinematic landscape of television unless we're looking at journalists. Even reality television, as the most over-represented genre in these films, takes the form of the more sensationalistic reality television of social experiments and bizarre contests, not the form of shows such as *Anthony Bourdain: Parts Unknown* (2013–2018) or such as National Geographic Channel series. Of course, these films were all written, directed, and produced by different people, and were never intended to serve as tiles in a complete mosaic of television; but combined the almost complete lack of interest shown in fictional or reality television that enters the "masculine" public sphere results in a conspicuously warped vision of television that seems determined to feminize the medium (and demeaningly to devalue it on that basis).

Dismissive commentary about reality television abounds in the films about reality in particular. Someone in *Cinema Verite* worries that putting a family's everyday life on television will look like "five hours of passing the salt," while in *EdTV* someone insists that toenail clipping is not exciting television. Reality television, in short, is framed as banal from the outset. What is more, though, it is framed as invasive—passing the salt and clipping one's toenails may be boring for others to watch but they are also private acts, and these films' judgment stems not only from the acts' boringness but from the belief that people deserve to be able to pass the salt or clip their nails without being watched. This violation of privacy is absolutely central to the critiques of *EdTV* and *The Truman Show* in particular, hammered home in countless scenes. Private lives, we're repeatedly told, should be private, both because they're not interesting, and because they're not "meant" to be shared.

Over-sharing is the centerpiece of *Welcome to Me*, as Alice manifests her poor mental health by needing to share everything with an audience. She eats an entire "meatloaf cake," keeping the camera on her the whole time, for example, and she calls up her therapist and has a session with him live (unbeknownst to the therapist). At one point, her entire apartment is transported to the set, an act that is clearly meant to suggest her inability to distinguish between private life and television. And this unwellness is directly feminized as she is at several points called a "crazy bitch." Over-sharing lies at the heart of *Little Black Book*, too, as protagonist Stacey goes searching for her boyfriend's exes. The "twist"—that her colleagues have made her the center of the story without her knowing it—only serves to underline the point that nobody is safe from this invasive reality gaze, and that everyone's secrets and private lives are fodder for television.

The gendered division between television that "matters" and television that doesn't is more clearly delineated in *Morning Glory*, in which the battle over the direction of the show sees the women, on one hand, opt for and prefer the feminized realm of "fluff," while Harrison Ford as paternal, respected journalist, on the other hand, wants a more "nutritious" diet. This diet figures in an argument Rachel McAdams' Fuller has with Ford's Pomeroy: Fuller's brand of light, entertaining news is likened to a donut, while Pomeroy's preferred serious news is likened to bran cereal. By the end of the film, Pomeroy has had to come around, and his surrender is marked by his promise to viewers to show them how to make a beignet, or a donut as he clarifies and underlines. The film, then, is not wholly critical of entertainment news, allowing it a modicum of respect; but Pomeroy's defeat is still framed as somewhat regretful, and the gendered stakes in this battle between donuts/entertainment/fluff/feminized stories and bran/"real news"/masculinized stories is clearly rendered.

If Pomeroy must ultimately accept a position between his old school masculinity and Fuller's feminized realm of televisual success, though, Wagner and MacLean note that *The Cable Guy* offers a more pronounced suggestion of television's feminization as demasculinization. As noted above, Chip's pathological behavior is posed as resulting from the absence of a father in total, and from his single mother leaving him in front of the television all day long. He has thus "had to cobble identifications together through the personalities he saw on television" (2008, 128), and Wagner and MacLean note how often the absurdities of Chip's behavior are framed in feminizing and/or homosexualizing terms, whereas the more clearly masculine Steven (played by Matthew Broderick, his masculine credibility established intertextually from his *Ferris Bueller's Day Off* [1986] fame) is threatened by the obsessive, "womanish" (127) Chip.

The TV Set also frames television as a feminizing medium. We see this at one level in the contrast between the diegetic sitcom's star and David Duchovny. The television show's star Zack (Fran Kranz) is inept at wooing Laurel, oscillating between bumbling and outright creepy, and yet he's framed as the kind of man television loves, while the film's star David Duchovny bathes in an aura of masculine cool (even if, ironically, that star image was born in television show *The X-Files* [1993–2002, 2016–2018]). More generally, though, the film offers a stark gender divide between the men dedicated to art and a message, and the women ruining it. Mike has the vision, Richard is one of only two people who get it, and two other male crew members are shown to at least have artistic leanings. But Mike's vision is destroyed by various women, prominently network exec Lenny and Mike's manager Alice. Even Lenny's sense of what works and what doesn't is revealed to come largely from her 14-year-old daughter's reactions to whatever Lenny shows her, and ultimately Mike's capitulation to their demands is required by his wife, who sees his vision but poses that having money for their new family is more important.

Meanwhile, several of the horror movies situate television's threat in feminized terms to the safety and balance of the home, not the public sphere or world at large. *Poltergeist* sees the domestic space terrorized by the poltergeist that first communes with Carol Ann, then takes her through the television. *Twilight Zone: The Movie* offers an image of a grotesque family ruled over by its television-obsessed child. Much of *The Ring*'s action occurs in the house. Television, in short, is a threat to the home, and to the safety of the family. In the parlance of horror films, the call came from inside the house. Even *Pleasantville*, though by no means a horror film, poses a threat of family sitcoms to the family, and the concluding sign that David learned this lesson is shown when he makes amends with his mother, accepting that no family is perfect.

Many television shows also mock and deride reality television, talk shows, tabloid news programs, and sitcoms as problematic because of their connections to femininity and the home, so these films are not alone in their criticisms. However, television regularly counter-balances these images with depictions of the television or film and television industries as masculinized. Thus, for example, David Duchovny virtually reprises his cool, masculinized Mike Klein from *The TV Set* as struggling artist Hank Moody in *Californication*; *Entourage* sprays testosterone all over Hollywood, making it a misogynist's playground; *Studio 60 on the Sunset Strip* makes heavy use of tropes of masculine creative genius to depict the titular program's diegetic creators Matt Albie and Danny Tripp (Matthew Perry and Bradley Whitford); *The TV Set*'s feminizing Lenny meets her match in *30 Rock*'s heavily masculinized network head Jack Donaghy

(Alec Baldwin); and *BoJack Horseman*'s titular figure follows a journey that is often marked as specifically male, and one of its stronger satirical attacks is on the film and television industries regularly needing to prop up and manicure the egos of many of its male stars. Though rare, too, television has offered a few narratives in which feminization and/or women's presence in the industry are positively valued, as in *BoJack Horseman*, *Better Things*, *GLOW* (2017–), and to a certain extent *UnREAL*. Thus, while television's allegation of feminization is often targeted at specific genres and has occasional moments of reprieve wherein women's presence and impact upon the industry are valued, film offers a more generalized and crude critique of the entire medium as feminine, domestic, and lesser because of it.

Movies about Other Media

In total, then, these films knock television around. It is a threat, artless, tawdry, exploitative, and feminized, where the latter is framed as inherently problematic. What of other media, though? One might expect that in an era of proliferating channels, platforms, devices, and options for entertainment, media might be inclined toward competitiveness and toward rivalries. In strict economic terms, such a strategy would be self-defeating for studios that often rely upon television revenues as much as on box office returns, even for their films, but we might expect writers and directors to engage in some low-level defense of what they perceive to be their field, craft, and realm. We might also expect writers and directors simply not to understand other fields, crafts, and realms, and hence to handle them clumsily. Do all other media suffer at the level of depiction? Though we do not have the data to answer this question with anywhere near the detail or resolution that we have drawn upon to answer the question of how movies portray television, we are struck by the comparative regard and respect we see directed toward several other media.

Book reading and literature in particular seem generally to be depicted with considerable respect in a variety of films. *The Guernsey Literary and Potato Peel Pie Society* (2018), for instance, offers a recent depiction of a book club formed in Guernsey following World War II. Based on a novel of the same name, the film portrays the book club lovingly, as a site for personal improvement, community-building, and healing for those involved in it. More famously, *Dead Poets Society* (1989) garnered Best Picture, Best Actor, and Best Director Oscar nominations for its tale of a private high school teacher inspiring his students to love literature. Also released in 1989, *Lean on Me* similarly offered another magic teacher tale, loosely based on the real-life experiences of inner-city high school teacher Joe Louis Clark. 1995's *Renaissance Man* introduced another magic teacher, this time working at an army training base. This message of books providing hope and healing is also on show in *The Shawshank Redemption* (1994), in which our protagonist Andy finds solace in the prison library (indeed, consider how commonly prison movies signal who are the "good guys" by showing them working in the prison library). Andy is not alone in letting books whisk him away, though, as the joy of getting "lost" in or enveloped by a good book is literalized in some other films, as in *The Never Ending Story* (1984) and *The Princess Bride* (1987). Meanwhile, one finds no shortage of films about literary figures, told in ways that hold the figures up, such as *Wilde* (1997), *Shakespeare in Love* (1998), *The Hours* (2002), *Sylvia* (2003), *Finding Neverland* (2004), *Capote* (2005), *The Brothers Grimm* (2005), *Becoming Jane* (2007), or *Bright Star* (2009). And even if not entering literature, movies' encounters with book stores can be loving, often quite literally, given the oversized role that book stores have often played as backdrops for meet-cutes and for burgeoning romance in romantic comedies—see, for instance, *Funny Face* (1957), *When Harry Met Sally* (1989), *You've Got Mail* (1998), *Notting Hill* (1999), *Before Sunset* (2004), *Dan in Real Life* (2004), and *They Came Together* (2014).

As alluded to earlier in the chapter, the newspaper industry often glows on film. Even when movies focus on corruption or malfeasance (witness *Citizen Kane* [1941] most famously), that corruption is painted as so egregious precisely because the general hopes expressed for newspaper journalism's potential to serve as the nation's beating heart are huge. As might be suggested by Hollywood's liberal use of comics as well for ideas, comics also do well. Even beyond drawing stories from comics, numerous comic book adaptations have very lovingly aimed to transfer or cite comic book style in ways that implicitly hold up and honor the medium and its artistry—most notably *Sin City* (2005), *300* (2007), *Scott Pilgrim vs. The World* (2010), and *Spider-Man: Into the Spider-Verse* (2018)—while comic book artists are themselves in films including *Crumb* (1994) and *American Splendor* (2003).

Radio has also fared well. Even when not the star of a film, radio often gets to play the voice and resolve of a nation in many World War II films, where speeches by Winston Churchill or Franklin Delano Roosevelt are shown as broadcast around England or the United States respectively. Witness, for instance, *Pearl Harbor* (2001), in which FDR's "A Day Which Will Live in Infamy" declaration of war against Japan carries over a montage of images of people suffering in Pearl Harbor, and people of different walks of life listening earnestly, tethered to their radios. Radio once again plays the voice of the nation in *The King's Speech* (2010), a film that is ostensibly about George VI overcoming his stuttering to lead England, but whose opening close-ups of radio microphones underscores is as much a tale about the power of radio. The film begins with George needing to make a speech to a stadium and live on radio, but as we hear radio announcers set up the importance of the address, we see a POV shot of him approaching the radio microphone up some stairs, and hence taking a low angle that allows the microphone to preside over him. He then looks out at the crowd, the out-of-focus microphone blocking his view. Radio obstructs his relationship with the nation, we're told visually, and yet in his radio speech that concludes the film, we now see his face reflected back off the shiny microphone, as the two have become one. He can now talk to the nation, it's suggested, and radio has made this possible.

Meanwhile, radio features prominently in a handful of other films, variously bringing information, messages of national importance, or simply fun to the masses. These include *Good Morning, Vietnam* (1987), memorably starring Robin Williams as real-life Vietnam radio personality Adrian Cronauer entertaining American troops; *Talk to Me* (2007), a biopic starring Don Cheadle as talk show personalist and activist Ralph "Petey" Greene; *Radio Days* (1987), Woody Allen's nostalgic look at the Golden Age of Radio; and *Do the Right Thing* (1989), in which Samuel L. Jackson's Mister Señor Love Daddy regularly speaks for and to the community. Radio on film is not a complete love affair—*Talk Radio* (1988), for instance, follows an abrasive, often hateful, radio host—but it receives nothing like the cold treatment its broadcast peer television does.

The music industry has certainly been satirized on film—from *This Is Spinal Tap* (1984) to *Frank* (2014)—but one need not struggle to find an abundance of romanticized depictions. Just as bookstores bring characters together in romantic comedies, record stores have regularly served as the fount springs of coolness, youthful edge, and friendship, as in *Empire Records* (1995), *Human Traffic* (1999), *High Fidelity* (2000), *Scott Pilgrim vs. The World*, *Good Vibrations* (2013), and *Hearts Beat Loud* (2018). Or films about the music industry and/or famous musicians are far too numerous to number, including recently *Yesterday* (2019), which imagines a world in which nobody else has heard The Beatles, allowing Jack (Himesh Patel) to take credit for their songs; *Bohemian Rhapsody* (2018), a biopic about Queen's Freddie Mercury; *A Star Is Born* (2018), the remake of a story of a seasoned musician who discovers a brilliant young talent; and *The High Note* (2020), about a personal assistant who longs to become a producer herself. Film and music are as reliant on each other as industries as are film and television, but film's regularly reverential, nostalgic, romanticized, and celebratory depiction of music and the music industry could thus serve as a film negative for the more suspicious, conflictual, critical, and pejorative images that film tends to offer of television. Films about the music industry also contrast with films about television in sheer number, as the music industry features prominently across film: IMDb, for instance, can include a fan's list of the "Best 100 Music Movies" (omidpacino 2012) or *Rolling Stone* can list, more specifically, the "30 Best Music Biopics of All Time" (Kreps et al. 2016), when there are nowhere near 100 films about television of any quality, and nowhere near 30 television biopics of any quality.

Newer digital media, from the Internet to video games to social media, have often been criticized on film. From *Existenz* (1999), a horror film about the dangers of virtual reality, to *Gamer* (2009), in which humans can control others' actions in a massive game called *Society*, and *Trust* (2010), in which a teenage girl is groomed for sexual abuse online, the threats of losing one's identity and sense of reality, and/or the dangers of digital media to one's safety center many a cautionary cinematic tale. The dangers that lurk behind the *business* of such networks of identity feature prominently in several films, too, from science fiction action film *Ready Player One* (2018) to Mark Zuckerberg biography, *The Social Network* (2010). But digital media are regularly the deus ex machina that allow heroes to "hack into the mainframe" and save the day, from *War Games* (1983) to *Jurassic Park* (1993), *Independence Day* (1996) to a variety of other films across genres. The sheer fun, style, and coolness of video games are on show elsewhere, too, starting with *Tron* (1982), in which a programmer ends up inside a computer, needing to escape it via highly stylized battles, and *The Last Starfighter* (1984), in which aliens get a teen to pilot a starship via game controls, and leading up to *Wreck It Ralph* (2012), an animated film that shows us the lives of a video game arcade's various digital characters at night, and its sequel *Ralph Breaks the Internet* (2018), in which they go online. The Internet itself has also brought together lovers in *You've Got Mail* (1998) and *Must Love Dogs* (2005), and thus as much as it appears as a den of catfishing rapists in some films, the Internet can also play a more innocent, benevolent matchmaker on film.

As this quick survey should show, one can find flattering, loving, and/or ennobling depictions of almost every other medium on film. Those depictions exist alongside peers that might criticize or outright villainize the medium, and a closer examination would surely reveal more determined patterns cutting across the totality of films about any given medium. But relevant for our purposes here is that better depictions of other media are far easier to find than of television. When television finds itself on film, we're either seeing a great journalist (who must fight their corporate bosses and "the system"), or we're seeing a depiction that at "best" is slightly unflattering (as in a film such as *Bewitched*), at worst is deeply unflattering (as in a film such as *The Truman Show*). Whether movies frame television this way through ignorance, a sense of rivalry, or both, this section's survey and its highlighting of several films that approach literary culture, the newspaper industry, comics, radio, the music industry, and digital media with more kindness, at least at times, suggest that television occupies a very particular place in that ignorance and/or competitive disdain.

Conclusion

As we write this, film and television have shared nine decades together in the United States. Young's survey of film's treatment of television in the latter's nascency, Wagner and MacLean's focus on film about television ranging from 1957 to the turn of the millennium, and our own survey of many films about television from the first two decades of the 21st century, though, struggle to find a single instance of an American film looking upon television outside journalism with much respect, much less with truly loving eyes, and instead document a long and ever-amassing history of suspicion and derision. Fred Rogers biopic *A Beautiful Day in the Neighborhood* (2019) might seem to come closest to offering a true, sustained exception of someone other than a journalist using television to do good, yet Rogers is framed as an utter anomaly—not just on television but in life—and as a unique figure, and the film focuses on journalist Lloyd Vogel (Matthew Rhys) learning from Rogers, not on Rogers' masterful use of television per se. Surely other exceptional moments of representing television exist, though, and our method of analysis didn't focus on one-off lines or scenes in films otherwise not at all about television, where perhaps some more respect is awarded television in passing. Or perhaps not. But the general rule has been well established and is hewn to with remarkable consistency.

We see similar representations offered repeatedly, even as the two industries have shared physical space with one another. Hollywood, Burbank, and the greater LA area are home and workplace to many execs, writers, actors, directors, producers, and all the below-the-line laborers who work on both. Actors increasingly move between the two media, as the list even of "A list" movie stars who have never worked in television dwindles, and as more writers and other creative talent similarly enjoy careers that span the two media (as we'll discuss in Chapter 4). And even at an everyday level, we should surely therefore expect "movie people" to be talking to "television people" all the time, hearing their stories as they watch their kids play soccer together, meeting through mutual friends, chatting to neighbors. And yet the world of television that is produced in LA is largely absent from or only partially rendered in films—gone are people working on television movies and on primetime scripted shows (save the rare sitcom), replaced by reality, game show, and talk show hosts and participants. Absent, too, is anyone considered a television artist. Even as television production has increased, even as its prestige has risen, television's artists are eerily missing from cinematic representations of television. Instead, as we've shown, when television goes to the movies as subject, it is often tawdry, exploitative, melodramatic, dangerous corporate plastic. Movies are not alone in representing television this way, so we are not arguing that they are the primary source of such images. But for a medium that shares space with and that in many ways is a colleague, peer, and friend of television, collectively film more often treats television like a particularly odious rival. In doing so, discursive distance is built between two creative industries, just as each is characterized and caricaturized as its own distinct entity.

3

TELEVISION STORIES GO TO THE MOVIES

Strategies of Adaptation

While the American film industry has long been centered on adaptation of novels, biographies, Broadway musicals, comic-book heroes, and other movies, recent decades have seen a rise in movies adapting television shows. Conversely, numerous television shows in recent years have adapted popular movies. But if the old (and highly problematic) adage, meme-ified throughout the Web, is that "the book was better than the film," what relationship are such adaptations and their promoters constructing between television and film? What is deemed possible in a film that wasn't in a television show, and vice versa? What is seemingly expected in one medium while not in the other? What do adapters need to add or subtract to ensure their adaptation thrives in a new media environment, and what does this tell us about their understanding of that environment? This chapter addresses these questions.

Cross-media adaptations are rich sites for exploring what is deemed possible and/or most appropriate in either medium, and hence for probing discursive constructions of what a medium "can," "cannot," or "should" do. Quite practically, a lot of decisions to adapt a television show into a film or vice versa will have been made with a desire to squeeze more cash out of a successful story. But the decision to change media is relevant: if a show was beloved on television, why not just produce more of that show, or reboot it as another television show; and given how many reboots populate cinematic culture in the 21st century—many of them wildly successful—if a film is beloved, why not just make another film? While in some cases the decision to cross over may have been made precisely with a desire to work around a former obstacle (such as a network that had tired of a show), the extra labor and challenges required to shift media beg the question of what the creative team hoped they would gain from the change. Admittedly, that question is hard to answer, requiring us to listen to creators' discussions about their work and somehow divine what was "really" intended versus what is simply being proposed for public relations strategy. An easier and more interesting question to answer is what do cross-media adaptations themselves suggest about perceived capacities and specialties of each medium? What can a show "finally" do now that it is a film? What has clearly been perceived necessary of the process of adapting film to television, or television to film?

We should avoid concluding too much from any single adaptation, for a whole host of large or mundane considerations may actually stand behind a decision to change this or that about a story, to focus on this or that element, and so forth. But recent years have delivered many television-to-film adaptations, and numerous film-to-television adaptations, thereby allowing us to look for patterns across them. In an effort to scour for such patterns, we watched the films and at least the pilots, often more, of television shows from many television-to-film adaptations of the last two decades:

Television Program	Film
21 Jump Street (1987–1991)	*21 Jump Street* (2012)
The A-Team (1983–1987)	*The A-Team* (2010)
Da Ali G Show (2000)	*Ali G Indahouse* (2002)
The Alvin Show (1961–1962) & *Alvin and the Chipmunks* (1983–1990)	*Alvin and the Chipmunks* (2007)
Avatar: The Last Airbender (2005–2008)	*The Last Airbender* (2010)
Baywatch (1989–2001)	*Baywatch* (2017)
Bewitched (1964–1972)	*Bewitched* (2005)
Charlie's Angels (1976–1981)	*Charlie's Angels* (2000)
Dark Shadows (1966–1971)	*Dark Shadows* (2012)
Dora the Explorer (2000–2014)	*Dora and the Lost City of Gold* (2019)
The Dukes of Hazzard (1979–1985)	*The Dukes of Hazzard* (2005)
Entourage (2004–2011)	*Entourage* (2015)
The Equalizer (1985–1989)	*The Equalizer* (2014)
Firefly (2002)	*Serenity* (2005)
Get Smart (1965–1970)	*Get Smart* (2008)
GI Joe: A Real American Hero (1983–1986)	*GI Joe: The Rise of Cobra* (2009)
Hannah Montana (2005–2007)	*Hannah Montana: The Movie* (2009)
The Honeymooners (1955–1956)	*The Honeymooners* (2005)
Inspector Gadget (1982–1986)	*Inspector Gadget* (1999)
I Spy (1965–1968)	*I Spy* (2002)
Land of the Lost (1974–1976)	*Land of the Lost* (2009)
Lizzie McGuire (2001–2004)	*The Lizzie McGuire Movie* (2003)
The Man from UNCLE (1964–1968)	*The Man from UNCLE* (2015)
Miami Vice (1984–1990)	*Miami Vice* (2006)
Mission: Impossible (1966–1973)	*Mission: Impossible* (1996)
My Little Pony: Friendship Is Magic (2010–)	*My Little Pony: The Movie* (2017)
Scooby-Doo (1969–1976)	*Scooby-Doo* (2002)
Sex and the City (1998–2004)	*Sex and the City* (2008)

(Continued)

Television Program	Film
The Simpsons (1989–)	*The Simpsons Movie* (2007)
South Park (1997–)	*South Park: Bigger, Longer, and Uncut* (1999)
The Smurfs (1981–1989)	*The Smurfs* (2011)
Star Trek (1966–1969)	*Star Trek* (2009)
Starsky and Hutch (1975–1979)	*Starsky and Hutch* (2004)
Teen Titans Go! (2012–)	*Teen Titans Go! To the Movies* (2018)
Tim and Eric Awesome Show, Great Job! (2007–2010)	*Tim and Eric's Billion Dollar Movie* (2012)
Transformers (1984–1987)	*Transformers* (2007)
Veronica Mars (2004–2007, 2019)	*Veronica Mars* (2014)

However, we wanted to be sure we weren't simply documenting changes made to all adaptations, and thus we found it important to watch and similarly document film-to-television adaptations, too. We found in the process that a two-part focus provided a more dynamic picture of what is deemed possible in each media environment, allowing us to examine not only how television shows go to the movies but how television goes to the movies for inspiration. As such, we also watched:

Film	Television Program
12 Monkeys (1995)	*12 Monkeys* (2015–2018)
About a Boy (2002)	*About a Boy* (2014–2015)
Psycho (1960)	*Bates Motel* (2013–2017)
Black Dynamite (2009)	*Black Dynamite* (2011–2015)
Clerks (1994)	*Clerks: The Animated Series* (2000–2001)
The Dark Crystal (1982)	*The Dark Crystal: Age of Resistance* (2019–)
Legion (2010)	*Dominion* (2014–2015)
How to Train Your Dragon (2010)	*Dreamworks Dragons* (2012–2018)
The Exorcist (1973)	*The Exorcist* (2016–2018)
Fargo (1996)	*Fargo* (2014–)
Friday Night Lights (2004)	*Friday Night Lights* (2006–2011)
From Dusk Till Dawn (1996)	*From Dusk Till Dawn: The Series* (2014–2016)
Manhunter (1986) and *Silence of the Lambs* (1991)	*Hannibal* (2013–2015)
Hotel Transylvania (2012)	*Hotel Transylvania: The Series* (2017–)
Kung Fu Panda (2008)	*Kung Fu Panda: Legends of Awesomeness* (2011–2016)
The Lion King (1994)	*The Lion Guard* (2016–)
Minority Report (2002)	*Minority Report* (2015)
Napoleon Dynamite (2004)	*Napoleon Dynamite* (2012)

Film	Television Program
Nikita (1990)	*Nikita* (2010–2013)
Tangled (2010)	*Rapunzel's Tangled Adventure* (2017–2020)
Stargate (1994)	*Stargate SG-1* (1997–2007)
Star Wars saga (1977+)	*Star Wars: Clone Wars* (2008–2020)
Teen Wolf (1985)	*Teen Wolf* (2011–2017)
Terminator (1984)	*Terminator: The Sarah Connor Chronicles* (2008–2009)
Westworld (1973)	*Westworld* (2016–)
What We Do in the Shadows (2014)	*What We Do in the Shadows* (2019–)

As these lists might suggest, we use the term "adaptation" somewhat loosely to allow room for reboots, reimaginings, and continuations that involve the same cast and many other creative personnel. The movement of stories from film to television and vice versa cannot be accounted for via theories of adaptation alone, demanding broader consideration as a process of media franchising in which intellectual properties travel and multiply across different markets and contexts of production over long periods of time (Johnson 2013). However, the concept of adaptation continues to prove useful in research oriented around media franchising, helping us to focus on the formal, narrative, and stylistic affordances perceived to be inherent to the individual media that share these complex and ongoing industry relationships. Adaptation can help us perceive some of the discursive boundary work that unfolds within media franchising. Slightly adapting Linda Hutcheon's definition of adaptations, then, we consider them as "deliberate, announced, and extended revisitations *or continuations* of prior works" (2006, xiv, words in italics added). These are not exhaustive lists, but were constructed to feature many of the more prominent adaptations of the last two decades. Some pairings both adapt a prior book (as with *About a Boy*, *Hannibal*, and *Friday Night Lights*, for instance), but whenever we saw ample evidence that the second adaptation was aware of and aimed also to adapt the first adaptation, we felt safe including it. And we should note that the watching and interpreting "we" here includes Nicholas Benson, who worked for two summers as a part-time research assistant for us. Benson watched many of these, highlighting specific elements for us to rewatch, and even suffering through *Entourage* for us. The authorial voice remains Derek's and Jonathan's, but we benefited remarkably from Benson's astute, thoughtful, probing observations made as he watched.

The last two decades of American media history, though, offer another gift to anyone interested in adaptation and cross-media movements in the form of the many films and television shows that *both* adapt comic books, most notably from Marvel Comics and DC Comics. These add an interesting spin to questions about conversion and adaptation, given that the characters and often plot elements within such adaptations began in another medium altogether. Long before any Avenger or member of the Justice League of America graced the silver screen or held their look of noble determination in a paused freeze-frame on one's television, they existed in Marvel and DC comic books. We could ask what the stories of their translation to film and television tell us about the discursive construction of distinction between comics and film, comics and television; but that is not our focus here, of course. Rather, we decided it would be productive to consider how Marvel and DC adaptations themselves spoke to what was possible in each medium, which were heroes and stories "best" for television, which for film, and how such stories "needed" to be told in each medium. Thus, we also examined the Marvel Cinematic Universe and its televisual counterparts of the 2000s and 2010s, some of Sony's and Fox's Marvel films and television shows, and DC's films and television shows. Given the thousands of pages of source material that had already mapped out not only many potential storylines, but often many alternate versions and interpretations of characters, Marvel, DC, and their partners in film and television had a lot to work with. What did they decide to send to film and what to television? Conversely, what was taken up by those in film and those in television?

Marvel Studios' films should be familiar to many readers of this book, as they have dominated the box office for the past decade. Beginning with Paramount Pictures' *Iron Man* (2008), *Iron Man 2* (2010), *Thor* (2011), and *Captain America: The First Avenger* (2011), and Universal Pictures' *The Incredible Hulk* (2008), four of the key Avengers were given their own standalone films before uniting in Walt Disney Studios Motion Pictures' *The Avengers* (2012). Disney then took the reins for *Iron Man 3* (2013), *Thor: The Dark World* (2013), *Captain America: The Winter Soldier* (2014), *Guardians of the Galaxy* (2014), *Avengers: Age of Ultron* (2015), *Ant-Man* (2015), *Captain America: Civil War* (2016), *Doctor Stranger* (2016), *Guardians of the Galaxy Vol. 2* (2017), *Thor: Ragnarok* (2017), *Black Panther* (2018), *Avengers: Infinity War* (2018), *Ant-Man and the Wasp* (2018), *Captain Marvel* (2019), and *Avengers: Endgame* (2019), with Sony Pictures adding *Spider-Man: Homecoming* (2017) and *Spider-Man: Far From Home* (2019) along the way. Having let the spider out of the bag, we also considered Sony's three *Spider-Man* films from 2002, 2004, and 2007, and its two *Amazing Spider-Man* films from 2012 and 2014 (none of which are part of the Marvel Cinematic Universe). In the same time frame, Marvel Television and ABC Studios added to the MCU franchise by producing *Agents of SHIELD* (2013–2020), *Agent Carter* (2015–2016), and *Inhumans* (2017) for ABC; *Daredevil* (2015–2018), *Jessica Jones* (2015–2019), *Luke Cage* (2016–2018), *Iron Fist* (2017–2018), *The Defenders* (2017), and *The Punisher* (2017–2019) for Netflix; *Runaways* (2017–2019) for Hulu; *Marvel's Cloak and Dagger* (2018–2019) for Freeform; and more are in development for Disney+ as we write. Twentieth Century Fox, meanwhile, had sole rights to the X-Men and Fantastic Four, producing its own healthy slate of films, of which we considered the *X-Men* films of 2000, 2003, 2006, 2009,

2011, 2013, 2014, 2016, 2017, and 2019. For television, we considered their *Legion* (2017–2019) and *The Gifted* (2017–2019).

DC's own adapted movies in the 21st century began with *Catwoman* in 2004, but we considered their DC Extended Universe (DCEU) titles, starting officially with *Man of Steel* (2013), and followed by *Batman v. Superman: Dawn of Justice* (2016), *Suicide Squad* (2016), *Wonder Woman* (2017), *Justice League* (2017), *Aquaman* (2018), *Shazam!* (2019), and *Birds of Prey* (2020). On television, following the successful *Smallville* (2001–2011), came *Birds of Prey* (2002–2003), with both launching on the WB Network and the former shifting to the CW when WB merged with UPN. The CW then rolled out several more, including *Arrow* (2012–2020), *The Flash* (2014–), *Legends of Tomorrow* (2016–), *Black Lightning* (2018–), *Swamp Thing* (2019), and *Batwoman* (2019–), all of which exist in shared diegetic space, dubbed the Arrowverse, and joined by *Supergirl* after its initial season on CBS starting in 2015. DC has other titles, of course, but we capped our viewing there.

Alongside these many films and television shows, we also studied the US pre-release posters advertising for each. As paratexts, posters are central to the early framing of a text (Gray 2010). In the case of an adaptation, posters provide evidence both of how the studios are approaching the adaptation—which elements do they think matter most?—and of how they imagine audiences to be approaching the adaptation—what appeals do they think will matter most to us?

What Adaptation Says about Media Capacities

Adaptation studies is a thriving field existing at the crossroads of literary, theater, art, film, and media/cultural studies. Far more numerous in that literature, though, are studies of adaptations from novels or plays to film (see, for instance, Corrigan 2012; Leitch 2009; Naremore 2000; Stam and Raengo 2005), of films to other films (see, for instance, Loock and Verevis 2012; Smith 2016; Verevis 2006; Wee 2014), and increasingly of transnational television adaptation/remaking (see, for instance, Fung and Zhang 2011; Hilmes 2013; Mikos and Perrotta 2011; Perkins and Verevis 2015). With adaptation studies, though, relatively little has been written on moves from television to film, film to television, and much that has been written either exists in the trenches of specifics and/or says little about the narrative's medial move (see, for instance, Grossman 2017; Loock 2014; McMahon-Coleman 2014; Scahill 2016). Constantine Verevis distinguishes between two types of film-to-television adaptation. The first

> attempts to create a circuit between a generation (or two) of viewers who encountered the tele-series as first runs and/or reruns through the 1960s and beyond, and a younger generation of filmgoers—children or grandchildren of the first group—who may have little or no knowledge

of the original tele-series but whose narrative image of that property is developed through the film's promotion,

while the second "revises 60-minute prime-time television dramas as big-budget, high concept remakes" (2015, 130), but his article on the topic is two pages and hence cuts short on this note.

Linda Hutcheon's *A Theory of Adaptation* (2006) similarly has little to say specifically about moves from television to film or vice versa. After classifying adaptations into those that move between or within the realms of "telling," "showing," and "interacting," Hutcheon surmises that film and television are both predominantly "showing" media, and both "relatively realist media" at that, and thus her attention is drawn elsewhere: "What happens," she continues, "when a manifestly artificial performance form like an opera or a musical is adapted to the screen?" (46), and with that she moves on. However, as her title promises, the book offers some general contextualizing commentary on adaptation that might help us set the scene for moves from film to television, television to film.

Hutcheon's approach is helpful for eschewing a crude technological determinism that she notes as another haunting figure in the history of adaptation studies and discourse. Hutcheon's categorization into telling, showing, and interacting risks its own determinism, which she variously submits to or fights at different points in her book, but it at least walks back from the overly simplistic McLuhanesque tendency to believe "the medium is the message" (see McLuhan 1964). She examines numerous clichés of adaptation—that only the telling mode can adequately render both intimacy and distance in point of view, for example (52–6)—and though she explores how some adaptations follow the clichés, in dubbing them clichés, she frames their nonnecessity. Hutcheon thus illustrates that pure technological determinism is unhelpful. Technological determinism allows for cute aphorisms, but ignores entirely the agency of artists, creators, industries, or even audiences. Hutcheon wisely notes, though, that some adaptors may be motivated precisely by the *challenge* of turning a seemingly most novelesque novel into a play or film, or so forth. Writing of the many adaptations of *Les Liaisons dangereuses*, for instance, she concludes that "the formal difficulties in dramatizing [the epistolary novel] are more likely to be seen as challenges than as disincentives for adapters" (40). The initial creative move in some adaptations may be an attempt to buck and refuse technological determinism.

Nevertheless, Hutcheon's discussion of telling, showing, and interacting points out that technologies and media will of course have some limiting factors. When a novel does not show pictures and a film is full of them, or when an opera is performed to those in seats watching while a video game is played with a controller in hands, we must allow for some limiting formal constraints. This chapter is not about those constraints, though, in part because film and television already flow into each other in technological and medial terms—as noted in our Introduction, many of the films we've all seen were on televisions. As Hollywood makes evermore sequels, and invests in evermore franchises, even the nominal difference that films are shorter in total running time, and hence over quicker than television shows, can be questioned. Freed from the requirement that episodes be 22 or 45 minutes, some television episodes on streaming and premium cable channels can now run as long as an average feature length film, while many film shorts run far shorter than the average television episode. But beyond changing rules and possibilities, both media are varied enough to provide us plenty of examples of texts that work against "rules" we might imagine to be medium-imposed: each season of *24* (2001–2010), for instance, covers just one day, meaning that the vast majority of films cover more time in 90 or so minutes than do the almost 17 hours of a *24* season. Or, while television might seem to allow more capacity for character development and identification, given all its time, some of media's most enduring, beloved characters are filmic.

Hutcheon follows much of adaptation studies by being primarily interested in form, but her approach is also helpful in repeatedly gesturing to a prevalent discursive framing of relative medial "value" that surrounds and envelopes both adaptation studies and public discussions of adaptation. She notes how often discussions of adaptations presume and rely upon a hierarchical ladder of which media are "best," which are "worst," with intense approbation attending all downward moves. She observes, for instance, that adaptations from novels or plays to film often suffer from film being considered lower and lesser than novels or plays, and she cites Charles Newman calling an adaptation of literature to film or television a move to "a willfully inferior form of cognition" (2006, cited on 3). In short, then, and even though this is not the point of her book, Hutcheon shows discussion of adaptation to be a rich site for the discursive positioning of different media, for the creation and reification of hierarchies of value and meaning imposed upon media. Certainly, while film may live on a supposedly lower rung of the cultural ladder than do novels, as the rest of our book shows, when film is instead pitted against television, it has regularly been presumed to exist on a higher rung. Television has long been derided as a lesser, "feminine" (Huyssen 1986), working class medium, and too often film's higher place on the ladder has been secured in relation to dismissive looks down upon television. Thus we should expect to see that moves from film to television will be seen as "downward" moves, while moves from television to film may be seen as graduations or promotions of a sort. And yet, as Michael Newman and Elana Levine (2011) powerfully document, some television producers, scholars, and fans have similarly proven themselves keen to distinguish between "quality television" and regular or ordinary television in order to rescue a place for *some* television, albeit at the expense of most television—witness, HBO's infamous slogan, "It's not television, it's HBO." Within such an environment—and they date this process to the 2000s and 2010s, concurrently with our sample—adaptations from film to serialized, "quality" television may be expected to fare better than before.

In considering discursive positionings, though, we should expect adaptations and the discussions about them to tell us more than simply which media are seen as best or worst. What other discursive boundary work is performed by adaptations? For the rest of the chapter, we look to television-to-film, film-to-television adaptations, and comics-to-either-film-or-television adaptations to see what cultural systems surround film and television. Working off the presumption that a good adaptation can overcome almost any formal "rule" that might be seemingly imposed by a medium, we consider that across multiple adaptations we will see patterns start to form about what is or isn't "supposed" to be on film or on television, about what a move from one medium to the other "requires," and hence about the discursive, not formal, boundaries that separate the two media. Hutcheon notes an analog in genetic adaptation, a "process by which something is fitted to a given environment" (31), so what does this tell us about those environments, and about the cultural "atmosphere" of each medium? Or if following Leo Braudy, the remake is a "meditation on the continuing historical relevance [...] of a particular narrative," "what its makers and (they hope) its audiences consider to be *unfinished cultural business*" (1998, 331), what parts of that business are repeatedly envisioned as being televisual, what parts filmic?

Commonalities of Adaptation

We begin with some observations about commonalities between cross-media movements and adaptations. First, many adaptations aim to offer additional backstory, prequel, and deep history. In this they follow a rich history of beloved cinematic sequels that go backward to go forward—think here of *The Empire Strikes Back* (1980) telling us that Vader is Luke's father, or of *The Godfather II* (1974) returning to Vito Corleone's past. Regardless of whether a story was moving to the movies or to television, many of the adaptations we considered aimed to offer backstory, or even an origin story. For example, television shows *Bates Motel* and *Hannibal* give us Norman Bates and Hannibal Lecter before they were infamous, while films ranging from *The A-Team* and *GI Joe: The Rise of Cobra* to *Starsky and Hutch* and *Inspector Gadget* offer origin stories of their heroes' fame.

Second, across all the adaptations we examined, many engaged in temporal updating and/or commentary. Those adaptations of properties from an earlier decade or moment in history that stayed in that moment frequently relished the opportunity to poke fun at the excesses and oddities of that moment, while those that moved the story to the current day often worked hard to make that story seem fresh and contemporary. *Bewitched* and *Psycho* each leave the 1960s, for instance, while *Charlie's Angels* and *The Exorcist* each leave the 1970s, and

Miami Vice and *Teen Wolf* each leave the 1980s. Meanwhile, *Starsky and Hutch* stays in the 1970s to make fun of it, and though none of the television shows exist largely to parody the decade of their film original (as will be discussed later), across both media some of the originals' more problematic identity politics, and active racism and sexism, are "cleaned up" for modern day. Ralph Kramden's notorious "to the moon, Alice" threat on *The Honeymooners*, thus becomes an inviting "I'll take you to the moon, Alice," in an all-Black remake. Or, moving from film to television, *Stargate* gains women characters in *Stargate SG-1*. Following Braudy's notion of "unfinished business," surely a key motivation of many adaptations, regardless of medium, is to comment upon and revisit the original's politics (see, for example, Butter 2015; Hassler-Forest and Nicklas 2015; Nielsen 1994). This is not to say they all "improve" per se— *The Last Airbender* notoriously whitewashes the story (Lopez 2012), and while *The Dukes of Hazzard* film tries to distance itself from the embedded racism of the show's iconic car, the General Lee, sporting a Confederate flag, its Daisy is also even more of an object than she was in the television show. But a general, if light, attempt to "update" scenery, style, and sensibility is evident across many adaptations.

Indeed, and finally, all but the most boring adaptations aim to play somewhat with form, even if only to justify their existence. Daniel Herbert states that adaptations "retell the story or transpose some crucial aspect of an existing text in another medium" (2017, 26), so the challenge for an adaptation's creative team lies in working out what is or are the "crucial aspect(s)" while engaging in some play with style and details, in order to allow for some form of innovation and novelty for audiences—a play of difference that is at the heart of contemporary franchising imperatives (see Johnson 2013). Thus we approached these adaptations fully expecting to see some movement between versions, and wanting to avoid attributing all movement to the cross-media shift or to discursively constructed notions of what each medium can or can't do. Rather, our focus lay on patterns of movement that flowed in the same direction without being countered by any such equal and opposite movement.

Television's Starless Skies

Turning now to differences, though, the relative focus on stars announces itself loudly before the shows even begin, and at the level of their advertising. Movies equal stars, it's suggested again and again, as the posters for adaptations of television shows feature the stars of the adaptations prominently, often with little more information deemed necessary. By contrast, many of the posters for adaptations of movies opt for iconic images or other images that evoke the tone of the film.

The posters for television shows made into films rely heavily, and at times almost solely, upon their stars. For instance, *21 Jump Street*'s backdrops, props, and costuming suggest a cop drama, but Jonah Hill and Channing Tatum preside over them, as do their names. One *A-Team* poster simply divides the space into four, pouring a close-up of each of the four stars into each quadrant, while a second shows them together, holding guns, with little extra information. *Bewitched* offers a clear blue sky with Nicole Kidman sitting on a broom, Will Ferrell hanging from it, their names breaking up the blue as much as the lone cloud depicted. *The Dukes of Hazzard* is dutifully reverent to the show's car but also careful to give its stars front-on smiling pictures. *Get Smart* loosely gestures to its playfulness by letting Anne Hathaway's hair blow across part of Steve Carell's face, but otherwise the poster simply depicts the two of them with a white background. *Land of the Lost*'s posters feature a T-Rex, but sandwiched between large print announcement of Will Ferrell and images of him. *Mission: Impossible* banks entirely on its star Tom Cruise, offering his face in silhouette profile and his name with little more. Several of the television to film adaptations also opted for several posters, one for each key character in ways that center the stars portraying these characters. *Baywatch*, *Dark Shadows*, *Entourage*, *GI Joe: Rise of Cobra*, *The Man from UNCLE*, *Miami Vice*, and *Starsky and Hutch* all took this approach. Even *Alvin and the Chipmunks*, a movie that might seemingly rely more intrinsically upon its computer-generated imagery (CGI)-animated chipmunks, allows Jason Lee's face to dominate the frame of one of its two key posters.

Across all the posters for our films, very few aimed—as did their televisual counterparts—to situate a world or tone, except via characters' faces. *Bewitched* provides a slight exception in its nod to Samantha's side saddle perching on her broom and nose twinkle, and *Dora and the Lost City of Gold* plays with the icons of Dora's backpack and pet monkey Boots, while concentrating more of the frame on the titular lost city than on Dora herself. And some of the animated films also felt freer to focus on tone and imagery, as with *The Simpsons Movie*'s image of Homer's hand reaching for a donut. But these exceptions generally proved a rule, or at least a strong pattern, of films featuring stars, banking their success on who was hired to play the characters, not on what the world looked like, on tone, on approach, or even on the use of iconic images and items. Frankly, many of the posters are boring, relying on the stars and titles alone to do the work of creating anticipatory excitement, clearly confident that they will do so, but thereby suggesting an improvement upon television by adding star power.

By contrast, the posters for films made into television shows were significantly more complex, rarely situating stars as central, and instead often aiming to communicate world, genre, and tone. Two key posters for *The Exorcist*, for instance, featured a silhouette of a man walking away from the viewer with a wide-brimmed hat and a large doctor's style bag, thus immediately evoking—for any who knew it—the poster of the film. A third poster offers a silhouette of a young woman whose head has rotated 180 degrees, thus evoking an infamous scene from the film in which the possessed Regan (Linda Blair) rotates her head

360 degrees. None of these posters list a star, and by opting for silhouettes they deprive us of sufficient details to glean one, or to be drawn in by characterization. All three, though, also mix their film iconography with clear symbols of horror in general—one sees the priest walking toward a door in a corridor bathed in blood red, another has him approaching a spooky cabin in the woods, while the third is set in an attic. Save for the title and broadcast information, the only words in each are, respectively, "Every soul is a battlefield," "Evil has a new home," and "There is a fate worse than death."

Bates Motel takes a similar approach. With text that identifies the channel (A&E), channel slogan ("Real Life. Drama"), title, and an offer to "Check in 3.18.13," a series of posters offer chilling images of a woman's arms handcuffed to a sink, someone probably hanging while on fire outside, and a severed hand washed up on a glum, pebbly beach. All of these communicate horror, but none offer much more information. Another poster borrows more clearly from *Psycho*, featuring a burning out neon sign for the Bates Motel in cold blue, with "Vacancy" attracting the eye in bright red. More text adorns this one, noting involvement by Carlton Cuse of *Lost* and Kerry Ehrin of *Friday Night Lights*, thereby establishing its "quality television" credentials. A modicum of casting information is offered—"Vera Farmiga as Norma Bates"—but omits any fuller list, not even noting Freddie Highmore's casting as the central character. Farmiga's presence thus appears to be offered less to sell a star, more to work alongside the iconic "Vacancy" sign to gesture to those who know *Psycho* that "Norman Bates' mother" features in the show, and hence that this is envisioned as a prequel. Yet another poster finally offers us images of Highmore and Farmiga, sitting on a motel bed expressionless. Their faces are dwarfed by the rest of the image, however, the actors' names are not listed, and thus little is done to situate them as stars. Rather, the poster's heavy lifting is performed by the words: "A boy's best friend is his mother."

The downplaying of Highmore as Norman Bates is notable, given Bates' role as one of horror's, and even film's, most iconic villains. And yet these posters are not alone, as *Hannibal*'s poster offers a close-up of Mads Mikkelsen's titular character well dressed and wiping his mouth with a fancy napkin, but the image cuts off his eyes and above. The effect, then, is to focus on the iconicity of the well-mannered cannibal, not on the person playing him. Though first acted on screen by Brian Cox in *Manhunter*, Anthony Hopkins' turn as Dr. Hannibal Lecter in *Silence of the Lambs* was much celebrated. To deny us a full view of Mikkelsen, though, refuses to situate his own performance as especially important. Once again, then, television appears as a starless medium, one that may be able to translate, adapt, and perhaps even amplify a world and a tone, but that stands in stark contrast to film, which is by contrast continually announced to be full of stars.

Fargo's apparent unwillingness to use Allison Tollman in its posters, an act that may have indicated her Molly Solverson was the show's closest analogue to Frances McDormand's iconic Marge Gunderson, also steps away both from nominating Tollman as a star and from suggesting stars even matter on television. Instead, *Fargo*'s television poster opted for graphic design set in needlepoint clearly meant to evoke the midwestern, "homey" setting yet interrupting its washed-out whites and blues with blood red lettering for the title. Amidst the patterned snowflakes, bordering, stag's head, and evergreens, moreover, are dollar signs, guns, axes, and (in a darker blue for emphasis) a figure with his own briefcase or doctor's style bag pointing a gun at a prone body that appears to be bleeding out the title. Again, then, the choice here is to indicate genre to those who might not know the original (murder in the Midwest) while gesturing to the bag that *Fargo* film viewers would recognize as Showalter's hidden money. No star is listed, only the channel, date of premiere, and title.

Terminator: The Sarah Connor Chronicles features the *bodies* of stars Lena Headey and Summer Glau more centrally, but diminishes their faces in ways that deny claims to stardom. Headey is looking down as she tends to her gun in one poster. Glau looks away from the camera in two other posters, the metal showing through a cut to the cheek in one, and an entirely metal skeleton in the other drawing the attention instead. A fourth gives us Glau's face, but atop a naked torso hung from electric apparatus, with metallic skeleton poking out of the arms. None list their stars' names.

We focus above on the posters of these five television shows since they adapt the most critically lauded and/or successful films, rich with iconography, but our analysis repeats itself across the other posters. Despite boasting a cast that includes Oscar-winning Ed Harris and Anthony Hopkins, *Westworld*'s posters all situate the immersive world and its genre hybridity, not the cast or its characters. *Dominion* offered a series of striking images, each modifying a Renaissance-style painting of an angel by adding machine guns, bullet belts, lingerie, a gimp mask, or other modern additions, but nowhere amidst these photos is any information on cast or characters. *Nikita* features Maggie Q prominently, but follows *Terminator: The Sarah Connor Chronicle*'s lead in focusing on her body, and in not identifying her. *Stargate SG-1* has one poster in silhouette, another showing the cast, but they are dwarfed in the latter by the more prominently featured image of the iconic stargate. Across several posters, *What We Do in the Shadows* adopts a black light and neon palette that partially obscures its cast's recognizability, while in another of its posters the three central vampires hang upside down. Only *From Dusk Till Dawn* used character posters (albeit without casting information), and *About a Boy* features the two central characters, but with sun glasses somewhat obscuring identification, and with no names listed.

In sum, the posters feature and amplify the importance of stars and characters in the films, while downplaying or outright ignoring and hiding stars and often characters in the television shows. Television, they suggest, is a world largely without stars, while film is posited as their home proper.

Admittedly, they are not alone in suggesting such a distinction. Anyone leafing through *Entertainment Weekly* in the past decade would notice a substantial difference in the way film and television advertisements emphasize their stars outside adaptations, too, so part of what we have documented here is a general division between the two media that extends into other genres of film and television. Certainly, star studies itself has long wrestled with whether television has "true" stars, at least as they are seen to exist in film. P. David Marshall writes of television as "generally an ancillary system" in star creation that is "less active in the generation of new celebrities than in the process of substantiating the significance of public personalities that have emerged in other domains" (1997, 130–1). Marshall is joined by many other scholars in seeing a categorical distinction between film's world of stars, television's "ancillary," secondary, and/ or inferior system (see, for instance, Ellis 1992; Langer 1997). These scholars often rely upon a self-generating syllogism, wherein because they don't personally acknowledge television as being as worthy and/or magical as film, they inevitably rate its stars as less worthy and/or magical than film stars. They are challenged by other scholars who've shown how television either is *now* more full of stars (Jermyn 2006) or was always (see, for instance, Doty 1990; Murray 2005), and by yet others who have examined the specificities of television's star, celebrity, and "personality" systems rather than simply judging them inferior (Bennett 2011). They are also challenged by the increasing cross-traffic of all but a few stars between film and television, and by especially Netflix's super-sized contracts of $60M and $100M respectively for television stars Dave Chappelle and Jerry Seinfeld. Regardless, that troubled logic clearly extends beyond these individual posters, framing how at least some, if not many, in the film and television industries consider stardom. Even if this is so, however, it is still revealing that these logics—based on imagined constructions of what film and television are, and of the relative value of their actors' auras—are allowed to overrule logics offered to a marketing and promotion team by the text and world itself. If, for instance, the belief that television is starless overcomes an understanding of *Psycho* and *Silence of the Lambs* as star- and performance-driven films, leading to a counter-intuitive (and perhaps counter-productive) choice not to bother announcing the new stars and casts for the television adaptations, we see a clear hierarchy of logics, wherein imagined constructions of media capacities outrank many other logics.

This focus on stars extends well beyond the posters, too, as across the films and television shows themselves, we regularly saw a pattern of film adding stars, television subtracting or losing them. At its purest, we can see this process of additive or subtractive stardom when we consider texts that continue rather than adapt per se. *Entourage* is especially telling here, a successful HBO show that ended in 2011, yet that followed up with a feature film in 2015. The film pulls back the original cast and stays firmly within the same diegetic world, yet also lays the celebrity cameos on thick, including actors Mark Wahlberg, Liam Neeson, Jessica Alba, Kelsey Grammar, and George Takei, sports stars Thierry Henry, Rob Gronkowski, Russell Wilson, Tom Brady, and Mike Tyson, singers Saigon and Pharrell Williams, famed rich people Mark Cuban and Warren

Buffett, and more. Granted, *Entourage* is set in a world of famous people, and the television show included its own prominent cameo appearances, but the sheer number of cameos in the film is a performance of wild excess, a clear attempt to add more. *Hannah Montana: The Movie* similarly adds Taylor Swift and Tyra Banks. This pattern repeated less starkly when Hasbro's successful *My Little Pony: Friendship Is Magic* moved briefly from television to film; the "Mane Six" were each voiced by their regular actors, but added to the cast were Uzo Aduba, Emily Blunt, Zoe Saldana, Kristin Chenoweth, and singer Sia. Contrast these examples to the cottage industry of animated children's television programs based on and continuing the diegesis of successful animated films, where it is more of a norm to *lose* stars. When *The Boss Baby* (2017) was adapted to *The Boss Baby: Back in Business* (2018–), for instance, gone was Alec Baldwin from the titular role, replaced instead by voice actor JP Karliak. And when *How to Train Your Dragon* was adapted to Netflix's *Dragons*, for instance, Jay Baruchel, America Ferrara, and TJ Miller remained, while Gerard Butler, Craig Ferguson, Jonah Hill, and Kristen Wiig were all replaced. Thus, even when an adaptation presumes that fans of the original will variously show up or tune in to see more of their beloved characters in the same diegetic world, movies are regularly seen to require the accretion of stars, while television is presumed not to need its stars, or at least not many of them.

Stars also rise in two animated television-to-film adaptations. The above-noted poster of *Alvin and the Chipmunks* that centers on Jason Lee faithfully indicates Dave's centrality to the plot, which now rotates as much if not more so around his reactions to the chipmunks, and their place in his own romantic and professional life, as around the CGI rodents. *Transformers*, too, spends little effort to flesh out its titular robotic aliens, instead offering Shia Lebeouf's Sam Witwicky as the frame through whom we're imagined to look (even as he and the camera together ogle Megan Fox). Both films, then, found it important to add a star and a human at their center, thereby gently implying that their television shows lacked such an anchoring or identificatory device (even though Dave appears in the cartoon originals, and even though the *Transformers* series featured the human companion Spike Witwicky, their roles are far less central on television).

An interesting tension exists here, though, and if we pull at that thread, we might dissemble these adaptations' apparent shared logic that movies are the realm proper of stars. For the posters of adaptations to movies to care so much about who is playing the central characters, and for the adaptations themselves to feature those characters so prominently, is to acknowledge that perhaps the characters were already central to the property in question. They suggest that a key pleasure of watching *The A-Team* movie, for instance, will be seeing new people inhabit and interpret BA Baracus, Hannibal, "Mad" Murdock, or Templeton "Faceman" Peck, which underlines the importance of George Peppard's, Dwight Shultz's, Mr. T's, and Dirk Benedict's original interpretations of those characters. Similarly, what above we have noted as television shows' coyness to nominate stars on the one hand betrays a belief that television does not run on a star system (at least in comparison to cinema), but on the other hand it risks implying that the stars and their characters were never really that important to the property—it was the "world" of *Psycho*, *Fargo*, *Terminator*, or *Westworld* that mattered most. In short, as much as we see this logic pervade adaptations and their marketing, it is a logic that crumbles upon further analysis and consideration.

We expected not to see the logic held up for the superhero films and television. As the genre name insists, after all, these films and television shows are filled with not just heroes but superheroes. Many are titled after single characters. We thus expected to see stars—or at the very least, the characters—placed as centrally, and to see the marketing and shows alike work hard to polish the star image of the actors playing these superhuman entities. At the level of the posters, few distinctions could be made, as star names were often absent from key posters in both media, and posters for both media also made heavy use of icons, whether Iron Man's mask, Captain America's shield, the energy trail that follows Flash, or stylized logos for Iron Fist, The Punisher, the Justice League of America, or Superman. Stars' faces and bodies featured prominently in many posters for both media, Tom Welling's pecs as prominently displayed in the poster for television's *Smallville* as Henry Cavell's are in the poster for film's *Man of Steel*, Gal Gadot's figure as central to the posters for the *Wonder Woman* film as Ashley Scott's is to the poster for television's *Birds of Prey*. Character poster series were common for both media, too, especially for any that focused on a superhero team, as with the Avengers or X-Men films, *Justice League*, *The Gifted*, *Inhumans*, and *Runaways*.

Daredevil's Netflix character posters gesture to a patterned difference within the films and television shows themselves, though, inasmuch as only one of them is for an actual superhero. Superhero shows on television regularly feature a broad supporting cast whose actions enable the hero's nobility. For *Daredevil*, then, Matt Murdock's hero is fashioned as much by non-superheroes Karen Page, Foggy Nelson, Claire Temple, and Father Lantom. The television shows regularly aim for broader casts, but this requires that dialogue and focus be shared between characters, rarely allowing the superhero to shine alone. By contrast, the films regularly give us the woman (or occasionally man) who loves the hero, and a lone friend, each of whom gets a scant few lines to set the hero straight in their hour of need, and/or to establish motivation when they are kidnapped or otherwise threatened by villainy. But by and large the films specialize in getting people out of the way to let the central characters shine. Thus even within the films and television shows, a star system is variously being built up in films and dissolved in television. This hierarchy of media's capacity to nurture stardom is spelled out in the early minutes of *Bewitched*'s adaptation to film, as Will Ferrell's Jack Wyatt is introduced as a movie star who is turning to television only because he has failed in the movies and needs a paycheck. Television cannot muster stars of the luminescence of film, we're told repeatedly by adaptations and their marketing, as well as in explicit terms here in *Bewitched*.

"This Is Not a Routine Expedition": Action, Gloss, and Subtle Re-Genrification

In writing this chapter, we realized that much of our commentary is glossed in the opening number, "Hey a Movie" from *The Great Muppet Caper* (1981). As the Muppets characteristically offer meta-commentary on the process of translating a hit television show to films, they promise a film "starring everybody ... and me," a line one can almost imagine Turtle from *Entourage* singing. But the song opens with the bolder promises: "There'll be spectacle / There'll be fantasy / There'll be derring do / And stuff like you would never see." As foretold by the Muppets, these lines gesture to another key implied transit route between the more mundane, everyday, procedural life of television and the grand, bold, action-filled, big stakes world of film.

Many films based on television shows have conspicuous, gratuitous action set-pieces. *Transformers* most obviously veered in this direction, hiring director Michael Bay to ensure a movie full of explosions, extended fight sequences, booming and shattering sound design, and a loving treatment and liberal use of the film's many cars, helicopters, and planes. With a budget of $150 million, Bay delivered a massive blockbuster. He also upped the stakes, as government agents feature far more heavily in the film than in the television show, and in general the threat to the planet is ever-present in the film, while the television show often focuses on the battle between rival transformer teams. *Charlie's Angels* also announces its heightened action, budget ($93 million), and gloss in its opening minutes. We open in the clouds, as a digitally rendered plane nears the camera. Cutting inside, a tracking shot follows an African man as he walks through the plane to the first-class cabin, seemingly negotiate payment for a hidden bomb strapped to another passenger, and then grab the passenger and jump out of the plane. Hurtling downward, he passes a helicopter, from which jumps someone else, soon joining him; they engage in a mid-air scuffle, release the bomb from the passenger just as it explodes, before our second hero retrieves the passenger, activates a parachute, and lands in a speed boat driven by a blonde woman in a bikini, before removing her helmet to shake out her hair. The African man lands in his own parachute and rips off his mask to reveal he is in fact the third "angel." Such an extravagant compilation of digitized imagery, tracking shot, elaborate stunts, aerial photography, and speed boats screams out a higher-budget, more breakneck-paced action *movie*.

Multiple other television-to-film adaptations tread similar paths. *The A-Team*, for instance, conspicuously pours money from its $110 million budget into a huge end sequence, and its stakes increase as the film allows characters to bleed, feel pain, and die. *Land of the Lost*, with a budget of $100 million, trades out the television show's practical effects for high-end CGI effects, even promising at the outset, through Will Ferrell's Dr. Rick Marshall: "This is not a routine expedition." *Bewitched* opens with aerial photography to announce its non-television-ness. *The Last Airbender* accompanies big action sequences on large sets with lots of digital effects and bombastic music, running a tab of $150 million. *Matrix*-style "bullet time" action sequences abound, as in *Charlie's Angels*. *Inspector Gadget* often seems little more than a vehicle for effects displays. *GI Joe: The Rise of Cobra* throws money from a $175 million budget at its action sequences and stunt work. *The Man from UNCLE* is a highly stylized, sleek visual treat, as is *Miami Vice*, with budgets of $75 million and $135 million respectively. And matching *Transformers* in grandeur and eventual box office haul and franchise success is *Mission: Impossible*, which, like *Charlie's Angels* and *The A-Team*, shows itself keen to "level up" from weekly problem solving to missions to save the nation or planet requiring complex stunts, extended chase and fight sequences, and exuberant displays of an $80 million budget.

We can see this leveling up of budget and spectacle in JJ Abrams' 2009 reboot of *Star Trek*. Although this film was the eleventh film produced in the franchise, it could be argued to be the first to fully engage in some of these processes of adaptation as media distinction. The previous ten films released between 1979 and 2002 had all served as continuations of television, featuring casts retained from series production. The budgets of these previous films reflected that television sensibility: the cheapest but also most critically acclaimed was *Star Trek II: The Wrath of Khan* (1982) made for only $12 million (in which Ricardo Montalbán, then star of television series *Fantasy Island* [1977–1984], reprises his 1967 *Star Trek* guest star role). Even when trying to embrace the cinema's demands for stars, with hopes of casting Sean Connery for a guest role in *Star Trek V: The Final Frontier* (1989) and Tom Hanks in *Star Trek: First Contact* (1996), the producers of these films settled for alternatives more befitting the presumed scale of television (Laurence Luckinbill and James Crowell, respectively). Given these resources, the space battles these *Star Trek* films could offer tended to be quiet, submarine-style cat-and-mouse games, not the all-out armadas and dogfights of *Star Wars* (1977). As a reboot, though, the Abrams film did not just recast Kirk and Spock with new, rising Hollywood stars; it also used an upgraded budget of $150 million to newly adapt the *Star Trek* television concept to expectations of cinema. That budget showed on screen not just through an abundance of lens flares, but also a revised focus on kinetic action, violent confrontations, and other forms of effects-driven spectacle as the protagonists seek to stop a "red matter" bomb with the stakes-raising potential to destroy whole planets. Unlike its rather talky, low-budget television continuation predecessors, this was a *Star Trek* film *adaptation* more comparable to *Star Wars*—and surely it helped to demonstrate JJ Abrams' suitability to direct *Star Wars: The Force Awakens* (2015) a few years later.

Although it too represents the continuation of a television program, even *The Simpsons Movie* aims for numerous animated sequences that involve more three dimensionality than seen in the television show, as Homer swings a wrecking ball, a huge mob approach the family with lit torches, and a sinkhole becomes a swirling whirlpool that sucks the family's entire house into it. The film offers many more high- and wide-angle shots of the town, too, than does the television show typically, as well as a 360-degree spin shot of Marge and Homer kissing triumphantly at the end. The stakes are grand, leading up to the government trying to bomb Springfield. Indeed, in typical *Simpsons* meta-commentary fashion, the plot gestures to how often television shows are expected to get bigger when moving to the movies, as the EPA installs a dome over the entire town of Springfield to protect America from its environmentally unsound practices. The Simpsons escape the dome in a clear metaphorical comment on many other television-to-film adaptations aiming similarly to escape a small "dome" supposedly imposed by television.

Far from just adding action sequences, we should more properly note a subtle modification of genre, becoming full-on summer action blockbusters whose generic formats are drawn from movies more than television. *21 Jump Street* most notably shifts from serious police procedural to cop buddy comedy. Both *Transformers* and *GI Joe* leap on the opportunity to turn Saturday morning cartoon into Saturday evening blockbuster. *Dora and the Lost City of Gold* and *Land of the Lost* veer from gentle adventure to Indiana Jones-style action-adventures. *Charlie's Angels*, *Mission: Impossible*, *The Man from UNCLE*, *Miami Vice*, *Baywatch*, *The Equalizer*, and *The A-Team* move from procedural action, a genre that often involves smaller level missions and problem-solving, to action movies with central missions, looming grand bad guys, and significant stakes. The first three in particular ape Bond films, their need for gadgets, and their act structures more than their televisual precedents. Inter-group tensions and remorse-and-recovery narratives feature heavily, driving the narrative more than when on television. In short, whereas all of these stories entered the adaptive process with their own narrative skins, those adapting them clearly felt a need to dress them up in movie clothing, believing they needed more action, stunts, CGI, gloss, resolution, and higher stakes. All were successful enough properties for execs to decide to adapt them, yet those adapting them clearly saw a need to "movie-fy" them, their genres, and their styles in the process.

We also see their transformations and positionings through their budgets and release dates. Considering the superhero movies, for instance, the budgets of the MCU films ranged from $140 million (for *Iron Man* and *Captain America: The First Avenger*) to $356 million (for *Avengers: Endgame*), averaging $191 million. Eighteen of the 23 were released between late April and August, and advertised aggressively worldwide, reaping box office revenues ranging from *The Incredible Hulk*'s $263.8 million to *Avengers: Infinity War*'s $2.048 billion, and averaging a stunning $944.6 million. All but one of Fox's ten *X-Men* films were also released between late April and August, averaging budgets of $150 million and worldwide box office revenues of $446.6 million. The DCEU films ranged in budget from *Birds of Prey*'s $84.5 million to *Justice League*'s $300 million, averaging $180 million. Half were summer releases, the other half targeting other holidays, but grossing $201.9 million worldwide on the low end (for *Birds of Prey*) and $1.149 billion on the high end (for *Aquaman*), averaging a yield of $685.6 million each. In short, the superhero films were released to be big, large, sweeping summer or holiday rides, and given the budgets to boot, while the releases of the superhero television shows were rarely touted as events, instead slotting into a channel's schedule or offerings as quotidian fare.

By contrast, none of the action films, or even hybrid action films, made into television programs maintained their genre. Science fiction action film *Minority Report* becomes a fairly standard police procedural, while action horror film *Legion*'s adaptation *Dominion* becomes a serialized fantasy show, *12 Monkeys* subtly shifts from science fiction action to science fiction mystery, *Terminator* becomes decidedly less action-centered in *Terminator: The Sarah Connor Chronicles* to embrace family melodrama, and *From Dusk Till Dawn* similarly loses its action-based core in its television show. Admittedly, action can cost money, and television shows rarely, if ever, boast the same budgets as films. But to see the de-centering of action as a product of budget alone would be to forget how much action *does* occur on television, and how many shows can still pack plenty of explosions, chases, fight sequences, or even battles into an episode while working creatively to limit the budget. Most of the superhero shows on television, for instance, manage to include plenty of action, albeit often working in the dark to limit the need for lavish sets and fully rendered CGI backdrops. Or, the only true exception in our sample, *Nikita*, arguably delivers every bit as much action as does Luc Besson's film of the same name, all while operating on a small CW budget.

In general, then, the adaptive routes leading between film and television suggest a pervasive lack of faith in television's ability to "do" action well. Conversely, they suggest not only an abundant faith in film's ability to "do" action, but perhaps even a belief that film *should* do action, that part of adapting something to film should require at least insertion of lots of action, if not complete re-genrification.

At first blush, the superhero television shows may seem to challenge this logic—many of them, we've noted, contain significant action. But if they on one hand remind us that action is absolutely possible on television, on the other hand they still subscribe to a division of the world into big action for the big screen and little action for the little screen. Superhero movies are, generally speaking, big budget affairs, garnering massive budgets, dominating the summer box office, and densely packing stunts, action set pieces, CGI, and grand sets into two- to three-hour rides. Many have relished the chance to depict grand battles not "just" one-on-one fights between superheroes and supervillains. Thus, for instance, each *Avengers* film includes battles of stunning magnitude, *Wonder Woman* finds the Amazonian in the middle of World War II, *Thor: Ragnarok* builds up to a battle between rival teams of Nordic gods, and each *X-Men* film features grand battles, too. And with many superheroes and supervillains developing robots to do their variously noble or evil bidding, even many "one-on-one" skirmishes call in a robotic cast of thousands, as in *Spider-Man: Far From Home*, for example, which sends Peter Parker on a trip to Venice, Prague, and London largely to enable huge set piece confrontations between Parker, villain Mysterio, and thousands of the latter's drones. Superhero films aim to be exhilarating, giving us everything from alien armies descending into Manhattan from a portal in the sky to gladiator fights on distant planets.

As if all these battles don't make it clear, too, superhero films have specialized in Big Stakes. The Avengers never waste their time with small-time criminals—they are protecting the world and eventually the universe from evil. Their ultimate super villain, Thanos, builds up to a plan to wipe out half of all living things in the universe, and succeeds in *Avengers: Infinity War*, requiring time traveling efforts to bring back that half of the universe in *Avengers: Endgame*. In the drumroll up to the Avengers assembling in their first film, though, the various character-centered films that preceded it similarly showed our heroes saving America, saving the world. *Guardians of the Galaxy* and *Captain Marvel* even introduce us to heroes whose precise purpose is to protect planetary systems beyond ours, Thor must protect the mythic realm of Asgard as much as Earth, and Doctor Strange must protect multiple dimensions. Over in DC, too, *Wonder Woman* sees our hero battle Ares the God of War, while *Justice League* sees our heroes unite to defeat Steppenwolf and his parademons who aim to destroy the planet, after having failed thousands of years prior when defeated by an assembly of Olympian gods, extraterrestrials, humans, and Atlanteans.

As if these stakes weren't already high enough, at the level of marketing and public reception, we have seen numerous superhero films take on various forms of discrimination. Beyond what its characters were doing, therefore, *Black Panther* was envisioned as fighting racism in Hollywood, as bringing Black pride and heroism to the masses, while *Wonder Woman* and *Captain Marvel* were similarly fighting for women and girls everywhere, so we were told. The *X-Men* films have long drawn the parallel between the diegetic persecution of mutants in their plots and real-life discrimination, with several of their stars prominently posing them as narratives about queer acceptance and power (Johnson 2008). At the levels of both the diegesis and of cultural context, superhero films regularly posit themselves as the most important, impactful texts in our cities, nation, planet, galaxy, universe, dimension, making it hard to even imagine texts with a grander sense of self-importance or stakes.

By comparison, the world of the televisual superhero is significantly more mundane. While their filmic counterparts are fighting onslaughts of alien invaders, encountering dark forces awakened after millennia, and doing what the world's combined military forces cannot in stunning set pieces, many of television's superheroes are fighting local criminals. Marvel Studios' Netflix shows stand out here, set in specific neighborhoods in New York. One of *Daredevil's* first season posters even used the eponymous DD logo to cordon off several city blocks in bright red lighting, announcing the significantly smaller scope. The show introduces us to characters fighting local bad guys committing petty crime, working up to organized crime and to the takedown of Wilson Fisk as a corporate bad guy. Luke Cage similarly faces a local bad guy, the worst Harlem (not another dimension) has to offer. Even though *Luke Cage* preceded *Black Panther*, and even though *Jessica Jones* preceded *Wonder Woman* and *Captain Marvel*, Cage and Jones aren't allowed to fight racism and sexism in as bold, national, or planetary terms as are their filmic counterparts. Although occasional moments in each of the Netflix Marvel series remind us we're in the same world as *The Avengers*, none of these characters are called upon to fight aliens (not even via cameos in the otherwise all-hands-on-deck battle in *Avengers: Endgame*), as instead their calling is humble, local, smaller. We also see them damaged more—*Daredevil's* fights are notorious for being knock-down, drag out affairs that leave the hero needing medical interventions. Even Jessica Jones and Luke Cage, whose powers give them super strength and invincibility respectively, are shown humbled, brought down, and cowed by their villains.

While Marvel's television shows exist in a smaller space, with much lower stakes, they are also significantly more intimate and personal. *Jessica Jones'* supervillain, the Purple Man, uses mind control to abuse women, and the narrative is centrally about overcoming abuse, about surviving in its long and painful aftermath. Jessica drinks heavily and is deeply scarred by the Purple Man. *The Punisher* delves deep into its character's fractured psyche to tell a story about post-traumatic stress disorder and the mental damage done to veterans. *Luke Cage* sees its hero fighting threats to his neighborhood. Meanwhile, Fox's *Legion* sets itself as much inside its protagonist's mind as outside it. David has remarkable powers of the mind but was continually told he was simply mentally ill, and as he struggles both to realize his powers and with villains who similarly work within his mind, the show often takes place in that mind. For its part, *The Gifted* focuses on a family on the run when the parents discover their children have special abilities, offering some echoes to *Runaways*, where a group of teens discover both their superhuman abilities and their parents' involvement in a criminal group. Both shows, in short, have family dynamics at their hearts. All of these shows have much smaller global stakes than the films, instead looking at personal, intimate stakes and issues. And thus between them and the films, we see a clear bifurcation wherein the films deal literally and figuratively with threats to the planet, the television shows deal with threats to the self and/or neighborhood.

DC's Arrowverse follows suit here, too, as its tales rarely move past a local frame. Like *Daredevil*, *Arrow* begins rather humbly, as its hero goes out at night to fight local bad guys. Even as his missions get bigger, and as successive series add characters and the ability to team up, the scope of villainy they must fight pales in comparison to the cinematic Justice League's adversaries. Generically, too, the Arrowverse's characters all have their romantic intrigues and challenges, friends who turn on them and must seek reconciliation, parents who lie, and so forth, in ways that invoke the melodrama of soap operas. Again, they are local stories about personal issues, battles, and triumphs, not about Saving the World. Cinema is encouraged to be the more masculine genre of big action, big stakes, and the public sphere, while Marvel, DC, and their co-producers alike have regularly directed stories about localized tribulations, the private sphere, and domestic issues to the presumed-to-be more feminine television.

Marge Simpson's Negligee Revealed: Sex, "Pervasive Language," and Adultification

The ratings for many of the adapted films reflect not just a plethora of action, however, for another pattern in TV-to-film adaptations is to add raunchier, bawdier jokes and scenes, and to add more sex. The MPAA lists many of these films as including "crude and sexual content," "pervasive language," "partial nudity," "innuendo and some sensuality/nudity," and "rude humor." Excluding *Ali G Indahouse*, *Entourage*, and *Sex and the City* as originals rated for adults, six of these adaptations are R-rated, and 19 are PG-13-rated, many for the inclusion of rude humor and sexual humor and/or content.

Charlie's Angels is instructive here, for as the above-noted opening tracking shot plays out, our second snippet of overheard conversation hears a flight attendant tell a colleague that he told a woman, "look, lady, it's not the seats that have gotten smaller, it's your ass that's gotten bigger," and a few seconds later, we see a young couple sneak into the bathroom together. The film also announces its intentions to situate itself wholly within the male gaze when our second shot of Cameron Diaz in her bikini has her stretching out in a way unnecessary to the scene, but so as to render her body a spectacle, while our first views of Lucy Liu and Drew Barrymore's faces come with slo-mo hair shakes. *The Dukes of Hazzard* is also replete with sexual humor, making Uncle Jesse significantly cruder than in the television show, and largely using Jessica Simpson's Daisy Duke for objectification—a point the airbrushing of her cleavage communicates in both of its posters, no less. Bo and Luke, meanwhile, shift from being clever troublemakers on television to being naïve, dimwitted, and prone to saying rude things on film. And *Land of the Lost* borrows more from its star Will Ferrell's history with rude humor than from its original, resulting in a film with significantly more adult content than the television show ever featured.

Thus, and curiously, adult humor suffuses many of these adaptations, even though their originals resided wholly within family television viewing blocks. Indeed, if we consider that many of the presumed viewers of adaptations of 1960s, 1970s, or 1980s television shows *21 Jump Street*, *The A-Team*, *Bewitched*,

Charlie's Angels, Dark Shadows, Dukes of Hazzard, The Equalizer, Get Smart, GI Joe, Inspector Gadget, I-Spy, Land of the Lost, The Man from UNCLE, Miami Vice, Mission: Impossible, Scooby-Doo, The Smurfs, Starsky and Hutch, and *Transformers* would have been young when the originals played, the common choice to "adultify" the humor, camerawork, and/or characterization is potentially risky, inasmuch as it takes the more "family-friendly" originals and transforms them for former fans. Even a show such as *Baywatch,* whose television original always peddled slomo shots of young people running in bathing suits, steps up to a film that includes, as the MPAA notes, "graphic nudity" and "crude sexual contact." Or whereas Solo's womanizing is subtly implied in *The Man from UNCLE* on television, his sexual encounters are more explicit in the film. And though the *Star Trek* continuation films that preceded the 2009 reboot often lacked the budget to transform television in terms of stars and visual scale, they too played along with this inexpensive means of communicating a cinematic graduation from the language restrictions of broadcast television; most notably, *Star Trek IV: The Voyage Home* (1986) generated a running gag from Kirk and Spock's experimentations with "colorful metaphors" like "double dumb-ass on you." In other films, Scotty calls the Klingon head of state a "bitch" and Data exclaims "oh shit!" as the *Enterprise* collides with a planet. The rebooted Kirk calling "bullshit" on Spock in 2009 only extends this tradition.

The *Simpsons Movie* veers this direction too. Early on, Bart skateboards naked through town in a sight gag that sees various framings conveniently cover his private parts, until all of a sudden he skates behind two bushes that reverse this framing, showing *only* his penis and testicles. Simpson neighbor Ned Flanders is in a fast food restaurant leading his boys in saying grace when he sees Bart, moreover, leading to first Ned and then Rod and Todd invoking Bart's "bountiful … penis." Later in the film, too, Marge and Homer lead into a sex scene, with Disney-esque animals surrounding them and disrobing them, a stag using his horns to rip off Marge's dress to reveal her negligee. Granted, everything in *The Simpsons* is played parodically and for laughs, but the joke in both cases is thus quite clearly that television-to-film adaptations are expected to be more crude, and to include more sex.

Also viewing the adaptive process with tongue firmly in cheek is *South Park: Bigger, Longer, and Uncut,* whose title alone mocks the expectations of television-to-film adaptations being bigger and more brazenly phallic, wrapped up in male bravado. *South Park* is a remarkably profane show already, thereby leaving seemingly few boundaries of rudeness and profanity left to cross, and yet the film gleefully and in self-aware fashion ups its ante with the musical number "Uncle Fucka," which strings together multiple "fucks," along with many other profanities in a song two best friends curse-sing to each other proposing they're each eager practitioners of incest. The song comes from a diegetic television-to-film adaptation of *The Terrance and Phillip Show* that outrages South Park's parents, setting off a moral panic, but in doing so it deftly makes fun of expectations that television shows—*Terrance and Phillip* and *South Park* alike—will find more edge when adapted to film.

By contrast, when films move to television, we see less ostensible infantilizing. Some darker threads were removed to make narratives safer for the whole family, as when *About a Boy* removes references to the mother's suicide attempts and clinical depression. But for the most part, television shows based on films held tone: *Fargo*, for instance, is no less dark than its original, and *Hannibal* is considerably *more* graphic than *Silence of the Lambs* or *Manhunter*. The superhero films and television shows, meanwhile, flip their chasteness, as superhero films rarely include more than a passionate kiss, whereas Netflix's Marvel shows include nudity and simulated sex, and even the broadcast CW network's Arrowverse allows for steamier sex scenes, albeit without nudity. Television absolutely *can* handle darkness, sex, and rudeness, in short, even if the logic of adaptation often suggests that film can handle such issues better.

A healthy collection of superhero television shows illustrates another part of the adultification picture, though, namely that television can often be rendered as a space for teens. Almost all of the superhero films are aimed squarely at a large audience. But superhero television is often aimed at teens, as in *Smallville*, *Arrow*, and the ensuing Arrowverse, all on teen-focused channel The CW, *Marvel's Cloak and Dagger* on teen-focused channel Freeform, or in *Runaways* and *The Gifted*. And yet, across the many superhero films we considered, only *Shazam!* and *Logan* take an interest in children with powers, while the latter's grim tone, violence, and R-rating signaled the film itself was definitely not for children. The *X-Men* franchise lends itself to telling more teen stories, given its potential setting at Xavier's School for Gifted Youngsters, and yet the films all focus on the guardian adults, introducing children only as wallpaper to scenes at the school, or as occasional troubled teens with poorly developed characters who exist for the adults to mentor. Spider-Man could also allow more storytelling for teens, given that Peter Parker is sometimes aged as a teen, yet the Tobey McGuire and Andrew Garfield Spideys were college age. Tom Holland's turn as the webslinger finally activates the character more clearly for teen appeal and interest, yet since his key narrative purpose in the MCU seems to be to activate (surrogate) paternal feelings in Tony Stark/Iron Man, even he is written with the adult viewer carefully in mind. *Spider-Man: Into the Spiderverse* offers a bolder exception, and yet tellingly is animated and set outside the MCU, thereby already framing it as exceptional. In general, across their multiple production teams, superhero films have rarely seen themselves as exclusively talking to teens, as instead superhero stories for teens have been envisioned as television stories.

Mocking Television

Some adaptations work on a short leash, loyally staying close to their originals, while others voyage farther from home, keen to explore the possibilities of the world more boldly. This much is common between film-to-television, television-to-film adaptations, and comic-to-either adaptations. However, we noticed a distinct trend, wherein many television-to-film adaptations enjoy making fun of television style, genres, and format, whereas even when film-to-television adaptations veered far from their originals, none actively mocked those originals or the medium from whence they came.

Winking at the camera happened far more often in filmic adaptations of television. Sometimes this took the form of gentle commentary or playing with the original's rules; sometimes it lurched more decisively into camp and parody. *21 Jump Street*, *Baywatch*, *Charlie's Angels*, *The Dukes of Hazzard*, *Get Smart*, *Land of the Lost*, *Scooby Doo*, *The Smurfs*, and *Starsky and Hutch* all premise themselves, no less, on a playful ribbing of their originals' supposed excesses. The above-noted opening scene of *Charlie's Angels*, for instance, is quite camp in being so overdone, from the bright red first-class cabin to the bawdy humor, the "angels" shaking their hair out in slow motion, and one "angel" wearing the skin and mask of a much larger African man: these all declare their overdoneness. We even hear a complaint from a passenger about the inflight movie, *TJ Hooker: The Movie*, suggesting television-to-film adaptations are bad ideas (echoed in Nick Offerman's Deputy Chief Hardy complaining about "recycled programs from the eighties" in *21 Jump Street*). *Charlie's Angels* allows its televisual roots to show, and seems to want to get away with it because it's "just parody," the same way that *Austin Powers: International Man of Mystery* (1997) and its sequels allow themselves sexist jokes and other excesses because they're "just parody" of a specific time and genre. This pattern repeats itself across the above-listed movies, to the point that one could note them forming a sub-genre of older television shows converted to films where part of the "fun" and play comes from camp exploitation of the supposed norms and values of the era, and of the implied crudeness of the medium. Several of these shows' use of the male gaze, reliance on crude humor, and obvious plot holes and absurdities (like Drew Barrymore convincingly passing as an African man played by LL Cool J) aim to license themselves because they're televisual. An interesting exception, *The Man from UNCLE* aims for a sleeker feel, but does so by becoming an homage to 1960s espionage *films*, not television.

By contrast, none of the film-to-television adaptations take the films to task for their or their medium's shortcomings, and none hide behind their filmness. By and large, these adaptations are more unequivocally loving toward their originals. Even when they veer in a different direction, as with *Fargo*, for instance, they still take great care to situate themselves within the "world" of the film. However, and notably, a few of these adaptations occasionally mock their new home of television. *Clerks* stands out here, as a film-to-television adaptation that often makes fun of the limits of the new medium. From the first frame, Randal announces "*Clerks* is filmed in front of a live studio audience" (even though it is animated), before offering a "previously on" segment that cuts to color bars, since as the first episode there was of course no previous episode. Its televisuality is thus triple underlined. Over-the-top and obvious cross-promotion for other ABC programs occur during the show, mocking television form, and the second episode is called a "clip show," in a swipe at the creative exhaustion that leads to such episodes. Each episode, moreover, ends with a PSA from Jay, Silent Bob, and Charles Barkley, ribbing the medium for its clumsy use of such "special messages."

Thus, the mockery of television is reasonably common in television-to-film adaptations, as is the use of television's supposed value system as a shield behind which lazy writing, objectification of women's bodies, and crude humor could stand. If film-to-television adaptations mock a medium, it too is television. Once again, though, there's a paradox in play here: some of these movies would have us believe that objectification of women, bad plots, and rude jokes are the brick and mortar of television, even while they are banking on those elements themselves. This paradox is evident in Roger Ebert's (2005) review of *The Dukes of Hazzard*, as he writes that

> It's a retread of a sitcom that ran from about 1979 to 1985, years during which I was able to find better ways to pass my time. Yes, it is still another TV program I have never ever seen. As this list grows, it provides more and more clues about why I am so smart and cheerful.

Ebert swipes at television's alleged stupidity and pointlessness as a means of damning an adaptation that is far bawdier and sophomoric than its original was (even if only somewhat less racist), and whose key crimes as he sees them, then, stem from the film.

The Simpsons Movie deserves special discussion here, as a film that gently parodies and plays with the conventions of adaptation, delivering sex, nudity, action, and big stakes. In doing so, however, the satire is Horatian, and never truly attacks film as medium. This comes in spite of the franchise regularly mocking its host genre—*The Simpsons Game* that spawned from the movie, for instance, is rife with ribbing of video games, often offering a deconstruction and critique of game conventions. The movie's most pointed comment on a medium, however, is directed at television. At one point, a crawl comes across the screen advertising a supposedly upcoming reality show, before admitting that, yes, "we" even advertise during movies now, complete with Fox network logo. The quick joke continues a long history of *The Simpsons* making fun of its host network; but here suggests that tawdry, inappropriate advertising *is* common for television, whereas movies should be free of such pitches. Thus, the movie's most barbed medium-focused comment aims at television, not film, which escapes the 90 minutes of parody unscathed. The nearest the film comes to mocking film is when, early on, Homer (watching an *Itchy and Scratchy* movie) complains that he can't believe "we" are paying to see something we usually see for free at home, saying "you're all suckers," both the diegetic audience and us. That comment, though, doesn't take film to task, just the economics of adaptation.

Conclusion

As noted at the outset of this chapter, some scholars of adaptation have seen a form of technological determinism speaking itself through adaptation, as various media announce what they are and aren't capable of, what they are more or less suited for. Our approach here instead has been to use adaptation to tell us what creators and executives collectively have allowed themselves to imagine as possible or impossible for different media. All of the distinctions we or others might see between film and television, after all, could be challenged by exceptions. We don't mean to be obtuse, and to ignore salient factors. A television season, for instance, may run between 10 and 20 hours, as opposed to the terser 90 to 150 minutes of most films; we could well expect that extra time allows certain storytelling conventions and possibilities. Even if many movies are watched on chair-back screens on planes, in living rooms, on mobile devices, and/or on laptops, just the prospect alone of some exhibition occurring in theaters surely entices certain forms of visual storytelling and storytellers. But both media are old enough, the range of possibilities within each wide enough, to show us that beyond technical distinctions between theatrical exhibition and viewing in a living room—which we insist is not the same thing as the distinction between movies and television as media—anything one can do, the other can do. Television has capacities for creating large narrative universes across many episodes, yes, but films can work in series, too, as the MCU, X-Men, or DCEU sagas show. Even at the level of individual films, some of the more celebrated immersive storyworlds exist in films (cf., *Blade Runner* [1982], *Brazil* [1985], *Mad Max: Fury Road* [2015], etc.). Film loves its stars, but television hardly lacks stars, as the cast of *Friends'* (1994–2004) bank accounts will testify, as Netflix's huge contracts show, or as half the content of *Entertainment Weekly* or *Entertainment Tonight* often attests. Action may look especially stunning on a large screen, but even before nominating any scripted television, we might note how many millions of sports fans turn dutifully to their televisions for weekly or nightly servings of action. Some television producers are more puritanical in allowing sex or rude humor, but HBO and Comedy Central can match (or often beat) anything R-rated films displays.

What we find far more interesting than asking what actual differences between movies and television adaptations tell us about is to ask—as we have here—what imaginary borders are announced by adaptations. And what we've found is that film is often imagined to be the proper realm for stars, for big stakes and big action, for the masculine public sphere and for stories set there, for bawdier humor and sex, and for adult fare, while television can often be imagined as more domestic, more teen or child-like, more intimate, and better suited to worlds than to stars. Beyond whether adaptations are any good, then, beyond whether they thrive in their allotted lane, and beyond what we see as their crimes or successes of fidelity and/or creativity, they serve as a site for policing a boundary between television and film.

Some of the exceptions we've considered point to shifting ground, as Comedy Central, HBO, Netflix, FX, and other channels aiming to be more boutique, "quality" venues might be considered to ignore the boundaries with more frequency. But are they? HBO's declaration that it wasn't television, it was HBO, was evidenced most clearly by a willingness or even eagerness to use profanity, to show nudity, and to employ grimmer, gorier violence. *Band of Brothers* (2001) and later *Game of Thrones* (2011–2019) each also aimed to up the ante of action and big set pieces on television. Each of these choices seem to have been quite strategic, intended as a way of distancing the channel from what television "is," moving closer to a style regularly dubbed by critics as "cinematic." Indeed, we don't even need to glean the strategy from afar, as numerous television producers have stated outright that their shows are actually more cinematic: joining David Benioff's and Richard Plepler's respective claims, already quoted in our Introduction, that *Game of Thrones* is movie-like is David Lynch's insistence that his *Twin Peaks: The Return* (2017) is an "18 hour movie" (Tizard 2017), for instance, or Sam Esmail's that the first season of *Homecoming* (2018) is a "five hour movie" (Sperling 2018). Delving further into such a strategy lies beyond the scope of this chapter and its focus on cross-media adaptations, and points to another key site where televisuality and the cinematic are discursively determined, but we note it here to underline that even the exceptions to our above-noted patterns and trends within adaptations and their imaginations of what is or isn't possible in film or television may be exceptions by strategic choice. Their producers may precisely be aiming to shift them closer to widespread notions of what cinema is and entails, and away from notions of what television is and entails.

And yet, ironically, with each television channel or producer that lunges toward that which they regard as more cinematic, and with each statement to the press that this or that television show isn't *really* a television show but is a movie, these producers are expanding the discursive imagination of what television is and what it's capable of. Television has always been capable of action, of gritty and impactful stories with high stakes directed at adults, and of all the other characteristics these adaptations collectively suggest exist more truly and authentically in the domain of film. But when high-profile cases remind us of this fact—even as their producers work to distance their product from the discursive domain of television—they challenge those discursive boundaries. They admit, perhaps under duress, that television is capable of that which film is and that the stylistic and thematic boundaries between their narratives have already crumbled. Many adaptations, though, cling to those crumbling boundaries, announcing, even while they try to squeeze more revenue from a franchise from another medium, that differences in medium matter, that film and television have different roles to play, different skillsets, and different abilities.

4

TELEVISION PRODUCERS GO TO THE MOVIES

Transforming Professional Identities

In the age of streaming, the increased prestige of television has attracted major Hollywood talent—from A-listers to beloved character actors—to series production. On HBO, *Big Little Lies* (2017–) boasts an all-star cast including Reese Witherspoon, Nicole Kidman, and Laura Dern. Perhaps most famously (and ultimately, infamously), *House of Cards* (2013–2018) on Netflix turned on the participation of Kevin Spacey, whose films had already sustained viewer attention on the service. More recently, Netflix has turned instead to film stars including Emma Stone, Charlize Theron, Chris Hemsworth, and many more. By 2018, Amazon Prime Video had secured Julia Roberts—still one of the top-paid actresses in Hollywood by some metrics (K. Elkins 2019)—to headline its *Homecoming* (2019–) series. With the onset of the COVID-19 pandemic in 2020 and the diminished prospects for film exhibition, even those A-listers who would refuse to work in television might soon find their work debuting on domestic streaming services rather than theatrically.

Despite these recent migrations of film talent to television, it is important to remember that television has long served as a stepping stone to the film industry. This is not to endorse the idea of film as some higher calling, but quite oppositely to recognize television as a training ground in which the craft of media making has been learned and a source of talent that can bring change and innovation to the film industry. Only the most obvious example is Steven Spielberg, who, despite his reputation as the master of cinematic spectacle, built his career on a foundation of television work. Spielberg directed episodes of series like *Night Gallery* (1970–1973), *Marcus Welby MD* (1969–1976), and *Columbo* (1968–2003) before making made-for-TV films like *Duel* (1971), cutting his teeth on television. In that light, one could consider whether his success as a filmmaker depended significantly on his televisual literacy. Spielberg was, of course, not novel or unique in having arrived in the film industry through a career in television; in fact, film historians Michael Pye and Linda Myles (1979) characterize Spielberg as part of a new generation of so-called "movie brats" whose film school educations distinguished them from an earlier cadre of television-educated filmmakers who had already come up through the broadcast medium. Well before Spielberg, directors like Arthur Penn, Robert Altman, and Bob Rafelson had become "notable innovators" in film after early careers directing television in the 1950s (Petrie and Stoneman 2014, 61). Moreover, Spielberg is not alone in having become a household name synonymous with the cinema by way of television. Before his production company Bad Robot took the reins of major film franchises like *Mission: Impossible*, the *Star Trek* reboot trilogy, and the *Star Wars* sequel trilogy, contemporary Hollywood visionary JJ Abrams established himself as a driving force behind television series including *Felicity* (1998–2002), *Alias* (2001–2006), and *Lost* (2004–2010). The professional trajectories of some of the most notable US filmmakers have thus run through television for decades.

This is not to say that television has been an in-road to film for everyone. Of course, we could name many notable filmmakers who have never worked in the television medium. But more importantly, the pathway to film production that runs through television is harder for some to tread than others. The exemplars mentioned so far all share in common not just success in leveraging television work into film careers, but also professional and social privileges as white cisgendered men. To ask how they reveal a pathway from television to film is also to consider what barriers might exist to get on that pathway in the first place and what inequalities might present obstacles along the way. The question of how the television industry supports film professionals is also a question of whose career aspirations that relationship does and does not support. According to *The Los Angeles Times*, only a dozen of the top-100 grossing films of 2019 were directed by women, who represented only 10.6% of all directors working overall, with less than 1% of those opportunities going to women of color (Sakoui 2020). This means that no matter what role television may or may not play, the pathways open to women and people of color to filmmaker careers are fewer and farther in between. An exploration of the way in which the professional pathway into film from television is constructed and made meaningful might therefore allow a better understanding of how such inequalities are produced. From that understanding of the way television has served as a meaningful gateway to career opportunity, we might also identify an opportunity to imagine how change and greater equity can follow.

With that in mind, this chapter develops several instructive case studies that reveal how some television professionals have transitioned into filmmaking careers, how these transformations of professional identity have come to be understood in the entertainment press, and how these professional advancements have transformed the way Hollywood filmmaking is understood. In doing so, it will be possible to identify the professional pathway from television to film both as one in which white men have been privileged in the past and as one that offers a path to greater inclusion in the future.

To support this examination, the chapter puts considerable focus on the way in which Marvel Studios has repeatedly turned to former television professionals to guide their extremely lucrative filmmaking enterprise (with a combined box office earning of over $8.5 billion over 23 films since 2008 as of this writing) (*Box Office Mojo* n.d.). As the centerpieces and culminations of their everything-is-connected Marvel Cinematic Universe strategy, the *Avengers* films have been consistently produced in collaboration between studio head Kevin Feige and a director whose most recent and most prominent credits were located in the world of television. The first *Avengers* film, released in 2012, was directed by Joss Whedon, then a cult-favorite television auteur known for the genre series *Buffy the Vampire Slayer* (1997–2003), *Angel* (1999–2004), *Firefly* (2002), and *Dollhouse* (2009–2010). While these shows attracted dedicated fan followings, none were mainstream hits, and Whedon's sole feature film directing credit prior to *The Avengers* was the continuation of *Firefly* in the form of the 2005 box office failure *Serenity*—offering less than definitive proof of his ability to translate television success to blockbuster filmmaking. Nevertheless, Whedon's *The Avengers* would deliver record box office returns, and he would carry on in this central creative role through the 2015 sequel *Avengers: Age of Ultron* (which meant not only directing the film, but consulting with directors assigned to Marvel's other projects). Following creative differences over that sequel, however, Whedon stepped away and Marvel sought new filmmakers to help steward the franchise. Next up were brothers Anthony and Joe Russo who, like Whedon, had some prior filmmaking credentials (most notably the 2002 indie release *Welcome to Collinwood* and the 2006 romantic comedy *You, Me and Dupree*), but hardly a track record proving their experience as stewards of a major action blockbuster. Yet like Whedon, the Russo brothers possessed a long list of television credentials, having directed the pilots for single-camera comedies, including *Arrested Development* (2003–2006, 2013–2019), for which they won an Emmy, and *Community* (2009–2015), for which they continued to serve as executive producers. After being hired by Marvel to direct the 2014 espionage thriller *Captain America: The Winter Soldier*, the Russo brothers directed the 2016 follow-up *Captain America: Civil War* and then stepped into the role vacated by Whedon to helm both *Avengers: Infinity War* (2018) and *Avengers: Endgame* (2019), released back-to-back in 2018 and 2019. Marvel has thus demonstrated a consistent pattern of entrusting its most valuable anchors in their film franchise to creators who honed their skills in television.

As much, then, as the success of the studio is a story of convergence between comics and film, we might also reconsider it as an industrial and creative crossover between film and television, where the production of blockbuster cinema relies extensively on the professional identities and creative skillsets of another entertainment field.

To explore these intersections, this chapter examines an archive of industry discourse that constructs meaning, identity, and value for these professional figures while trying to make some kind of sense out of the practices and decision-making processes of studios and other employers. As media industry scholars, including John Caldwell, have argued, trade journals can serve as "deep texts" that enable the communication and circulation of knowledge within and across different communities of industry workers (2009, 202). As publications that attract a professional readership (although surely non-professionals can read them, too), trade journals help generate shared, commonsense perceptions about how industries work, producing what Timothy Havens has called the "industry lore" (2006, 123) that regulates and shapes the way practitioners engage in and understand their work. While they often parrot press releases and adopt celebratory perspectives toward the industries they cover, trade journals nevertheless represent only one site of critical and reflexive discourse through which industry cultures are constructed. To examine the culture of professional development that extends from television to film through Marvel Studios, this chapter extends from an extensive review of stories published primarily in Hollywood trade journals from 2010 to 2020 that work to make sense of the hiring of figures like Whedon and the Russos as well as their career trajectories following their filmmaking successes. Although many publications like *Variety* and *Deadline* contribute to this discourse, as well as popular venues like *The New York Times*, *The Atlantic*, and many fan sites, the scope of this chapter limits what all could be examined, so emphasis has been placed on *The Hollywood Reporter* because of the greater resources it tends to devote to covering superhero films and other genre fare. Of course, the things that these directors and others say about their careers to *The Hollywood Reporter* are performative; but it is a specific kind of performance given in one of the preeminent venues in entertainment industry reporting, aimed at generating meaning and value from media work.

From this archive, the chapter first explores the advancement of the Russo brothers from their work in television, revealing the ways in which their television credits were positioned as commonsense, logical qualifications for Marvel's film enterprise. In doing so, this analysis demonstrates both efforts to make sense of this remarkable career trajectory and the strategies used to construct and assign value to television work within filmmaking practice. From there, the chapter next traces similarities surrounding the hiring of Joss Whedon, but with a focus much more on the ways in which the television-creator-turned-filmmaker is narrativized as the subject of transformation. Both Whedon and the Russos emerge in trade reporting not as television-film hyphenates who maintain a position in both industries, but instead as figures who have transitioned into new roles and spaces exclusive to film with their television pasts behind them. Even when these directors did, in fact, continue working in television, this industry discourse often did the counterfactual work of suggesting they continued to work exclusively as film professionals. The resulting professional culture is not one in which the lines between television and film become blurred so much as one in which professionals accrue value by crossing from one side to the other. At the same time, however, this crossover potential carries the possibilities of transforming film itself, and thus the chapter reveals the ways in which these career trajectories destabilize perceptions of the cinema and invite new kinds of professional experiences and competencies. After examining the value that industry lore ascribes to the perspectives that figures like the Russos bring to television, the chapter ends by reflecting on the potential for this professional pathway to diversify film production. While the white men at the center of this industry lore evince the film industry's continued refusal to look for value in a more diverse pool of contributors, this interest in the value of television creativity creates a parallel opportunity to imagine more inclusive forms of professional transformation. Women of color including Ava DuVernay have developed career narratives in which movement between television and film figures less as a step up between hierarchical fields and more as a fluid and non-hierarchical form of creative agency. While dominant industry narratives position professional movement from television to film work as a permanent upgrade for the worthy, these messier and more flexible arrangements reveal that these hierarchies need not remain intact.

Scorsese Was Right

In November 2019, acclaimed US film director Martin Scorsese ruffled feathers by claiming first in *Empire* magazine and then in a *New York Times* op-ed that, as much as the entertainment output of Marvel Studios had been a commercial success, it did not qualify as cinema. Since getting into the business of producing its own movies, rather than licensing that right out to major Hollywood studios, Marvel had released 23 films over an 11-year period that had consistently—and profitably—won over many fans and critics alike. Scorsese, however, was not among them: after trying to "watch a few" of Marvel's films, he concluded, "I tried, you know? But that's not cinema" (de Semlyen 2019). Although the director did not seem to openly begrudge their commercial success, and even acknowledged that the films could be "well made," he nevertheless sought to distinguish the spectacle that Marvel's superhero narratives offered from a cinematic art form that could deliver a sense of the "unexpected" while being grounded in everyday reality (Scorsese 2019). "It isn't the cinema of human beings trying to convey emotional, psychological experiences to another human being," he explained (de Semlyen 2019). Having drawn this boundary between the cinema and the outsized, spectacular images demanded of the superhero world, Scorsese invoked a longstanding criticism of blockbuster fare to liken Marvel product to the thrill ride: "Honestly, the closest I can think of them, as well made as they are, with actors doing the best they can under the circumstances, is theme parks" (de Semlyen 2019). Of course, Marvel's supporters in both fandom and the entertainment industries rushed to the defense, characterizing Scorsese as disappointingly elitist and out-of-touch (*Hollywood Reporter* 2019). Debate quickly followed to reassert the psychological and emotional reality behind characters like Iron Man and Thor, reaffirming Marvel's status as cinema on Scorsese's own terms. In adapting comic book narratives to the medium of film, Marvel product triggered a discourse on the nature of the cinema while inviting comparisons to theme parks and other entertainment forms.

While there is little point in trying to resolve that debate here, its terms do reveal productive possibilities for exploring the collision of industry worlds and rethinking what we think we understand when we invoke media like "film," "comics," or "television." Indeed, it is particularly ironic that Scorsese's platform to wax philosophical on the true nature of cinema in venues like *Empire* emerged from publicity surrounding *The Irishman* (2019) and its distribution deal with Netflix. Although the Scorsese-directed film had a limited theatrical release earlier in the month, it premiered on the streaming service on November 27. Its branding on the platform marked it as a "Netflix Film" to be more closely associated with the streaming service than other acquired content, almost disavowing that earlier theatrical release. To be sure, Netflix and Scorsese continued to call *The Irishman* a film—and yet its disarticulation from traditional distribution and exhibition contexts (and articulation to all the television content in the Netflix library) could certainly destabilize assumptions about the nature of cinema as a medium. However, rather than try to uncover the contradictions in Scorsese's statements or otherwise push back against his refusal to see the markers of cinema in what many would acknowledge as the biggest, most visible films of all time, we could alternatively embrace his polemic and consider the value of rejecting the assumption that all movies are cinema. Without agreeing with Scorsese's conclusion that Marvel films are best understood as theme parks, we can take his rejection of their claim to the cinema as an invitation to consider their strong relationship to other media (even beyond the comic books upon which they are narratively adapted).

Here, then, we can consider the value of understanding the Marvel Studios project in relation to television. This is not merely to acknowledge that Marvel Studios often engages in television-related extensions of their brand—although series like *Agents of SHIELD* (2013–2020) and *Daredevil* (2015–2018) might certainly be part of the story. Instead, it is to recognize that despite the distribution and exhibition of Marvel films to be screened theatrically by paying audiences, the creative and industrial dynamics that generate this product owe significantly to the forms, practices, and communities of television.

Only most obviously, the serialized nature of Marvel films invites comparison to television. Character arcs unfold not within films, but across them: Tony Stark, the "genius billionaire playboy philanthropist" of *Iron Man* (2008) and *Iron Man 2* (2010), enters into the narrative of *The Avengers* as a figure of self-assuredness; but his encounter with an overwhelming alien invasion force at the end of that film leads him to grapple with new anxieties and feelings of inadequacy in *Iron Man 3* (2013). As this arc progresses, he succumbs to fears that put the world at greater risk in *Avengers: Age of Ultron* and destabilize his primary alliances in *Captain America: Civil War*. Although he tries to build new alliances as a mentor in *Spider-Man: Homecoming* (2017), the weight of prior failures leads to crushing defeat in *Avengers: Infinity War* and the death of his protégé. His final appearance in *Avengers: Endgame* resolves this arc of compounded defeat: Stark finally finds redemption by sacrificing himself to eliminate the overwhelming threat foreshadowed in *The Avengers*, thereby achieving the security he had sought since that film, restoring broken alliances, and even resurrecting his protégé—whose arc now continues by taking on the mantle of the mentor in *Spider-Man: Far From Home* (2019). Considering this unfolding narrative between 2008 and 2019, it is easy to make comparisons to the long-form storytelling strategies of television in which soap operas and other generic forms have accustomed viewers to following characters' storylines for years across episodic installments. That said, such an analysis would recognize the qualities of narrative seriality as an essential element of television, despite the fact that not all television forms are so serialized, and television does not possess a monopoly on stories told by installment. Indeed, we should be cautious about ascribing a televisuality to the seriality of Marvel Studios' films in that the comic book medium being adapted has long been serialized, and the project of building a shared story world across different ongoing titles is a strategy that Marvel's films have drawn from these periodical publishing industry origins.

Instead of looking solely at the textual level of narrative form and strategy, then, we might find deeper connections between film and television by examining more carefully the intersections of creative cultures at a production level. Here, attention to creative labor and professional communities that cross the boundaries between film and television can reveal how the making of this billion-dollar blockbuster content depends in significant part on the experiences, skills, and sensibilities of those who have navigated the demands of television storytelling. Marvel Studios' relationship with Joe and Anthony Russo provides an excellent example of the film industry's reliance upon television producers and their experience as a means of delivering a particular kind of cinema.

Television Creators for Hire

Prior to their engagement by Marvel to direct *Captain America: The Winter Soldier*, the Russo brothers had established themselves as expert television directors with a reputation for shepherding the creative process of producing pilot episodes. Although television directing is transitory work—where a director might come in to direct one or two consecutive episodes before another steps in to tackle the next installment—this work directing pilots meant that the Russos often set the look, sound, and tone of series that future directors would follow in subsequent episodes. The Russos did not begin their careers in television work, however. Their first post-graduate project was the self-financed 1997 film *Pieces*, which did not see wide release in the United States, but caught the attention of film director Steven Soderbergh when screened at the Slamdance Film Festival. In 2002, Soderbergh produced their next film, *Welcome to Collinwood*. It was at this point that their careers shifted to television, as 20th Century Fox hired the Russos to direct the 2003 pilots for both the FX cable crime series *Lucky* and the FOX network comedy *Arrested Development*. For the latter series, the duo would win an Emmy, and they continued to direct subsequent episodes before its cancellation in 2005. Meanwhile, they lent their talent to other pilots like ABC's dramedy *What About Brian* (2006–2007) and stepped in as directors on NBC's airport drama *LAX* (2004–2005). This is not to suggest that television had eclipsed film in the Russo brothers' ambitions. While engaged in this TV work, the Russos directed the 2006 film comedy release *You, Me, and Dupree* for Universal. However, this one major studio release represents the Russos' sole film directing credit between their 2002 *Welcome to Collinwood* debut and their emergence on the blockbuster scene with 2014's *Captain America: The Winter Soldier*. The Russos thus spent over a decade engaged primarily as television creators, working across a number of different genres and networks. A closer examination of their selection as the directors of *The Winter Soldier* can therefore reveal how the skills and professional sensibilities associated with television creation came to be understood as a valuable and essential component of filmmaking under Marvel's banner.

In October 2006, on the heels of the summer release of *You, Me, and Dupree*, *The Hollywood Reporter* reported on a follow-up deal with Universal and Imagine Entertainment in which the Russos and partner Phil Johnston would develop new film and TV projects, including one called "A Friggin' Christmas Miracle." Simultaneously, the report noted, the Russos had secured a development agreement with Touchstone TV for the single-camera comedy project "Life Is Super." Lest this sound like a superhero project that presaged their later work for Marvel, "Life is Super" focused on a woman raising five adopted and unremarkable children; but if greenlit, the Russos would have directed the pilot and served in a continuing capacity as executive producers. Surely the release of *You, Me, and Dupree* had helped attract attention to the Russos, but nevertheless they continued to work in the arena of television and descriptions of them in trade reports emphasized their value as "Emmy winners" for the *Arrested Development* pilot (Andreeva and Kit 2006). This emphasis on their television accomplishments continued the next year as the Russos signed on to direct the pilot for the ABC comedy *Carpoolers* (2007–2008). By 2007, *The Hollywood Reporter* described the Russos as experienced pilot directors, citing not only their accolades for *Arrested Development*, but also their accomplishments getting *Lucky* and *What About Brian* off the ground. Their film credits were certainly acknowledged, but this trade reportage presented the Russos as less accomplished in that regard: this film work is noted as a feather in their cap, to be sure, but also as a sidenote to their greater television accomplishments. The superlative account of their pilot work as having "earned them an Emmy" outshined the more descriptive acknowledgement that they "most recently helmed the comedy feature" (Andreeva 2007). As the length of time since the release of *You, Me, and Dupree* increased, in fact, the Russos' expertise came to be framed more exclusively in terms of television accomplishments. In April 2008, the Russos signed to direct the pilot for "Courtroom K," a single-camera comedy for ABC, at which point *The Hollywood Reporter* ignored their film credits entirely and explained their qualifications by virtue of their experience on *Arrested Development* and *Lucky*, as well as, of course, their Emmy award (Nordy and Andreeva 2008). Collectively, these trade reports worked to endorse the qualifications and value that the Russos brought to the various projects they developed in this period, ultimately situating their talents within the world of television. In these reports' contributions to industry lore, it made sense that the Russos would be in line for these opportunities given their television credits.

In 2009, the Russos signed with NBC-Universal to direct the pilot and serve as executive producers for the comedy series *Community*—an opportunity that further situated the Russos within the generic traditions of episodic television. Although each episode of the series focused on a core cast of six community college classmates, these installments could vary significantly in style and genre while borrowing from the traditions of other media like film and video games. When the characters engaged in a campus-wide paintball match in the episode "Modern Warfare," for example, *Community* embraced the conventions of the action film. In another episode, "Digital Estate Planning," the action unfolded in the virtual space of a side-scrolling video game. "Critical Film Theory" spoofed Quentin Tarantino films, while "Intermediate Documentary Filmmaking" adopted mockumentary camera work and editing styles. In discussing their work on *Community*, the Russos insisted that the variability in genre and style made the series distinct from most television content. "We look for opportunities to be different from episode to episode in style," Joe Russo explained to *The Hollywood Reporter*. "It's running against the grain of what's traditional in television." In the same article, Anthony added, "it just lent itself to a wide range of exploration because you're at a community college—anything could be going on there, any type of class, any type of subject" (Hueso 2011).

Yet while the Russos figured this variability as a means of distinguishing *Community* from other television series, their interest in experimentation with different conventions and styles in each episode reflects the strategies that have long been central to television series production as creators face the challenge of producing dozens, if not hundreds, of episodes in succession. As Jeffrey Sconce writes, the art of television lies in balancing "differentiation amid repetition"; although all generic forms involve some kind of variation on repeated conventions, television "faces a unique challenge. Rather than produce potentially infinite variations on a common structure [...] television must produce 'parts' that each week embody the whole while also finding, within such repetition, possibilities for novel and diverting variations" (2002, 101). Sconce identifies "stock plots" held in common across different television series—such as characters meeting evil twins or getting amnesia in ways that cause them to behave in new ways—not as evidence of unoriginality, but instead as opportunities to "revel in a familiar character inverted and defamiliarized without consequence" (102). In that sense, the stylistic and generic play of *Community* represents the continuing evolution of these televisual efforts to balance difference and repetition, allowing the world of the series to be rebuilt around an array of different—but familiar and legible—storytelling formulae. Considered in this way, the work that the Russos (and many others) did on *Community*—and subsequently highlighted in their public reflections on their craft in the trade press—could be considered television *par excellence*.

These publicly visible claims about the value of episodic differentiation to television, and the Russo brothers' ability to excel in that practice, provide significant context for understanding their move from television back to film. In June 2011, the Russos signed an overall deal that would supposedly "bind" them to the NBC-Universal studio for the next two years with the charge of developing new projects while staying on as *Community* executive producers. Noting the nine pilots successfully brought to series production by the Russos over the previous decade, *The Hollywood Reporter* framed this deal as a boon for NBC, quoting entertainment chairman Bob Greenblatt who remarked:

> Our new deal with the Russo brothers shows that NBC is looking for creative producers who are both successful and not afraid to take chances [...] Their unique vision and ingenuity should result in some very edgy content that will capture everyone's attention.
>
> *(Rose 2011)*

While it is unclear whether the Russos saw this two-year deal to its completion, their next contract would seemingly turn on the value that their unique vision and ingenuity could have for supporting a sequence of blockbuster films.

In June 2012, *The Hollywood Reporter* announced that the Russos had entered negotiations with Marvel to direct *The Winter Soldier*. According to the commentary offered by the trade publication, "the brothers continue Marvel's strategy of finding unorthodox helmers for their movies. The Russos are known more for their work in comedy" (Kit 2012). The competition for the director's chair was described as a "bake-off" in which the contenders had to "study *The Avengers* as part of their exam." These contenders included George Nolfi, who had previously directed the sci-fi thriller *The Adjustment Bureau* (2011), and F. Gary Gray, whose seven previous film directing credits included *Friday* (1995) as well as the action thrillers *Set It Off* (1996), *The Negotiator* (1998), *The Italian Job* (2003), and more. While *The Hollywood Reporter* informed its readers about this process by which candidates proved themselves to Marvel, it also implicitly assured its readers that this process made sense and that, despite their lack of experience in directing action thrillers, the Russos' knowledge of *The Avengers* seemingly made them a good fit. The Russos were a counterintuitive choice that demanded explanation and reflection—despite years of credits in film and television alike. Even as the success of *Avengers: Endgame* seemed to confirm the wisdom of Marvel's choice in 2019, popular reflections still mused that theirs was "an unlikely journey." An *Atlantic* article commented that "Before the two were brought into the Marvel fold by the company's chief producer, Kevin Feige, nothing about the Russo's resume suggested that they'd be particularly suited to big-budget superhero storytelling" (Sims 2019). So with this lack of relevant experience, what creative perspective is it that the Russos could have been seen to offer Marvel?

It's easy to imagine that white privilege would have played some role here as the Russos' list of film credits was certainly dwarfed by Gray, an African American film veteran whose oeuvre much better matched the espionage-thriller tone of *Winter Soldier*. However, Gray reportedly removed himself from contention in order to direct the hip-hop biopic *Straight Outta Compton* (2015), a move that *Forbes'* Scott Mendelson (2015) speculates could have worked out to Gray's advantage:

> Had he directed *Captain America 2*, he likely would have been one of Marvel's many 'one and done' filmmakers with merely a guaranteed smash hit comic book movie to his name. That's not nothing, but the success of *Straight Outta Compton* belongs to him.

The *Winter Soldier* job could have been Gray's to lose; but as long as we're entertaining speculation, it's worth noting that for the Russos, *Winter Soldier* was not a one-and-done job, but the first step on a journey to producing two of the five highest grossing films of all time. One could imagine whether Gray missed out on more than one directing role, or whether the Russos' whiteness somehow positioned them to remain in a position that might otherwise have been a one-and-done deal for a non-white director. Of course, these are not issues on which one would expect any of the parties involved to make public comment.

Instead, what the Russos have publicly disclosed about how they secured the directors' chair involves capitalizing on the value of their skills as managers of television narrative. Although many of these claims have been made in the years since, the Russos have in several interviews explained the rationale by which they were able to convince Marvel of their potential, and those stories of professional accomplishment invariably identify the relevance of their television experience to contemporary mainstream cinema. First, the Russos have foregrounded the utility of their experience as managers of generic difference within series repetition to the franchise model of filmmaking that drives Marvel and, increasingly, blockbuster cinema as a whole. "Another thing we learned from working on *Community* is that we were just constantly exploring and subverting genre," Joe Russo explained. "It seemed every week we were changing up our style and our tone, the look and feel of it, the score, the way the characters behaved. We were able to explore genre on a very deep level" (Mancuso 2020). Russo echoed popular criticism around the Marvel films that attribute their success in large part to their generic flexibility, where every installment distinguishes itself by drawing on a different genre formula (Phillipson 2019; Prell 2016). While they all involve superheroes, one film might place those characters in the confines of a war film, the next in a spy thriller, the next in space opera, and the next in a comedy. As Joe Russo explained, it was the experience of working in episodic television that made them stand out as potential creative collaborators for Marvel: "When you're subverting genre, you're studying to an extent that you're really understanding the nuances of it. This was critical and certainly the paint ball episodes [of *Community*] were a huge part of our Marvel career" (Mancuso 2020). Russo posited that their television careers made them genre experts, and this made them a match to Marvel's filmmaking needs above and beyond their list of film credits.

That generic expertise supported a second claim about how the Russos' television experience matched the needs of contemporary film. Regardless of whether series are set in space, in hospitals, in domestic settings, or elsewhere, conventional US television narratives have frequently revolved around ensemble casts and relationships between characters that evoke a sense of family (even if those families are not bound by kinship but by shared workplaces and other shared social contexts). Here, too, the Russos figured their strong experience in managing television ensembles and complex family dynamics as attuned to the needs of Marvel's filmmaking enterprise. While the character of Tony Stark may have a serialized arc, his is only one of many that Marvel Studios developed over the course of over 20 films—a narrative balancing act that television creators have experience navigating. As Joe Russo noted:

> you'll see that we've worked with ensembles almost exclusively throughout our career. Eccentric ensembles with diverse characters [...] Certainly we learned how to tell stories with many characters [...] in a compressed time frame. Sometimes we'd have 20, 30 speaking roles in an episode of *Community* that's 21 minutes long. There's certainly a lot of time spent,

and energy spent, training ourselves to do that [...] in a credible way where the story and characters hold together.

(Mancuso 2020)

In a separate interview, Anthony Russo similarly framed the skill of managing television ensembles as the edge they needed to thrive in their filmmaking for Marvel:

We spent about a decade in television [...] and I think that background helped to prepare us for the serialised stories that we have going in the MCU [...] If you look at all of our work, Joe and I have always been drawn to ensemble work [...] From our very first movie, and through all of our television work, we love working with ensembles.

(Cashin 2019)

Notably, Anthony Russo traced this talent for ensemble work as something that stretched back beyond their television projects to their earliest film projects. In doing so, he argued that the link between television and film goes beyond the specific, interconnected superhero universes of Marvel Studios, where the management of ensemble casts is a skill demanded of directors in both media in the 21st century. Joe Russo even suggested that this skill is required in response to generational shifts in which a younger generation of viewers "is more invested in serialized storytelling than they are in two-hour narratives" (Sims 2019). From that perspective, the Russos portrayed television as the best training ground for that learning skill, permitting them a valuable perspective compared to filmmakers more strictly defined by and limited to film work conceived as a one-off.

In framing *The Avengers* as ensemble, moreover, the directors figure the character relations in terms of the serialization of television family dynamics. As Anthony described their second Marvel film, *Captain America: Civil War*:

That movie was so much about examining the Avengers as a family unit, and breaking them up, basically divorcing them in that movie. And that was the setting for Thanos to arrive [in *Avengers: Infinity War*], because what better moment for the greatest threat the Avengers are ever gonna face than having the Avengers at their absolute lowest point ... because we have these skills for television and this taste for ensemble storytelling that I think complimented [*sic*] where we were going with the narrative in the MCU. (Cashin 2019)

In statements like these, the Russos tied the management of family relations to the serialized arc of the narrative as it is parceled out in each film installment. This sense of family required attention to character relations not just in specific moments, but also as they evolved and deepened over time. Anthony Russo thus explained to *The Atlantic* that the process of managing these ensembles meant considering the "depth of emotion" that audiences might develop for characters over time, which in television production requires tracking sizable casts of characters over many years, seeding and paying off narrative threads that might develop across seasons, and hiding clues and Easter eggs to support fan speculation and excitement (Sims 2019). In this emphasis on the serialization of film, the Russos identified as their inspiration for breaking the story not the structures of previous film sequels and trilogies, but instead serialized works of television like *Breaking Bad* (2008–2013):

> we always talked about *Breaking Bad* as a modern example of writing yourself into a corner [...] I remember watching it over that period of time and thinking at the end of every episode, how the hell are they going to move this show forward into the next episode?
>
> *(Molloy 2019)*

While the Russos self-reflexively defined their value as filmmakers in terms of the management of genre, ensemble casts, and serialized storytelling, they also inserted into the discourse on contemporary blockbuster filmmaking an insistence of the value of television production practices and techniques. With *Infinity War* and *Endgame* shot back-to-back for release in 2018 and 2019, respectively, Marvel's release model demanded quicker, more multitasked directorial roles than those enjoyed by one-off film directors. As Anthony Russo stressed to attendees of the Milken Institute conference in 2019, television production requires pre-production, production, and post-production to overlap, where one episode might be in the process of editing while another is shooting and another is still at the script stage; he likened the making of these *Avengers* films to that cyclical, simultaneously multiple mode of television production, and postulated that it was television experience that enabled this kind of filmmaking: "We had the training from TV to do that" (Frost 2019). At the level of production planning and execution, then, television offers a model and arena of expertise that accorded professional value to the Russos as filmmakers.

The result of this discourse is a reading of *The Avengers* films as television and the Russos as the "TV guys" (Frost 2019) who brought its serialized storytelling together on screen. In some accounts, the Marvel Cinematic Universe could be understood as a form of watercooler media through the creative trajectories it shared with the Russos' earlier television work:

> the original fans of *Community* or *Arrested Development* had no choice to watch en masse: piled into the living room, clustered around the television, phone off the hook [...] It's a collective experience of this ilk [...] that draws audiences into movie theaters.
>
> *(Frost 2019)*

Forgiving the overly nostalgic and ahistorical nature of the claim (as if *Community* and *Arrestment Development* hailed from an era prior to DVRs, DVDs, and online video), it credits the Russos' television experience with making Marvel's product into must-see cinema. Other critics have posited that the Russos' work with the Avengers franchise is merely retelling of *Community*, where the television series presaged everything that the Russos would do in their films, tracing similarities down to character beats and plot devices tied to quantum realities (Gumeny 2019). Interestingly, this view renders invisible all the collaborators involved in these film and television projects alongside the Russos—from *Community* creator Dan Harmon, to Marvel creative chief Kevin Feige, to the directors of the 17 Marvel films the Russos did not direct. Yet this exaggerated assessment of the Russos' creative power, authorship, and influence nevertheless reveals the commonsense acceptance of the value that their television experience can bring to the world of blockbuster filmmaking.

Transforming into a Filmmaker

Just because television skills can accrue value in the world of filmmaking, however, this does not mean that the professional identity of being a "filmmaker" does not still carry its own value, status, and prestige compared to the world of television. As much as the Russos leveraged their television experience to position themselves for success in Marvel's filmmaking enterprises, the trade press and other sites of industry lore-making portrayed them as "TV guys" who had now become fully-fledged film professionals. Nor were they the only creative figures in the Marvel stable with significant television credits that trade reporting figured as having transformed into creatures of the cinema. Like the Russos, Joss Whedon developed a significant reputation for himself in television before leveraging that success into an opportunity to work with Marvel's serialized character ensemble as director of *Avengers* and *Avengers: Age of Ultron*. While this chapter so far has focused on the claims made during and about the Russos' initial attempts to cross (back) over into filmmaking following a long television career, this section now explores how the careers of the Russos and Whedon alike came to be narrativized in the entertainment trade press following the achievement of that professional crossover. After these directors proved the value of their television experience to filmmaking endeavors, industry discourse about their careers suggested that they had undergone some kind of transformation. While they had built on their television skillsets to succeed in their filmmaking pursuits, that process had been one of metamorphosis where the "TV guys" were now movie guys.

Although he has been more recently accused of abusing his power to engage in inappropriate relationships, Joss Whedon was once considered a feminist icon and cult hero, celebrated for his work bringing series like *Buffy the Vampire Slayer*, *Angel*, *Firefly*, and *Dollhouse* to television screens. Even after these allegations became public in 2017, trade discourse about Whedon commonly adopted a celebratory tone, describing him in terms such as "a pioneering voice for female-focused genre fare, having created the hit TV show Buffy the Vampire Slayer two decades ago" (Kit 2018). Such descriptions acknowledged his status as a cult figure and the feminist ideals that once seemed at the foundation of his strong female heroines. Many media scholars shared this assessment of Whedon as a televisual god, with an entire journal and conference devoted to research involving his works. In short, Whedon's television career had made him a revered cult figure. Thus when *The Hollywood Reporter* previously reflected on his growing status thanks to the visibility of the 2012 *Avengers* film, it similarly noted that "The Marvel blockbuster is about to make him a household name, but to some, he's long been an icon" (Zakarin, "Exploring" 2012). That iconic status owed to television and the cult following he was able to cultivate in niche genres like fantasy and science fiction as well as in more narrowcast networks like the WB and UPN that had targeted younger viewers. "Owing more to comic book storylines and feminist literature than any past or present TV show at the time," *The Hollywood Reporter* explained of Whedon's signature 1996–2002 television series, "*Buffy* mixed fantasy and teenage drama to produce both emotional connections to characters and complex, engrossing mythology" (Zakarin, "Exploring" 2012). On at least one instance, Whedon identified the medium of television as being more amenable to this sort of content than the contemporaneous film industry—although he acknowledged that this was not always the case. "Female-driven stories are a part of TV in a way that they used to be part of movies," Whedon explained, before suggesting that women have now come to find greater opportunities on-screen in television, even if equality lags behind the camera: "Even before it was respectable, a great film actress could make a home in TV and get much more to work with—especially after a certain age" (O'Connell 2017).

Like the Russos after him, Whedon entered into his relationship with Marvel Studios with a reputation based in television, which seemed to mesh with his particular storytelling interests. Unlike the Russos, however, Whedon had previously crossed paths with Marvel projects outside of television at earlier points in his career: he had written an early version of the screenplay for the 20th Century Fox production of *X-Men* (2000) and had leveraged the cult fandom surrounding his television series to attract interest from the comic book industry. Among projects for other publishers, he was hired by Marvel to write *Astonishing X-Men* in 2004 and *Runaways* in 2007. Whedon thus had significantly more direct prior experience in the world of superheroes and comic books than did the Russos before directing a Marvel film. Yet despite this cult credibility, Whedon's film directing experience remained comparable. The trade press thus responded somewhat skeptically to Whedon's suitability to manage a feature film on the scope of *The Avengers*; *Variety*'s review for the film remarked that "With only one feature directorial credit to his name, the middling 2005 sci-fier *Serenity*, Whedon of *Buffy* fame would not have been the first name on most people's lists to tame such a potentially unwieldy project." In the face of the film's success, however, publications like these engaged in a sense-making project to explain how, "from a logistical point of view alone," these television credentials allowed Whedon to impose "a grip on the material that feels like that of a benevolent general, marshaling myriad technical resources while juggling eight major characters" (McCarthy 2012).

However, as much as Whedon's creative identity had been constructed in and around television, the start of his filmmaking relationship with Marvel brought with it a narrative of professional transformation. Although Whedon may have been a "TV guy" when he signed on to direct *The Avengers*, that crossing of boundaries into film brought with it a recalibration of his professional identity and the values ascribed to creative skillsets developed in the training ground of television. In this recalibration, the move from television to film is figured more as a break, a passage from one realm to another, rather than the professional occupation of a middle ground between them. In this narrative of transformation, the creator wraps himself in a cocoon woven from the silky skills of television production and emerges on the other side as a beautiful filmmaker. The process is imagined as metamorphosis, not hybridity. For example, in 2010, when reporting on Whedon's career trajectory at the conclusion of his Fox television series *Dollhouse* and the beginning of his work on *The Avengers*, *The Hollywood Reporter* explained that the director "swears off TV—for now" (Hibberd 2010). Although this framing did allow for Whedon to return one day, it figured his move into filmmaking as one that involved an imposed distance from television. No longer a caterpillar, the butterfly must be a butterfly. After the release of *The Avengers* in 2012, a letter that Whedon wrote to thank his fans captured the trade paper's attention by showing that Whedon "isn't letting the blockbuster success of his Marvel film change him." Yet despite that instance of continuity, *The Hollywood Reporter* commented on this letter by insisting that "his TV days are seemingly in the past" (Zakarin, "Joss Whedon" 2012). Despite promising not to change, the TV guy was no longer a TV guy.

Of course, this narrative is complicated and rendered somewhat counter-factual by the fact that Whedon's relationship with Marvel in no way precluded continuing investment in the medium of television. Most obviously, the success of *The Avengers* led Marvel to begin experimenting with TV production, and Whedon was asked to play a major creative role in the making of *Agents of SHIELD*, a 2013–2020 espionage adventure program made for broadcast network ABC that spun off a minor but recurring character from the Marvel films, Agent Phil Coulson, and introduced a new team of characters to become his television family. Whedon co-created the series alongside brother Jed Whedon and Maurissa Tancharoen, directing the pilot but handing them the role of showrunners. Sharing news of the development of the series and the deals made to establish these roles, *The Hollywood Reporter* wrote that "*S.H.I.E.L.D.* marks Whedon's return to the small screen" (Goldberg 2012). At this point, it had only been two years since Whedon had "sworn off" television at the end of his last series, yet this language of a return suggested that there was significant distance to be crossed to bring him back from his filmmaking pursuits. Indeed, this notion of a return persisted in discussing Whedon's post-*Avengers* television interests, reinforcing the idea that a break had occurred even in the face of significant professional continuity. Much of the press surrounding *SHIELD* revealed considerable concern with establishing the extent of Whedon's involvement in the series even as he continued in his role as Marvel filmmaker in preparations for the 2015 sequel *Avengers: Age of Ultron.* When asked "how big" his involvement with the television series would be, Whedon tempered expectations by responding "As much as an exec producer can who is also making a movie [...] I got the best writers and actors I could so I could do this and that's the best way to run a show" (Goldberg 2013). Although Whedon positioned himself between film and television, the comments belied the primacy of his filmmaking role and the proxies he claimed he would be using to maintain a presence on television. He thus created reason to consider his supposed return to television with some uncertainty, and in some ways the interview proceeded to suggest that as an extension of *The Avengers* film franchise, *SHIELD* did not constitute a completely legitimate reinvestment in television on Whedon's part. "Will Whedon look to return to the TV with his own property after *SHIELD*," it asked, to which he responded by throwing cold water on the idea that television might be one of his priorities: "The goal is never about the medium, it's always about the next story" (Goldberg 2013). Whedon certainly positioned himself as having the potential to work wherever he wanted, free of constraint to any one medium—yet this is also an implicit affirmation that he had transformed and moved on from his previously close association with television.

There is a difference, then, between the credits that figures like Whedon continued to amass across film and television alike and the way that industry lore constructed the relationship of crossing those boundaries as one of transformation from one state of professional creativity and fixed media identification to the next. The issue is not just whether Whedon and others continued to work in television as they explored filmmaking careers, but how trade stories circulated to make sense of and give value to that work. In this case, industry lore could insist on constructing professional identities in terms of transformations and returns between fixed, binary states. So in 2018, when Whedon signed a new executive producer deal to help develop a television comedy project for Freeform called "Pippa Smith: Grown-Up Detective," *The Hollywood Reporter* navigated this boundary crossing, explaining its exceptional status as a

> rare small-screen project for Whedon, who last exec produced ABC's Agents of SHIELD, though he is not considered to be closely involved in the Marvel drama on which his brother and sister-in-law, Jed Whedon and Maurissa Tancharoen, serve as showrunners.

The article further underlined that Whedon "most recently has focused on features" and listed his TV credits as *Firefly* and *Angel*, rather than the more recent *Dollhouse* (Goldberg, "Developing" 2018). The image of Whedon as filmmaker persisted, thanks to caveats that downplayed his involvement in *SHIELD* and other more recent television projects, creating the impression of a more unbroken commitment to cinema. This insistence on Whedon's transformation could even be counter-factual. In a 2018 story about the development of the Joss Whedon–created HBO series *The Nevers* (2020–), *The Hollywood Reporter* used very similar language about a "return to the small screen" and emphasized the difference between his distant executive producer role and the day-to-day showrunner roles on *SHIELD*. Yet it disavowed Whedon's co-creator role on *SHIELD* to claim that *The Nevers* would be "the first show he has created since Fox's *Dollhouse*" (Goldberg, "Sci-Fi" 2018). At some level, this was a simple error or difference of interpretation in what counts as "creating" a series, perhaps distinguishing creation from co-creation; but whatever the cause, the result reinforces the notion that Whedon stepped away from television and became a fully-fledged filmmaker in the interim. The insistence on the exceptional status of projects like "Pippa Smith" and *The Nevers* confirmed the extent of this transformation.

Returning to the "unlikely" film career of the Russo brothers, we can see a similar narrative of transformation from TV guys to "Marvel's main movie executors" (Siegemund-Broka and Kit 2015). Following the success of *The Winter Solider* in 2014, the Russos had developed sufficient bankability to stretch beyond their relationship with Marvel and command a first-look deal with Sony Pictures in March 2015. The announcement of this deal in trade reports made clear that it represented a contract commensurate with their new roles in Hollywood rather than a television deal that would extend their previous professional identities. First, the statement supplied by the Russos themselves foregrounded their identities as filmmakers: "The studio has created an environment that is not only collaborative but truly filmmaker-friendly, and we're excited to begin developing both new and ambitious material with them." Meanwhile, in its own framing, *The Hollywood Reporter* invoked the same notion of transformation with which filmmaking careers like Whedon's had previously been understood: "The duo reinvented themselves as action and genre moviemakers after years of working in television comedy," it explained (Kit 2015). Here transformation figured as a process of reinvention, where the Russos drew upon their television skillsets to make *Winter Soldier*, but emerged on the other side as filmmakers. Such an account imagines the move between television and film not necessarily as a natural or intuitive one, nor one easily reversed.

This Sony deal did not preclude the Russos from continuing to work with Marvel to direct *Captain America: Civil War*, and after Whedon stepped away from directing any more Marvel films in 2015, they had further opportunity to take on development duties for *Avengers: Infinity War* and *Endgame*. "The Infinity get is a massive feather in the duo's cap," wrote *The Hollywood Reporter* in

March 2015, "and marks the latest in an incredible career trajectory" stretching from television to film, where "It was their work on some of the geeky episodes of *Community*, however, that led to *Winter Soldier*" (Siegemund-Broka and Kit 2015). Yet the transformation of the Russos into filmmakers was perhaps made clearer by the way in which they framed their forays into "branded entertainment" (Jarvey 2014) less as an extension of television's commercial imperatives and more as part of their new status as filmmakers. Along with film director Justin Lin, the Russos created in 2014 a company called Bullitt. Named after the 1968 Steve McQueen film and inspired by the way that film showcased the Ford Mustang as one of the "greatest commercials" ever made, the new company aimed to produce "commercials and longform entertainment" that might perform the same function (Jarvey 2014). Although this commercial function arguably fit with the Russos' television experience, the endeavor was embedded in cineaste pleasures and positioned as a "filmmakers' collective" involving partners like directors Louis Leterrier and Troy Miller, cinematographer Phedon Papamichael, and Tony Scott's RSA Films. Even when directly involved in the seemingly more televisual work of producing commercials—such as a three-and-a-half-minute project for Smirnoff Vodka made while working on *Civil War*—the Russos' post-Marvel work accrued alternative value as part of a filmmaking enterprise.

Meanwhile, like Whedon, the Russos' ongoing relationship as directors of Marvel's films did not preclude continuing work in the realm of television, despite their seeming transformation. In July 2014, for example, Marvel announced that the Russo brothers had agreed to direct the second and third episodes of *Agent Carter* (2015–2016), an ABC television series with thematic tie-ins to *SHIELD* that created a starring vehicle for Hayley Atwell's Peggy Carter character from the *Captain America* films. The same report said Joe Johnston, director of the first *Captain America* (2011), was interested in directing his own episode "if the scheduling works out." In actuality, only Joe Russo would make time in his schedule to direct a single episode. Yet the possibility of either of the Russos participating in the series was envisioned less as a return to the television arena in which they were expert, and instead as "Captain America: Winter Soldier directors … headed to ABC's Agent Carter" (Couch 2014). The story being told was one of film professionals chipping in to help get a new television endeavor off the ground, rather than entertaining the possibilities that the Russos are still TV guys at heart (indeed, only one of them ended up delivering on this promised return).

Instead, the Russos now functioned as filmmakers in the stories of creativity and professionalism circulated in the media industries. In July 2014, for example, they were honored by the 10th Annual HollyShorts Film Festival. Event spokespeople told *The Hollywood Reporter* that they were

> proud to present Joe and Anthony Russo with the 2014 HollyShorts Visionary Award […] We've seen their meteoric ascent through the years,

and what's special about them is how they always look to inspire the next generation of filmmakers—and that's what our festival is all about.

(Ford 2014)

These claims about their "rise" and "ascent" suggested that the incredible trajectory their career followed had not been a value-neutral one, but a move from the less prestigious field of television to the level of success they had only just recently found as filmmakers. "Meteoric" suggested a marked difference from their earlier status to the one they now enjoyed. *The Hollywood Reporter* confirmed this in their commentary when they explained that the Russos "got their start as indie filmmakers and later went on to direct and produce shows like *Arrested Development* and *Community*. *Captain America: The Winter Soldier*, which hit theatres in April, has earned a stellar $713.2 million worldwide to date" (Ford 2014). Their television credentials were not disavowed by any means, but they were also sandwiched in between a romantic indie identity and their recent blockbuster filmmaker success; television was invoked as the realm of relative obscurity in which they toiled before finally ascending to their earliest filmmaking dreams.

Following the record-breaking performance of *Avengers: Endgame* in 2019, the Russos traded on a professional identity firmly situated in the world of filmmaking. Make no mistake—they still spoke profusely about their television production roots, the value of it, and the power it had given them to prosper in contemporary Hollywood, as the first part of this chapter made clear. However, that television experience was simultaneously framed as part of a transformation in which the Russos had now become something else. The same interviews in which they spoke of the value of their television experience could also help secure their credibility as filmmakers, where the special effects–driven spectacle of *Endgame*, for example, could be related by Joe Russo to their life-long love of Michelangelo Antonioni. The Russos cited inspiration from his strategies of using the environment to reflect "the psychology of the characters. We use the digital internegative in our real set design and in our CG set design to reflect psychology, but not in a way that's as highly expressionisitic as 'Red Desert' " (Desowitz 2019). While those references to the film canon might not read to many Marvel fans—and are certainly less likely to resonate than nods to *Community* or *Arrested Development*—they help secure a claim to this newer, transcendent professional identity. Their television references create value out of where they have been, while the film references generate value out of the position in which they have arrived at the end of that transformative trajectory. Having finished their obligations to Marvel, the Russos and their AGBO Films company established a new partnership with storied Hollywood film studio MGM aimed at leveraging its library to support a host of new film remakes (Fleming 2019). Meanwhile, even while looking fondly back at the television series, Joe Russo envisioned his potential future involvement with *Community* as a movie rather than something that would unfold on television (Mancuso 2020).

Ultimately, the story of professional success under construction in this industry lore is one that can begin with television, but seems to end with film.

The Spaces between Filmmakers and TV Guys

These cases make clear that television has served as a pathway to film careers. While Whedon and the Russos are perhaps, echoing Steven Spielberg, upper-limit examples where television skillsets provide opportunities to manage the most expensive and visible Hollywood productions of the 21st century, we could list any number of other film professionals who launched their careers working in network or cable television. With a simple Google search, it is not hard to find long lists of renowned directors who learned their craft in television's training grounds over the past 70 years (Hall 2013; *MeTV* 2016). These resources ask us to consider alongside those directors already mentioned here a long list of TV professionals turned film auteurs, including Jonathan Demme, Sam Peckinpah, James L. Brooks, Sidney Lumet, Brad Bird, Mel Brooks, Ridley Scott, Tim Burton, Sydney Pollack, and Edgar Wright (who, incidentally, was originally slated to direct Marvel's *Ant-Man*). Thus, while Marvel presents a very particular, 21st-century style and system for filmmaking, it is hardly unique in Hollywood for seeking out the talents of those who have worked in television. Moreover, as more and more Hollywood content managers look to Marvel as a model for building their own "cinematic universes" (Kit 2019; McMillan 2018; Shanley 2018; Wardlow 2018), it stands to reason that Marvel's specific experience of looking to the talent of television producers to help manage franchise filmmaking practice would gain broader relevance. We can therefore expect film futures to be built on the serialized and professional histories of television.

Yet looking at these lists of television professionals who got their start in television, we can also see that the pathway into filmmaking offered by television is not equally accessible to anyone who wants to travel it. These lists tend to be comprised exclusively of white men. In this way, they merely reflect the overall inequalities of Hollywood filmmaking in which, according to the Center for the Study of Women in Television and Film, women made up only 20% of all directors, writers, producers, executive producers, editors, and cinematographers working on the top 100 box office grossing films of 2019. Unfortunately, this unequal number represented an "historic high," up from 16% the previous year. In terms of directing alone, women made up only 12% of directors for these 100 films, compared to only 8% in 2018 (Lauzen 2020). UCLA's 2019 "Hollywood Diversity Report" offered comparable data in terms of gender and also revealed that only 12.6% of all film directing opportunities and 7.8% of all film writing credits were held by people of color in 2017 (Hunt, Ramón, and Tran 2019)—a considerable underrepresentation given that almost 40% of the US population is non-white (US Census Bureau

2020). Considering such significant gender and racial imbalances, these lists of television creators-turned-filmmakers are unsurprising, as the data suggests that Hollywood employers would look disproportionately to the white men in that pool of television trained aspirants.

The television industry plays an equal role in barring some creators from traveling this road to filmmaking—and yet there is also reason for some very muted optimism in terms of relative opportunity.

On the one hand, employment data offers some equally depressing figures for television employment. According to UCLA's Diversity Report, people of color have had disproportionately few opportunities to create television shows: only 9.4% of broadcast scripted series, 11.2% of cable scripted series, and 16.5% of digital scripted series. In addition, these numbers were framed as "noticeable gains" from the previous report (Hunt et al. 2019). By comparison, UCLA's data seemed more positive for women, who comprised around 22% of scripted broadcast and cable series creators and almost 35% on digital television platforms. Yet those numbers, too, reflected a television industry that continued to afford significantly greater opportunities to men. Research from Alton Carswell and the Think Tank for Inclusion and Equity and (2020) further showed that even when hired, 64% of women and people of color reported experiencing bias, discrimination, or harassment: even if they got their feet in the door, they confronted a culture of isolation and failure to support their careers. If television is to be a training ground for opportunities across the media industries, then these failures and inequalities have significance beyond just the television industry itself. They work to reproduce privilege and inequality along all the pathways that might extend from television (whether to film or to other employment opportunities).

On the other hand, it is also worth recognizing that while television is hardly an equal playing field, it has offered somewhat greater opportunities for women and people of color than film. Although the phenomenon of "peak TV" seems to have been imploded by the COVID-19 production shutdown of 2020, the last half of the 2010s saw a massive increase in demand for television content, with more hours of original scripted programming being produced than ever before to meet the demands of a booming number of streaming services looking for content to attract new audiences. It is in this context that we might understand the "noticeable gains" reported by UCLA. In the 2014–2015 season, for example, only three women of color were employed as directors across the entirety of US programming produced for cable networks AMC, FX, HBO, and Showtime, as well as streaming service Netflix. This was across hundreds of hours of content across dozens of series. Although some broadcast series like *Grey's Anatomy* (2005-) proved exceptional by comparison—hiring 21 non-white women to direct during this same period—many other broadcast series like *NCIS* (2003-) and *Law & Order: SVU* (1999-) offered no better records than their cable and streaming competitors. While *Variety*'s Maureen

Ryan (2015) called this "peak inequality," the production boom of peak TV slowly created opportunities (beyond *Grey's Anatomy*!) to close the gap. In late 2019, the Directors Guild of America reported that women and people of color had directed half of all episodic television programs that year, an increase from 42.5% in 2018, and just 21% in 2014. Broken down by gender and race, women directed 31% of television episodes (an increase of 100% over five years) and people of color directed 27% (an increase of 40% over five years) (Robb 2019). Industry analysts saw measurable changes attributable to the expanded opportunity created by the television industry's increased production output. These gains could be had for women and people of color and "it didn't cost white men any work," claimed one *IndieWire* article in 2017, even as it recognized that these gains "haven't come out of nowhere; in the last two years, diversity hiring initiatives have begun making real progress in holding showrunners and studios accountable for real improvement" (Miller 2017). While activists pushed for greater equity, the conditions of peak TV allowed a redistribution of opportunity to be imagined as something other than a zero-sum game.

Indeed, these improvements followed not just hiring initiatives, but industry investment in genres and programming forms that created more opportunity to center women and people of color. In comedy alone, this more inclusive programming boom included *The Mindy Project* (2012–2017), *Girls* (2013–2017), *Broad City* (2014–2019), *Better Things* (2015–), *Catastrophe* (2015–2019), *Atlanta* (2016), *Fleabag* (2016–2019), *Insecure* (2016–), *Lady Dynamite* (2016–2018), *One Mississippi* (2016–2017), *SMILF* (2017–2019), *Patriot Act with Hassan Minhaj* (2018–2020), *Random Acts of Flyness* (2018–), *A Black Lady Sketch Show* (2019–), *Pen15* (2019–), *Ramy* (2019–), *Shrill* (2019), *Never Have I Ever* (2020–), and more. From this body of work emerged new television auteurs like Mindy Kaling, Issa Rae, Lena Dunham, Donald Glover, Phoebe Waller-Bridge, and Hassan Minhaj, to name just a few. Far from being lone voices on the margins in the rooms where white male professionals created television stories about white men for white male viewers, women and people of color could find an increasing (but, unfortunately, still insufficient) number of opportunities to contribute to programs that aimed to center their experiences and perspectives. Seeing their target audiences as increasingly diverse, television distributors like FX, HBO, and Comedy Central offered a shared context and multiple outlets in which this work could develop.

Make no mistake—the television industry has only begun to address these inequalities. The point is only that the industry lore circulating in and around television began to recognize change in action (however limited or problematic). This recognition, moreover, often pit television against film, celebrating the former by comparison to the persistence of the status quo in the latter. *Deadline* described the gains toward equality in 2019 television as "much better than in feature films," where people of color were actually directing 46% fewer films with budgets over $250,000 than five years prior (Robb 2019). Comparable analyses of perceived progress in television explained that "by contrast, the film industry barely seems to be moving forward" (Liao 2017).

Taking these comparisons into account, the question of transforming television careers into film careers is one that must grapple with the conditions and cultures of inequity in each medium. At the same time, we cannot assume that the process of crossing over is itself neutral. While each industry may have its own practices and strategies for managing equality of opportunity, the points of intersection may be defined by privileges and inequities of their own. For example, if television provides more opportunities for women and people of color than film, we might expect the process of professional crossover to help diversify the film industry. Yet while television has afforded opportunities for women and people of color to develop creative careers, it is not always doing so in a way that provides equal access to doorways that lead to the film industry. In March 2020, *Den of Geek* profiled 26 female film directors readers "should know about" (Bonner 2020). The choice to highlight 26 (not 30 or some larger, rounder number) and the inclusion of several international and documentary filmmakers underscored the relatively small number of women directors working in Hollywood at that time. Another similar list marshals only 67 names (*StudioBinder* 2020). While *Den of Geek*'s list usefully brought visibility to directors ignored in dominant industry narratives, not a single profile mentioned prior work in television.

However, several of these featured directors have worked in both television and film, despite it going unmentioned. Karyn Kusama directed *Girlfight* in 2000 and *Aeon Flux* in 2005 before directing a 2007 episode of *The L Word* (2004–2009). She then continued to direct films like *Jennifer's Body* (2009), *The Invitation* (2015), and *Destroyer* (2018) while taking on occasional episodic directing duties for *Halt and Catch Fire* (2014–2017), *Chicago Fire* (2012–), *The Man in the High Castle* (2015–2019), *Casual* (2015–2018), and *Billions* (2016–). Over a decade, Melina Matsoukas built a career making commercials and music videos, until 2016 when she directed seven episodes of *Insecure*. She would direct two episodes of *Master of None* (2015–2017) the following year, before helming the feature film *Queen & Slim* (2019). While Academy Award winner Kathryn Bigelow has enjoyed a prestigious film career including *Blue Steel* (1990), *Point Break* (1991), *Strange Days* (1995), and more recently *The Hurt Locker* (2008), *Zero Dark Thirty* (2012), and *Detroit* (2017), she engaged in a mid-career exploration of television, directing three 1998 and 1999 episodes of *Homicide: Life on the Street* (1993–1999), as well as an episode of *Karen Sisco* (2003). As writer, director, actor, and producer, Lorene Scafaria has occupied many roles across a two-decade career in film and television. She wrote and directed the films *Seeking a Friend for the End of the World* (2012), *The Meddler* (2015), and *Hustlers* (2019), while on television writing for *Ben and Kate* (2012–2013) and directing episodes of *New Girl* (2011–2018) in 2013 and 2014. Although moving outside the US production system to do so, *Little Woods* (2018) and *Candy Man* (2021) director Nia DaCosta also directed episodes of the British Channel 4 series *Top Boy* (2011). It is thus clearly the case that the Russos and Whedons of the world are not the only film directors to cross over to and from television, despite receiving much more attention for it.

Perhaps most analogous to these figures are Patty Jenkins and Ava DuVernay, both of whom have directed for television while also being handed the reigns of a major Hollywood franchise. Jenkins' career carries many parallels to the Russos in particular: after directing the short film *Velocity Rules* (2001) and the feature *Monster* (2003), she found herself developing a career in television. In this period she worked as a director for *Arrested Development* in 2004 and *Entourage* in 2006. By 2011, she was similarly entrusted to set the look and tone of new series, directing the pilot and second episode of *The Killing* (2011–2014). The next pilot she would direct for *Betrayal* in 2015 would also come with an executive producer credit, evincing her success in building a solid television career. By 2017, Jenkins earned significant plaudits as the director of the Warner Bros. superhero film *Wonder Woman*, which was praised not only for bringing needed gender diversity to the genre, but also for being an exception to the dour and uneven installments that had so far comprised the DC Comics film universe. Even as she stayed on to manage the franchise as director of *Wonder Woman 1984* (2020), Jenkins maintained an investment in her TV work, directing the pilot and executive producing *I Am the Night* in 2019. Nominated for many awards as a documentary and feature director, Ava DuVernay has also worked in parallel across film and television in a highly visible way. Her 2014 film *Selma* was nominated for the Golden Globe for best director and the Academy Award for best film—making DuVernay the first African American woman to be recognized in those categories. She also earned an Academy Award nomination for her 2016 documentary *13th*, and Disney looked to her to direct the 2018 fantasy film *A Wrinkle in Time*. All the while, DuVernay cultivated a significant career in television. First, she directed a 2013 episode of *Scandal* (2012–2018), then the pilot of a project called "For Justice" in 2015. Following the success of her films, however, she had new power to create her own television projects. She has served as creator, writer, and director on the OWN series *Queen Sugar* (2016–) and *Cherish the Day* (2020). In addition, she earned a Peabody award as well as an Emmy nomination for the Netflix miniseries *When They See Us* (2019), which she also created, wrote, and directed. The professional accomplishments of Jenkins and DuVernay demonstrate that the pathway between television and film is traveled by a more diverse set of creators than just white men.

Yet this road does not always seem to be traveled in the same way. If the industry stories about the Russos and Whedon narrated a journey of being pulled toward filmmaking and transformed from one creative state to another, the tales told about DuVernay suggested that she could move between film and television while maintaining a more liminal creative status. In a 2019 feature on the "modern Hollywood empire" that DuVernay built from her success, *The Hollywood Reporter* remarked not on her transformation into a fully-fledged filmmaker, but instead on her status as the manager of a new enterprise in which television had become increasingly central. Although film remained central to her work—she owned the production company Array Filmworks with its own indie distribution provider Array Releasing—much of that creative energy was devoted to television projects: "DuVernay runs a company that now employs about 50 people at work on 14 TV shows in various states of production and development, as well as her independent film distribution arm, which has released 22 movies in theatres" (Keegan 2019). Indeed, while figures like the Russos and Whedon often embody romanticized values of filmmaking as creative end in trade reporting, DuVernay could appear impatient at that suggestion, embracing the medium of television and partners like Netflix that might help her reach her goals. Asked by *The Hollywood Reporter* about her partnership with Netflix and uncertainty in the Academy of Motion Picture Arts and Sciences about how to treat "films" released through that platform, DuVernay responded:

> We'll look back in a very short number of years and it'll all sound ridiculous […] I can't show *Straight Outta Compton* in Compton, and I can't show *Selma* in Selma because there are no movie theaters. Now you have a platform [... that] will make sure that audiences, not only in this country, but in 190 countries, for the price of a hamburger can see your movie, your TV show, your whatever.
>
> *(Keegan 2019)*

DuVernay appeared uninterested in ascending from television to film, looking instead to how she could work in the spaces between media to make her voice and those of the creators she now worked with heard. Managing this vast empire, DuVernay is clearly a "TV Gal"—and yet, it seems unlikely she would adopt such an identity, seeing strength not in alliance with media-specific cultural identifications, but instead in working in in-between spaces that serve her goals best.

It is also worth noting that directors like Jenkins, Matsoukas, and others also continue working in television after finding some filmmaking success. Oprah Winfrey, too, emerged as a creative force in television, and even after developing a significant amount of cultural capital from her acting in *The Color Purple* (1985) and *Beloved* (1998), maintained her significant investments in television through ventures like her cable channel OWN. On one level, this is no different from figures like Whedon or the Russos, who continue to operate in television even after they find success with film projects. However, less evidence exists that these female creators, or the trade reporting surrounding them, lay claim to a professional identity tied exclusively to filmmaking. This may be in part because of gender biases that lead to an oversized amount of attention in the trade press and other spaces of industry loremaking to male creators; with that space comes more room to groom professional identities associated with the status and power of the cinema. At the same time, while women and people of color may slowly win more opportunities to direct, the structures that provide support and career advancement may not enable the kinds of professional moves and creative security that would make such permanent transformation an attractive goal. Cultivating opportunities equally across film or television is a sound strategy for creator communities who face uncertainty and who are unequal in the arenas in which they work. White men may enjoy the privilege of fantasies of transformation in the crossover between film and television, while women and people of color may find themselves developing strategies of flexibility and fluidity to take advantage of every opportunity.

This is not to say, though, that there is a clear dividing line based on gender (or race) when it comes to how these fantasies of transformation play out. The competing list of 67 best female filmmakers, for examples, does offer the television credits of some of its nominees. And in doing so, directors like Gail Mancuso are said to be "shifting" as she "makes the jump" from the world of directing television comedies like *Modern Family* (2009–2020) to feature projects like *Besties* (*StudioBinder* 2020). Kathryn Bigelow, too, was "thrust back into the spotlight" with *The Hurt Locker* following her time working in television. In that equation, her time in television was by suggestion a lesser period in her career out of that spotlight. Similarly, and perhaps more dismissively, the profile of Mary Harron carries an air of disappointment in noting that after making the cult "classics" *I Shot Andy Warhol* (1996) and *American Psycho* (2000) "she worked mainly in television," replacing superlatives with descriptors. Mimi Leder, too, "transitioned back to television," a shift that suggests some kind of transformation—and a disappointing one at that. So women, too, have clearly been figured in the industry narratives that position work in film as more prestigious and accomplished than television and thus filmmaking as an aspirational professional identity. By contrast, though, the transgender duo of Lana and Lilly Wachowski appear in this list to have "pushed into television" as if it was a new frontier rather than a mere training ground (*StudioBinder* 2020).

Instead of drawing hard binary divisions, it may suffice to say that the pathway from television to film is one that is traveled unequally, and that journey is one that is tied up in the identities constructed for professionals working in these industries. Some travelers are able to reach the path, while others are barred from it. Once on the path, some may decide to move toward a destination that figures some professional outcomes and some cultural formations— often, the romanticized "cinema"—as the ultimate goal. However, others may linger in the space between, whether because they are barred from reaching the destination, or because they find the crossover space to be a productive one. In this way, the question of who gets to cross over—who is a "TV guy," who is a filmmaker, and who even cares about such labels—tells us something important about the power of moving between media industries and the way that mobility can shape and be shaped by creators' identities.

Conclusion

As the serialized production of their film franchises continues, studios like Marvel must look for new talent. Filmmakers like the Russo brothers and Joss Whedon have moved on—perhaps in pursuit of transcendence to whatever the next cinematic plane of existence might be. In the space they leave behind is an opportunity for other creators who honed their skills in the world of television to make their own journey to the movies. As long as the blockbuster and franchise production strategies continue to favor serialized stories featuring large casts of characters, it is highly likely that Hollywood will continue to look to former television professionals to bring their experience to bear on the filmmaking enterprise—particularly as the trade narratives explored in this chapter have established these qualifications as part of an industrial common sense. Moreover, there is reason to hope that the heroes of those trade stories need not continue to be white men like Whedon and the Russos. Marvel has already employed Chinese filmmaker Chloe Zhao to direct *Eternals* (forthcoming) while signing African American director Nia DaCosta to helm the sequel to *Captain Marvel*.

What remains to be seen, however, is whether the same stories of professional success and tales of transformation from television producer to filmmaker will be told. These stories are built around a sense of hierarchical identities, tied explicitly to distinctions between media and also implicitly to social privileges. On the one hand, baked into the idea of transformation from television creator to filmmaker is an endorsement of the kind of media hierarchies at play throughout this book. Although television experience may offer expertise in serial storytelling as well as a chance to build valuable cult followings, film still appears as a higher calling, a promotion, an upgrade. In this frame, going to the movies, for television producers, manifests as the attainment of greater professional power and standing. This is not to say that Whedon or the Russos themselves look down upon television; on the contrary, we believe they share a genuine love for the medium, repeatedly pulled back to it despite whatever assertions that they have left it behind. Instead, in the perspectives they share with trade reporters—and the way those perspectives get activated as part of longer stories of career trajectory—industrial figures like the Russos and Whedon serve as characters in a story that affirms the value of cinema as the higher plane to be reached. Such narratives of professional trajectory need to be read alongside the lionization of theatrical exhibition in Chapter 1, the on-screen film narratives that devalue television in Chapter 2, and the practices of adaptation in Chapter 3 that seek to upgrade television. The path from television to film cannot be traveled without grappling with the unequal value placed on each medium.

On the other hand, the stories of television's journey to the movies can vary depending on who it is that might be going to the movies. The path that leads from television to film is not one that all can yet equally travel. Studios like Marvel look to hire a more diverse pool of creative talent to support their blockbuster films, and the production cultures of television are slowly becoming more inclusive; but until there is an equitable distribution of creative power within television, the idea that television careers can serve as a launching pad for greater success in blockbuster film is one that will reinforce existing privileges. Especially when viewed as a means of creative ranking up, the path from television to film is one that will be more frequently passable by those with more power. Beyond career advancement, there is also the question of who gets to be at the center of the narratives produced by trade reporting. Even if the power to translate television skill into filmmaking opportunity is enjoyed more widely, there remains the risk that the storytelling practices of industry lore will continue to tell the tales of some of the travelers on that professional path, but not others. Directors like Nia DaCosta may be on a similar professional path to the one white men like Whedon and the Russos traveled, but even then the persistence of racism and sexism in the telling of trade stories could ignore her comparable insights on television training, the nature of blockbuster filmmaking, and their intersections. That is a story remaining to be written, but for now we are left with trade reporting largely preoccupied with the ability of white men to leverage their television experience as a way of making permanent upward moves in the hierarchies between media industries.

However, as that industry lore continues to be revised, there is the potential for different kinds of stories in which professionals craft alternative forms of identity that do not depend on the hierarchies of media at the heart of this book. As we see in the case of Ava DuVernay, working in television and film need not be presented as a binary choice. The stories of permanent transformation from television professional to filmmaker do not determine the path for all. Instead, television and film could be envisioned as equal parts of a creative portfolio without, as DuVernay suggests, all this unnecessary investment in distinctions and status that limit where media can be shown and experienced. Filmmaking need not be an endpoint; instead, when television producers go to the movies, they can move back to television without losing anything. In fact, that return might bring many gains. Of course, as noted at the very beginning of this book, many media professionals regularly move between these realms already. But as they do so, they move between fields to which industry cultures have ascribed different cultural and social values. That process should continue, but the stories that get told about television going to the movies should change.

CODA

Let It Go?

Cultural boundary crossing is rarely uncontested. And while this is evident in the arguments that regularly envelope discussions of who can cross national borders and how, of what constitutes citizenship, and of queered and/or hybrid identities, this book has found it no less true of the discussions that surround the collisions of products, people, and perceptions across the boundaries of television and film. At first glance, the task of determining where television ends and film begins, and of why anyone should care, may seem remarkably mundane. Yet, the previous chapters have shown that the maintenance and transformation of boundaries between film and television do matter to a great many. At times, the terms of mattering are vocalized explicitly—in purple prose articles about how television will never "beat" film, for instance—but they are always implicitly being reified and repeated by the many other discursive guard rails placed around each medium and their interactions with one another, some of which this book has illuminated.

For theatrical exhibitors, the distinction between these media has real economic consequences, as the premium placed on the idea of going to the movies rather than staying home to watch television proves crucial to their survival. The transformation of those boundaries thus represents a disruption of existing industry practices. For many critics, the idea of fixed boundaries between media can anchor aesthetic world views and justify beliefs about value and quality. At stake in challenging the boundaries between media is the possibility of upsetting fundamental ways of seeing and criteria of judgment. For storytellers, the boundaries between media set normative terms, conventions, and expectations that govern the creative process. While the adaptation of a television series into a movie represents an opportunity to transform a story in fundamental ways, the process also tends to be limited by assumptions about what different media can and cannot do. Creativity is both enabled and confined by these boundary crossings. And for the professionals who do this creative work, moving across the boundaries of television and film can represent something more than the next gig. Instead, the act of crossing from one medium to another can have real impact on perceptions of professional worth and prestige.

What this book has revealed then is the energy, preoccupation, and urgency that surround these border crossings between film and television. This is a boundary that gets regularly crossed, as so many of our examples have shown, and yet that movement continues to generate excitement, anxiety, concern, criticism, exaggeration, investment, and more as producers and consumers alike try to make sense of it. The collisions of television and film are mundane, and yet they take on great meaning.

There is more to be said about why that might be. We have traced the collisions, weighed their impacts, and interrogated responses to television's movement into the realm of the cinema. We have shown how the transformation of television in its collision with film matters to a great number of individuals and institutions within media culture. But at the end of the day, it is still possible to struggle with the question of why this all has to matter at all. Asking this question is not to surrender the importance of the pages you've just read; instead, it is to acknowledge the possibility of imagining a world where these boundaries do not have to matter in the way they do now. We understand how and why they matter in the specific cultural contexts of the United States examined here, but we also hope to keep open the possibility that we could challenge the assumptions at the foundation of these discourses about media boundaries in order to envision other possibilities. If nothing else, this book has shown how these borders are porous, and how that porous nature allows them to be transformed. So we hope a search for a stronger answer to the question "why?" might lead not to further rationalization of these boundaries but instead to more transformation of them.

In that light, the televisual journey we have mapped here goes to its final destination. Our fundamental concern has been with television's ability to "go" to the screens, styles, texts, and work worlds of the cinema. The story we've been told is one of movement, and in that movement lies possibility. When looking at those movements, we see value in being able to "let it go." On the one hand, this means holding out some excitement for the possibilities of television's ability to go to the movies. Let's embrace that mobility and hope for the potential that television and film alike could be transformed for the better in that movement. In that transformation might lie new possibilities for exhibition, for storytelling, for work, and for recognizing the unrealized value and potential of media. On the other hand, maybe there's a lot that we should be letting go in the sense that a therapist or animated ice princess might recommend. Can we embrace television's mobility into the realm of the cinema without replicating the discursive hierarchies that dominate our thinking about these boundary crossings? Can we imagine a convergence of film and television without assessing losses and gains of capital, aesthetic value, or professional status? Can television's ability to go to the movies be harnessed for its productive power to tell new kinds of stories, make cultural resources more accessible, and both multiply and amplify the voices of those who are too often unheard?

Let go of the obsession with the maintenance of these boundaries and the fears of what might be lost in their crossing. Instead, next time television goes to the movies, consider going along.

WORKS CITED

Academy of Motion Picture Arts and Sciences. "93rd Academy Awards of Merit." *Oscars.org*, June 15, 2020. https://www.oscars.org/sites/oscars/files/93aa_rules.pdf.

Albasi, K. "The Coming Drought of New Movies and TV Shows." *Medium*, May 6, 2020. https://medium.com/@kayalbasi/the-coming-drought-of-new-movies-tv-shows-19b6f6e8addd.

Alexander, Julia. "Netflix Adds Another Whopping 10 Million Subscribers, But Warns Growth May Slow." *The Verge*, July 16, 2020. https://www.theverge.com/2020/7/16/21326434/netflix-second-quarter-earnings-tv-shows-movies-originals-subscribers-adds-ted-sarandos.

AMC. "Game of Thrones: The IMAX Experience." *amctheaters.com*, January 30, 2015. https://www.amctheatres.com/movies/game-of-thrones-the-imax-experience-47250.

Anderson, Christopher. *Hollywood TV: The Studio System in the Fifties*. Austin: University of Texas Press, 1994.

Andreeva, Nellie. "Russos Shuttle 'Carpoolers.'" *The Hollywood Reporter*, February 5, 2007. https://www.hollywoodreporter.com/news/russos-shuttle-carpoolers-129406.

Andreeva, Nellie and Borys Kit. "Trio Team for TV, Film Projects." *The Hollywood Reporter*, October 30, 2006. https://www.hollywoodreporter.com/news/trio-team-tv-film-projects-141109.

Balio, Tino, ed. *Hollywood in the Age of Television*. New York: Unwin Hyman, 1990.

Bart, Peter and Mike Fleming, Jr. "One of Us Has Oscar Vote And Is Reluctant To Cast It On a Netflix Film." *Deadline*, February 20, 2018. https://deadline.com/2018/02/netflix-oscar-votes-mary-j-blige-scott-stuber-ted-sarandos-1202296132/.

Baysinger, Tim. "Coronavirus Could Lead to Studio Mergers and End of 'Peak TV,' Analyst Says." *The Wrap*, April 24, 2020. https://www.thewrap.com/coronavirus-could-lead-to-studio-mergers-and-end-of-peak-tv-analyst-says/.

Bennett, James. *Television Personalities: Stardom and the Small Screen*. New York: Routledge, 2011.

Bennett, Lucy and Booth Paul, eds. *Seeing Fans: Representation of Fandom in Media and Popular Culture*. New York: Bloomsbury, 2016.

Benson-Allott, Caetlin. *Killer Tapes and Shattered Screens: Video Spectatorship from VHS to File Sharing.* Berkeley: University of California Press, 2013.

Benson-Allott, Caetlin. *The Stuff of Spectatorship: Material Cultures of Film and Television.* Berkeley: University of California Press, 2021.

Bielby, Denise and C. Lee Harrington. *Global TV: Exporting Television and Culture in the World Market.* New York: NYU Press, 2008.

Bonner, Hannah. "26 Women Directors You Should Know About (and Why You Might Not)." *Den of Geek*, March 7, 2020. https://www.denofgeek.com/movies/women-directors-you-should-know-about/.

Bourdieu, Pierre. *Distinction: A Social Critique of the Judgment of Taste.* Translated by Richard Nice. London: Routledge and Kegan Paul, 1984.

Bowenbank, Starr. "Here's What the Cast of *Game of Thrones* Wore on the Season 8 Red Carpet." *Elle*, April 5, 2019. https://www.elle.com/fashion/celebrity-style/g27045485/game-of-thrones-cast-season-8-premiere-red-carpet/?slide=31.

Box Office Mojo. "Franchises." n.d. https://www.boxofficemojo.com/franchise/?ref_=bo_lnav_hm_shrt.

Braudy, Leo. "Afterword: Rethinking Remakes." In *Play It Again, Sam: Retakes on Remakes*, edited by Andrew Horton and Stuart Y. McDougal, 324–7. Berkeley: University of California Press, 1998.

Brody, Richard. "Why Movies Still Matter." *The New Yorker*, August 30, 2016. https://www.newyorker.com/culture/richard-brody/why-movies-still-matter.

Brueggemann, Tom. "As 'Tenet' and 'Mulan' Finally Open, Studios Make It Difficult to Judge Their Box-Office Success." *IndieWire*, September 4, 2020. https://www.indiewire.com/2020/09/tenet-and-mulan-box-office-success-1234584337/.

Buckman, Adam. "Oscars and Emmys Ask: Is Netflix A Movie or TV Company?" *MediaPost*, April 5, 2019. https://www.mediapost.com/publications/article/334064/oscars-and-emmys-ask-is-netflix-a-movie-or-tv-com.html.

Bureau of Labor Statistics. "The Employment Situation – June 2020." July 2, 2020. https://www.bls.gov/news.release/pdf/empsit.pdf.

Butter, Michael, "Exit Gender, Enter Race: Jonathan Demme's 'Update' of *The Manchurian Candidate*." In *Remakes and Remodeling: Concepts—Media—Practices*, edited by Rüdiger Heinze and Lucia Krämer, 41–56. Bielefeld, Germany: Transcript Verlag, 2015.

Caldwell, John. "Cultures of Production: Studying Industry's Deep Texts, Reflexive Rituals, and Managed Self-Disclosures." In *Media Industries: History, Theory, and Method*, edited by Jennifer Holt and Alisa Perren, 199–212. Malden, MA: Wiley-Blackwell, 2009.

Carswell, Alton and the Think Tank for Inclusion and Equity. "Behind the Scenes: The State of Inclusion and Equity in TV Writing." *womeninfilm.org*, 2020. https://womeninfilm.org/wp-content/uploads/2020/05/TTIE_BTS2020_Printable-Version_FINAL.pdf.

Cashin, Rory. "The Russo Brothers on How Directing Episodes of Community Made Them the Perfect Fit for Avengers: Endgame." *Joe*, 2019. https://www.joe.ie/movies-tv/russo-brothers-directing-episodes-community-made-perfect-fit-avengers-endgame-666156.

Copple Smith, Erin. "The Logics of Synergy: Media Conglomerates and Cross-Promotional Practices." PhD diss., University of Wisconsin-Madison, 2012.

Corrigan, Timothy, ed. *Film and Literature: An Introduction and Reader*, 2nd edition. New York: Routledge, 2012.

Couch, Aaron. "Comic-Con: 'Captain America: Winter Soldier' Directors Heading to 'Agent Carter.'" *The Hollywood Reporter*, July 25, 2014. https://www.hollywoodreporter. com/live-feed/captain-america-winter-soldier-directors-721320.

Dahl, Roald. *Charlie and the Chocolate Factory*. New York: Puffin, 2016.

Davis, Rebecca. "China Box Office: 'Mulan' Is No Hero with $23 Million Debut." *Variety*, September 13, 2020. https://variety.com/2020/film/news/ disney-mulan-china-box-office-1234768301/#article-comments.

Deeb, Gary. "The Season's Hits, Flops, In-betweens." *Chicago Tribune*, October 12, 1978: A7.

de Semlyen, Nick. "The Irishman Week: Empire's Martin Scorsese Interview." *Empire*, November 6, 2019. https://www.empireonline.com/movies/features/ irishman-week-martin-scorsese-interview/.

Desowitz, Bill. "The Russo Brothers Explain How 'Avengers: Endgame' Was Inspired By Antonioni-Level Darkness." *IndieWire*, April 25, 2019. https://www.indiewire. com/2019/04/avengers-endgame-finale-russo-brothers-vfx-1202127637/.

Dibdin, Emma. "The *Game of Thrones* Cast Attends the Season 8 Premiere in New York City." *Bazaar*, April 3, 2019. https://www.harpersbazaar.com/celebrity/latest/ g27033699/game-of-thrones-season-8-premiere-red-carpet/.

Doty, Alexander. "The Cabinet of Lucy Ricardo: Lucille Ball's Star Image." *Cinema Journal* 29, no. 4 (1990): 3–20.

Ebert, Roger. "Race Humor Creates Road Hazard." *RogerEbert.com*, August 4, 2005. https://www.rogerebert.com/reviews/the-dukes-of-hazzard-2005.

Elkins, Evan. *Locked Out: Regional Restrictions in Digital Entertainment Culture*. New York: NYU Press, 2019.

Elkins, Kathleen. "George Clooney, the World's Highest Paid Actor, Earns More Than the 10 Highest-Paid Actresses Combined." *CNBC News*, February 24, 2019. https://www.cnbc.com/2019/02/22/the-worlds-highest-paid-actors-and- actresses.html.

Ellis, John. *Visible Fictions: Cinema, Television, Video*. New York: Routledge, 1992.

Epstein, Adam. "'Game of Thrones' Is the Most Cinematic TV Show Ever Made." *Quartz*, June 21, 2016. https://qz.com/712430/game-of-thrones-is-the-most- cinematic-tv-show-ever-made/.

Epstein, Adam. "Disney's Streaming Service Is Booming While Its Other Businesses Are on Hold." *Quartz*, April 9, 2020. https://qz.com/1835770/disneys- streaming-service-is-booming-thanks-to-coronavirus/.

Faughnder, Ryan. "Movie Theaters Face 'Existential Threat' from COVID-19." *Los Angeles Times*, July 11, 2020. https://www.latimes.com/entertainment-arts/ business/story/2020-07-11/movie-theaters-hollywood-reopening-new-films.

Fleming Jr., Mike. "'Avengers: Endgage' Helmers Joe & Anthony Russo's AGBO to Godfather Remakes of MGM Library Title IP." *Deadline*, April 9, 2019. https:// deadline.com/2019/04/avengers-endgame-agbo-joe-russo-anthony-russo-mgm- library-the-thomas-crown-affair-1202591932/.

Ford, Rebecca. "'Captain America: The Winter Soldier' Directors to Be Honored at HollyShorts Festival." *The Hollywood Reporter*, July 29, 2014. https://www. hollywoodreporter.com/news/captain-america-winter-soldier-directors-721931.

Fox Business, "AMC Movie Theaters Close to Deal to Avoid Near-Term Bankruptcy." July 7, 2020. https://www.foxbusiness.com/economy/amc-movie-theaters-close-to-deal-to-avoid-near-term-bankruptcy.

Fraser, Nancy. "Rethinking the Public Sphere: A Contribution to the Critique of Actually Existing Democracy." In *Habermas and the Public Sphere*, edited by Craig Calhoun, 109–42. Cambridge, MA: MIT Press, 1992.

Frost, Natasha. "Avengers Became the Biggest Movie Franchise in the World By Acting Like a TV Show." *Quartz*, April 30, 2019. https://qz.com/quartzy/1608091/the-russo-brothers-tv-experience-helped-produce-avengers-endgame/.

Fung, Anthony and Xiaoxiao Zhang. "The Chinese Ugly Betty: TV Cloning and Local Modernity." *International Journal of Cultural Studies* 14, no. 3 (2011): 265–76.

Gemmill, Allie. "Here's Why 'The New Mutants' Can't Premier on Disney+ or Hulu." *Collider*, July 27, 2020. https://collider.com/new-mutants-hulu-disney-plus-release-reason-why/?fbclid=IwAR1pODktNq1YX_oJjKK2OXt1wWUSf7ARnM6-WhplGiDD1idec-x5rL7kd2cA.

Gennis, Sadie. "HBO Rules Out Airing Any of *Game of Thrones'* Final Season in Theaters." *TV Guide*, July 12, 2017. https://www.tvguide.com/news/game-of-thrones-season-8-movie-theaters-imax/.

Glieberman, Owen. "Steven Spielberg vs. Netflix: A Preview of the War for Cinema's Future." *Variety*, March 10, 2019. https://variety.com/2019/film/columns/steven-spielberg-vs-netflix-a-preview-of-the-war-for-cinemas-future-1203159522/.

Goldberg, Lesley. "ABC Orders Marvel's 'S.H.I.E.L.D.' to Pilot from Joss Whedon." *The Hollywood Reporter*, August 28, 2012. https://www.hollywoodreporter.com/live-feed/abc-marvel-joss-whedon-shield-pilot-365884.

Goldberg, Lesley. "'Agents of SHIELD' Cast, Creators on Movie Synergy, Joss Whedon's Involvement." *The Hollywood Reporter*, August 4, 2013. https://www.hollywoodreporter.com/live-feed/agents-shield-cast-creators-movie-599354.

Goldberg, Lesley. "Joss Whedon Developing Comedy for Freeform." *The Hollywood Reporter*, June 5, 2018. https://www.hollywoodreporter.com/live-feed/joss-whedon-developing-comedy-freeform-1117283.

Goldberg, Lesley. "Joss Whedon Sci-Fi Drama Ordered Straight to Series at HBO." *The Hollywood Reporter*, July 13, 2018. https://www.hollywoodreporter.com/live-feed/joss-whedon-sci-fi-drama-nevers-ordered-straight-series-at-hbo-1126951.

Gray, Jonathan. *Show Sold Separately: Promos, Spoilers, and Other Media Paratexts*. New York: NYU Press, 2010.

Gray, Jonathan. "Mobility Through Piracy, or How Steven Seagal Got to Malawi." *Popular Communication* 9, no. 2 (2011): 99–113.

Gray, Jonathan. *Dislike-Minded: Media, Audiences, and the Dynamics of Taste*. New York: NYU Press, 2021.

Greenwood, Peter. "'Battlestar Galactica' Shook Up Audiences—Literally—With Its Theatrical Releases." *MeTV*, June 20, 2017. https://www.metv.com/stories/battlestar-galactica-shook-up-audiences-literally-with-its-theatrical-releases.

Grossman, Julie. "Fargos." In *Adaptation in Visual Culture*, edited by Julie Grossman and R. Barton Palmer, 193–212. New York: Palgrave Macmillan, 2017.

Gumeny, Eirik. "Community Was Basically the Russo Brothers' Avengers Before the Avengers." *SyFy Wire*, September 17, 2019. https://www.syfy.com/syfywire/community-was-basically-the-russo-brothers-avengers-before-the-avengers.

Guyette, Natalie. "In the Era of Peak TV, We Might Run Out." *Wisconsin Public Radio*, July 22, 2020. https://www.wpr.org/era-peak-tv-we-might-run-out.

Haglund, David. "Stop Saying That TV Is Better Than Movies These Days." *Slate*, July 18, 2013. https://slate.com/culture/2013/07/tv-is-not-better-than-movies-so-stop-saying-so.html.

Hall, Jacob. "Their First Gig: The Television Beginnings of Major Film Directors." *Screen Crush*, June 28, 2013. https://screencrush.com/film-directors-tv-beginnings/.

Hartley, John. *Popular Reality: Journalism, Modernity, Popular Culture*. London: Arnold, 1996.

Hassler-Forest, Dan and Pascal Nicklas, eds. *The Politics of Adaptation: Media Convergence and Ideology*. New York: Palgrave Macmillan, 2015.

Havens, Timothy. *Global Television Marketplace*. London: BFI, 2006.

Havens, Timothy. *Black Television Travels: African American Media around the Globe*. New York: NYU Press, 2013.

Herbert, Daniel. *Film Remakes and Franchises*. New Brunswick, NJ: Rutgers University Press, 2017.

Hibberd, James. "Joss Whedon Swears Off TV—For Now." *The Hollywood Reporter*, July 23, 2010. http://heatvision.hollywoodreporter.com/2010/07/joss- whedon-direct-avengers.html.

Hibberd, James. "*Game of Thrones* Producers Confirm Final Season Only 6 Episodes." *Entertainment Weekly*, March 12, 2017. https://ew.com/tv/2017/03/12/game-of-thrones-sxsw/.

Hibberd, James. "The End of Game of Thrones: An Exclusive Report on the Epic Final Season." *Entertainment Weekly*, November 1, 2018. https://ew.com/tv/2018/11/01/game-of-thrones-final-season-ew-cover-story/.

Hilmes, Michele. *Hollywood and Broadcasting: From Radio to Cable*. Urbana: University of Illinois Press, 1990.

Hilmes, Michele. "The Whole World's Unlikely Heroine: Ugly Betty as Transnational Phenomenon." In *Reading Ugly Betty: TV's Betty Goes Global*, edited by Janet McCabe and Kim Akass, 26–44. London: IB Tauris, 2013.

Hoffman, Jordan. "The Best of Both Worlds In-Theater Event – A Fan Perspective." *Star Trek*, April 26, 2013. https://www.startrek.com/article/the-best-of-both-worlds-in-theater-event-a-fan-perspective.

The Hollywood Reporter. "James Gunn, More Directors Take Issue with Scorsese Calling Marvel Movies 'Not Cinema.'" October 6, 2019. https://www.hollywoodreporter.com/heat-vision/scorsese-marvel-movies-not-cinema-theme-parks-spark-backlash-1245730.

Hoyt, Eric. *Hollywood Vault: Film Libraries before Home Video*. Berkeley: University of California Press, 2015.

Hueso, Noela. "How the 'Community' Season Finale Is Going Out with a Big Bang." *The Hollywood Reporter*, May 5, 2011. https://www.hollywoodreporter.com/news/how-community-season-finale-is-185835.

Hunt, Darnell, Ana-Christina Ramón, and Michael Tran. "Hollywood Diversity Report: Old Story, New Beginning." University of California, Los Angeles, 2019. https://socialsciences.ucla.edu/wp-content/uploads/2019/02/UCLA-Hollywood-Diversity-Report-2019-2-21-2019.pdf.

Hutcheon, Linda. *A Theory of Adaptation*. New York: Routledge, 2006.

Huyssen, Andreas. *After the Great Divide: Modernism, Mass Culture, Postmodernism*. Bloomington: Indiana University Press, 1986.

IMDB. "Mission Galactica: The Cylon Attack." *IMDB.com*, n.d. https://www.imdb.com/title/tt0077937/releaseinfo?ref_=tt_dt_dt.

IMDB. "Roots—Release Info." *IMDB.com*, n.d. https://www.imdb.com/title/tt0075572/releaseinfo?ref_=tt_dt_dt.

IMDB. "Roots: The Gift—Release Info" *IMDB.com*, n.d. https://www.imdb.com/title/tt0096009/releaseinfo?ref_=tt_dt_dt.

Ivanova, Irina. "US Economy Suffers Biggest Quarterly Decline on Record." *CBS News*, July 30, 2020. https://www.cbsnews.com/news/gdp-drop-q2-32-9-us-economy-suffers-biggest-quarterly-decline-on-record/.

Jarvey, Natalie. "'Captain America' Directors, Justin Lin Launch Branded Entertainment Firm." *The Hollywood Reporter*, April 30, 2014. https://www.hollywoodreporter.com/news/captain-america-directors-justin-lin-699600.

Jay, Robert. "A Tale of Two Battlestars." *Television Obscurities*, April 20, 2018. https://www.tvobscurities.com/articles/two_galacticas.

Jenkins, Aric. "Disney Q3 Earnings: Streaming a Bright Spot as Parks and Cruises Plummet." *Fortune*, August 4, 2020. https://fortune.com/2020/08/04/disney-q3-earnings-2020-coronavirus/.

Jenkins, Henry. *Convergence Culture: Where Old and New Media Collide*. New York: NYU Press, 2006.

Jermyn, Deborah. "Bringing Out the Star in You?: SJP, Carrie Bradshaw and the Evolution of Television Stardom." In *Framing Celebrity: New Directions in Celebrity Culture*, edited by Su Holmes and Sean Redmond, 96–117. New York: Routledge, 2006.

Johnson, Derek. "A Knight of the Realm vs. the Master of Magnetism: Sexuality, Stardom, and Character Branding." *Popular Communication* 6 (2008): 214–30.

Johnson, Derek. *Media Franchising: Creative License and Collaboration in the Culture Industries*. New York: NYU Press, 2013.

Keegan, Rebecca. "The Mogul for This Moment." *The Hollywood Reporter*, May 22, 2019. https://www.hollywoodreporter.com/features/ava-duvernay-tackling-central-park-five-netflix-series-they-see-us-1212466.

Kilday, Gregg. "Average Price of a Movie Ticket Rise to $8.97 in 2017." *The Hollywood Reporter*, January 17, 2018. https://www.hollywoodreporter.com/news/average-price-a-movie-ticket-soars-897-2017-1075458#:~:text=While%20the%20average%20price%20of, National%20Association%20of%20Theatre%20Owners.

Kit, Borys. "Russo Brothers in Final Talks to Direct 'Captain America 2.' *The Hollywood Reporter*, June 6, 2012. https://www.hollywoodreporter.com/heat-vision/russo-brothers-final-talks-direct-334218.

Kit, Borys. "Joe and Anthony Russo Sign First-Look Deal with Sony Pictures." *The Hollywood Reporter*, March 3, 2015. https://www.hollywoodreporter.com/news/joe-anthony-russo-sign-first-778917.

Kit, Borys. "Joss Whedon Exits 'Batgirl' Movie." *The Hollywood Reporter*, February 22, 2018. https://www.hollywoodreporter.com/amp/heat-vision/joss-whedon-exits-batgirl-movie-1087384.

Kit, Borys. "Paramount Picks Up Comic Books Movie 'Harbinger' from Sony." *The Hollywood Reporter*, September 11, 2019. https://www.hollywoodreporter.com/heat-vision/paramount-picks-up-comic-book-movie-harbinger-sony-1238972.

Klinger, Barbara. *Beyond the Multiplex: Cinema, New Technologies, and the Home*. Berkeley: University of California Press, 2006.

Knight, Arthur. "Review: Battlestar Galactica." *The Hollywood Reporter*, November 17, 1978. https://www.hollywoodreporter.com/news/battlestar-galactica-read-thrs-1978-749702.

Kohn, Eric. "'Game of Thrones' Premier Makes a Case for the Future of Theatrical Exhibition." *IndieWire*, April 4, 2019. https://www.indiewire.com/2019/04/game-of-thrones-premiere-theatrical-exhibition-future-1202055987/.

Kompare, Derek. *Rerun Nation: How Repeats Invented American Television.* New York: Routledge, 2005.

Kreps, Daniel et al., "30 Best Music Biopics of All Time." *Rolling Stone*, March 24, 2016. https://www.rollingstone.com/movies/movie-lists/30-best-music-biopics-of-all-time-78623/.

Lane, Sylvan. "Netflix Shares Sink as Company Sees Growth Slowing after Coronavirus-Driven Subscriber Surge." *The Hill*, July 17, 2020. https://thehill.com/policy/technology/507801-netflix-shares-sink-as-company-sees-growth-slowing-after-coronavirus-driven.

Lang, Brent, Adam Vary, and Matt Donnelly. "Show Stopper: Coronavirus Sends Hollywood into Unprecedented Crisis." *Variety*, March 23, 2020. https://variety.com/2020/biz/news/hollywood-coronavirus-entertainment-industry-movies-festivals-1203529795/.

Langer, John. "Television's Personality System." In *The Media Studies Reader*, edited by Tim O'Sullivan and Yvonne Jewkes, 164–72. London: Arnold, 1997.

Lauzen, Martha. "The Celluloid Ceiling: Behind-the-Scenes Employment of Women on the Top 100, 250, and 500 Films of 2019." *Center for the Study of Women in Television and Film*, 2020. https://womenintvfilm.sdsu.edu/wp-content/uploads/2020/01/2019_Celluloid_Ceiling_Report.pdf.

Lee, Wendy. "Record High Netflix Subscriptions in Coronavirus Crisis." *Los Angeles Times*, April 21, 2020. https://www.latimes.com/entertainment-arts/business/story/2020-04-21/netflix-usage-profits-surge-during-coronavirus-crisis.

Leitch, Thomas. *Film Adaptation and Its Discontents: From Gone with the Wind to The Passion of the Christ.* Baltimore, MD: Johns Hopkins University Press, 2009.

Liao, Shannon. "The Emmys Showed That Peak TV May Help Solve Cinema's Diversity Problem." *The Verge*, September 21, 2017. https://www.theverge.com/2017/9/21/16330190/emmys-2017-diversity-representation-netflix-hulu-amazon-poc-women-lgbtq.

Lindahl. Chris. "Disney Didn't Just But 'Hamilton' for $75 Million; It Bought a Potential Franchise." *IndieWire*, February 4, 2020. https://www.indiewire.com/2020/02/hamilton-movie-disney-lin-manuel-miranda-1202208283/.

Littleton, Cynthia. "HBO Boss Has Seen All the Final 'Game of Thrones' Episodes: 'They're Like Six Movies.'" *Variety*, January 7, 2019. https://variety.com/2019/tv/news/game-of-thrones-season-8-episodes-like-movies-1203101806/.

Littleton, Cynthia and Elaine Low. "Hollywood Braces for Coronavirus Financial Hit That Could Change the Industry Forever." *Variety*, March 18, 2020. https://variety.com/2020/biz/features/hollywood-coronavirus-financial-festivals-film-television-production-1203537442/.

Loock, Kathleen. "'The Past Is Never Really Past': Serial Storytelling from *Psycho* to *Bates Motel*." *Literatur in Wissenschaft und Unterricht* 47, nos. 1–2 (2014): 81–95.

Loock, Kathleen and Constantine Verevis. *Film Remakes, Adaptations, and Fan Productions: Remake/Remodel.* New York: Palgrave Macmillan, 2012.

Lopez, Lori Kido. "Fan Activists and the Politics of Race in *The Last Airbender*." *International Journal of Cultural Studies* 15, no. 5 (2012): 431–45.

Maerz, Melissa and Chris Nashawaty. "Are TV Shows Better Than Movies Right Now?" *Entertainment Weekly*, September 11, 2015. https://ew.com/article/2015/09/11/great-debates-are-tv-shows-better-movies-right-now/.

Maly-Bowie, Barbara. "'Home Is Where Your Netflix Is'—From Mobile Privatization to Private Mobilization." *Literary Geographies* 5, no. 2 (2019): 216–33.

Mancuso, Vinnie. "Joe Russo Believes There Will Be a 'Community' Movie." *Collider*, April 20, 2020. https://collider.com/community-movie-update-joe-russo/.

Marshall, P. David. *Celebrity and Power: Fame in Contemporary Culture*. Minneapolis: University of Minnesota Press, 1997.

McCabe, Janet and Kim Akass. "It's Not TV, It's HBO's Original Programming: Producing Quality TV." In *It's Not TV: Watching HBO in the Post-Network Era*, edited by Marc Leverette, Brian Ott, and Cara Louise Buckley, 83–95. New York: Routledge, 2008.

McCarthy, Todd. "The Avengers." *The Hollywood Reporter*, April 24, 2012. https://www.hollywoodreporter.com/news/avengers-315593.

McClintock, Pamela. "Box Office Calendar in Chaos: 'Next Year Is Becoming a Cage Match.'" *The Hollywood Reporter*, August 1, 2020. https://www.hollywoodreporter.com/news/box-office-calendar-chaos-next-year-is-becoming-a-cage-match-1304963.

McLuhan, Marshall. *Understanding Media: The Extensions of Man*. New York: McGraw-Hill, 1964.

McMahon-Coleman, Kimberley. "'I Was Hoping It Would Pass You By': Dis/ability and Difference in *Teen Wolf*." In *Remake Television: Reboot, Re-use, Recycle*, edited by Carlen Lavigne, 141–54. Lanham, MD: Lexington, 2014.

McMillan, Graeme. "Can 'Pacific Rim' Support Its Own Cinematic Universe?" *The Hollywood Reporter*, March 22, 2018. https://www.hollywoodreporter.com/heat-vision/pacific-rim-can-it-support-own-cinematic-universe-1096495.

McNair, Brian. *Journalist in Film: Heroes and Villains*. Edinburgh: Edinburgh University Press, 2010.

Mendelson, Scott. "F. Gary Gray Traded 'Captain America' for 'Straight Outta Compton.'" *Forbes*, August 17, 2015. https://www.forbes.com/sites/scottmendelson/2015/08/17/well-f-gary-gray-was-right-to-make-straight-outta-compton-instead-of-captain-america-2/#5172567f2e94.

MeTV. "11 Acclaimed Directors Who Got a Start on Television." March 28, 2016. https://www.metv.com/lists/11-acclaimed-directors-who-got-a-start-on-television.

Mikos, Lothar and Marta Perrotta. "Traveling Style: Aesthetic Differences and Similarities in National Adaptations of *Yo Soy Betty, La Fea*." *International Journal of Cultural Studies* 15, no. 1 (2011): 81–97.

Miller, Liz. "Women and People of Color Directed More TV Than Even This Year and It Didn't Cost White Men Any Work." *IndieWire*, November 14, 2017. https://www.indiewire.com/2017/11/tv-directors-diversity-2016-2017-1201897411/.

Molloy, Tim. "Joe Russo Reveals How Breaking Bad Influenced Avengers: Endgame." *MovieMaker*, November 8, 2019. https://www.moviemaker.com/joe-russo-breaking-bad-avengers-end-game-avengers-infinity-war/.

Molnar, Phillip. "Can Movie Theaters Survive in a COVID-19 World?" *San Diego Union Tribune*, June 26, 2020. https://www.sandiegouniontribune.com/business/story/2020-06-26/can-movie-theaters-survive-in-a-covid-19-world.

Murray, Susan. *Hitch Your Antenna to the Stars: Early Television and Broadcast Fame*. New York: Routledge, 2005.

Naremore, James, ed. *Film Adaptation*. New Brunswick: Rutgers University Press, 2000.

Newman, Michael Z. and Elana Levine. *Legitimating Television: Media Convergence and Cultural Status*. New York: Routledge, 2011.

Nielsen, Aldon L. *Writing between the Lines: Race and Intertextuality.* Athens: University of Georgia Press, 1994.

Nordy, Kimberly and Nellie Andreeva. "Russos Put Order in the 'Courtroom.'" *The Hollywood Reporter*, April 11, 2008. https://www.hollywoodreporter.com/news/russos-put-order-courtroom-109144.

O'Connell, Michael. "'Buffy' at 20: Joss Whedon Talks TV Today, Reboot Fatigue, and the Trouble with Binging." *The Hollywood Reporter*, March 10, 2017. https://www.hollywoodreporter.com/live-feed/buffy-at-20-joss-whedon-talks-tv-today-reboot-fatigue-trouble-binging-984885.

omidpacino. "100 Best Music Movies." *IMDB*, July 6, 2012. https://www.imdb.com/list/ls009668187/.

Pallotta, Frank. "AMC Bans Universal Films from Its Theaters over 'Trolls World Tour' Spat." *CNN*, April 29, 2020. https://www.cnn.com/2020/04/28/media/trolls-world-tour-universal-amc/index.html.

Pallotta, Frank. "Here's Why You Can't Watch 'Mulan' On Disney+ Right Now." *CNN*, July 25, 2020. https://www.cnn.com/2020/07/24/media/mulan-tenet-delay-digital/index.html.

Pedersen, Erik. "Steven Spielberg Misses Academy Meeting on Oscar Eligibility for Netflix Films But Offers Some Opinions." *Deadline*, April 23, 2019. https://deadline.com/2019/04/steven-spielberg-netflix-oscar-eligibility-comments-1202600879/.

Perkins, Claire and Constantine Verevis, eds. *Transnational Television Remakes* special issue of *Continuum: Journal of Media and Cultural Studies* 29, no. 5 (2015).

Petrie, Duncan and Robert Stoneman. *Educating Film-Makers: Past, Present, and Future.* Chicago: Intellect, 2014.

Phillipson, Daisy. "Every Movie Genre the MCU Has Had a Go At So Far – From Romcom to Period Drama." *Digital Spy*, July 25, 2019. https://www.digitalspy.com/movies/a28504196/marvel-mcu-every-genre-horror-comedy/.

Polone, Gavin. "The Main Reason TV Is Now Better Than Movies." *Vulture*, September 12, 2012. https://www.vulture.com/2012/09/why-tv-is-better-than-movies-gavin-polone.html.

Prell, Sam. "Every Marvel Movie Is a Different Genre, and That's Why the MCU Works." *Games Radar*, January 15, 2016. https://www.gamesradar.com/every-marvel-movie-different-genre-and-s-why-mcu-works/.

Prudom, Laura. "'Game of Thrones' Comes to Theatres to Distract You from the Long Wait for Season 7." *Mashable*, December 7, 2017. https://mashable.com/2017/12/06/game-of-thrones-fan-screening-season-7-movie-theater-dvd-blu-ray/.

Pye, Michael and Linda Myles. *The Movie Brats: How the Film Generation Took Over Hollywood.* New York: Henry Holt & Co, 1979.

Rafferty, Brian. "Could This Be the Year Movies Stopped Mattering?" *Wired*, August 26, 2016. https://www.wired.com/2016/08/do-movies-still-matter-2016/.

Renfro, Kim. "Inside HBO's Star-Studded World Premiere and After-Party for the Final Season of 'Game of Thrones.'" *Insider*, April 4, 2019. https://www.insider.com/game-of-thrones-season-8-premiere-after-party-photos-2019-4.

Robb, David. "DGA Report: Female & Minority Episodic TV Directors Have Another Record Year." *Deadline*, November 19, 2019. https://deadline.com/2019/11/dga-report-female-minority-episodic-tv-directors-have-another-record-year-direct-half-of-all-shows-for-first-time-ever-1202789379/.

Rose, Lacey. "Anthony and Joe Russo Ink Overall Deal with NBC." *The Hollywood Reporter*, June 20, 2011. https://www.hollywoodreporter.com/news/anthony-joe-russo-ink-deal-203438.

Ryan, Maureen. "Peak Inequality: Investigating the Lack of Diversity among TV Directors." *Variety*, November 10, 2015. https://variety.com/2015/tv/features/diversity-directors-tv-amc-fx-hbo-netflix-showtime-1201633122/.

Sakoui, Anousha. "Female Directors in Hollywood Are Still Underrepresented, But the Gap Is Narrowing." *Los Angeles Times*, January 2, 2020. https://www.latimes.com/entertainment-arts/business/story/2020-01-02/women-directors-working-reaches-highest-level-in-a-decade-but-still-underpresented.

Santo, Avi. "Para-television and Discourses of Distinction: The Culture of Production at HBO." In *It's Not TV: Watching HBO in the Post-Network Era*, edited by Marc Leverette, Brian Ott, and Cara Louise Buckley, 19–45. New York: Routledge, 2008.

Scahill, Andrew. "Serialized Killers: Prebooting Horror in *Bates Motel* and *Hannibal*." In *Cycles, Sequels, Spin-offs, Remakes, and Reboots: Multiplicities in Film and Television*, edited by Amanda Ann Klein and R. Barton Palmer, 316–34. Austin: University of Texas Press, 2016.

Schwartzel, Erich. "'Trolls World Tour' Breaks New Records and Charts a New Path for Hollywood." *The Wall Street Journal*, April 28, 2020. https://www.wsj.com/articles/trolls-world-tour-breaks-digital-records-and-charts-a-new-path-for-hollywood-11588066202#:~:text=Universal%20has%20made%20more%20than,Tour%E2%80%9D%20domestic%20customers%20so%20far.

Sconce, Jeffrey. "What If? Charting Television's New Textual Boundaries." In *Television After TV: Essays on a Medium in Transition*, edited by Lynn Spigel and Jan Olsson, 93–112. Durham, NC: Duke University Press, 2002.

Scorsese, Martin. "I Said Marvel Movies Aren't Cinema. Let Me Explain." *New York Times*, November 4, 2019. https://www.nytimes.com/2019/11/04/opinion/martin-scorsese-marvel.html.

Scott, A.O. "Are Films Bad, or Is TV Just Better?" *New York Times*, September 9, 2010. https://www.nytimes.com/2010/09/12/movies/12scott.html?pagewanted=all&mtrref=undefined.

Shales, Tom. "ABC's Fall Shakeup." *Washington Post*, May 2, 1978: B1.

Shanley, Patrick. "Can Anyone Besides Marvel Make a Cinematic Universe Work?" *The Hollywood Reporter*, March 29, 2018. https://www.hollywoodreporter.com/heat-vision/marvel-cinematic-universe-why-is-it-one-works-1096504.

Siegel, Tatiana, Borys Kit, and Lesley Goldberg. "Hollywood Could Take $20 Billion Hit from Coronavirus Impact." *The Hollywood Reporter*, March 13, 2020. https://www.hollywoodreporter.com/news/hollywood-could-take-20-billion-hit-coronavirus-impact-1284582.

Siegemund-Broka, Austin and Borys Kit. "Russo Brothers to Direct 'Avengers: Infinity War' Parts 1 and 2." *The Hollywood Reporter*, March 23, 2015. https://www.hollywoodreporter.com/heat-vision/russo-brothers-direct-avengers-infinity-war-parts-1-2-783685#:~:text=Joe%20and%20Anthony%20Russo%2C%20who,as%20Marvel's%20main%20movie%20executors.

Sims, David. "What It Was Like Making the Biggest Movie of 2019." *The Atlantic*, May 7, 2019. https://www.theatlantic.com/entertainment/archive/2019/05/russo-brothers-interview-avengers-marvel-endgame/588832/.

Smith, Iain Robert. *The Hollywood Meme: Transnational Adaptations in World Cinema*. Edinburgh: Edinburgh University Press, 2016.

Spangler, Todd. "Disney Plus: Half of US Homes With Kids Under 10 Have Already Subscribed, Data Shows." *Variety*, March 17, 2020. https://variety.com/2020/digital/news/disney-plus-half-us-homes-kids-subscribe-1203536676/.

Spangler, Todd. "Netflix Packs on Record 16 Million Subscribers in Q1, Getting Huge Lift in Coronavirus Lockdowns." *Variety*, April 21, 2020. https://variety.com/2020/digital/news/netflix-record-16-million-subscribers-q1-2020-coronavirus-1234586125/.

Spangler, Todd. "Quarantine Life: Staying at Home Can Drive Up TV Viewing 60% of More, Nielsen Says." *Variety*, March 16, 2020. https://variety.com/2020/digital/news/coronavirus-quarantine-life-media-consumption-data-increase-1203535472/.

Sperling, Nicole. "TV's Top Show-Runners Give Rare Peek behind the Scenes." *Variety*, June 1, 2018. https://www.vanityfair.com/hollywood/2018/06/hottest-tv-showrunners.

Spigel, Lynn. *Make Room for TV: Television and the Family Ideal in Postwar America*. Chicago: University of Chicago Press, 1992.

Stam, Robert and Alessandra Raengo, eds. *Literature and Film: A Guide to the Theory and Practice of Film Adaptation*. Malden, MA: Blackwell, 2005.

Star Trek. "The Best of Both Worlds in Theaters April 25." February 14, 2013. https://www.startrek.com/article/the-best-of-both-worlds-in-theaters-april-25.

Stone, Nora E. "Marketing the Real: The Creation of a Multilayered Market for Documentary Cinema." PhD diss., University of Wisconsin-Madison, 2018.

Straubhaar, Joseph. *World Television: From Global to Local*. London: Sage, 2007.

StudioBinder. "The Best 67 Female Film Directors Working Today." May 31, 2020. https://www.studiobinder.com/blog/best-female-directors/.

Sullivan, Andy. "US TV Viewing Is Increasing During Coronavirus Pandemic." *Comscore*, March 24, 2020. https://www.comscore.com/Insights/Blog/US-TV-Viewing-Is-Increasing-During-Coronavirus-Pandemic#:~:text=Viewing%20of%20the%20big%20four, %25%20and%2035%25%20increases%20vs.

Thomas, Zoe. "Netflix Gets 16 Million New Subscribers Thanks to Lockdown." *BBC News*, 22 April, 2020. https://www.bbc.com/news/business-52376022.

Tizard, Will. "David Lynch on 'Twin Peaks,' 'Arthouse' Television, 'Lynchian Fear.'" *Variety* November 14, 2017. https://variety.com/2017/film/global/david-lynch-twin-peaks-camerimage-1202615377/.

Truitt, Brian. "Disney-owned Theaters? Mask with Your Ticket? Moviegoing Could Look Quite Different Post-Pandemic." *USA Today*, June 14, 2020. https://www.usatoday.com/story/entertainment/movies/2020/06/14/future-moviegoing-could-coronavirus-kill-movie-theaters/3186292001/.

Tryon, Chuck. "TV Got Better: Netflix's Original Programming Strategies and Binge Viewing." *Media Industries* 2, no. 2 (2015). https://quod.lib.umich.edu/m/mij/15031809.0002.206/--tv-got-better-netflixs-original-programming-strategies?rgn=main;view=fulltext.

Tuchow, Ryan. "Nick Greenlights Two Made-from-Home Series." *Kidscreen*, May 6, 2020. https://kidscreen.com/2020/05/06/nick-greenlights-two-made-from-home-series/.

Uricchio, William. "Television, Film and the Struggle for Media Identity." *Film History* 10, no. 2 (1998): 118–27.

US Census Bureau. "Quick Facts." July 31, 2020. https://www.census.gov/quickfacts/fact/table/US/PST045219.

Verevis, Constantine. *Film Remakes*. Edinburgh: Edinburgh University Press, 2006.

Verevis, Constantine. "TV to Film." In *American Hollywood 2*, edited by Lincoln Geraghty, 129–30. Bristol: Intellect, 2015.

Wagner, Jon Nelson and MacLean, Tracy Biga. *Television at the Movies: Cinematic and Critical Responses to American Broadcasting*. New York: Continuum, 2008.

Wardlow, Ciara. "When a Cinematic Universe Is Built Around Something New." *The Hollywood Reporter*, March 24, 2018. https://www.hollywoodreporter.com/heat-vision/pacific-rim-a-cinematic-universe-is-built-around-something-new-1097004.

Wasko, Janet. *Hollywood in the Information Age*. Austin: University of Texas Press, 1994.

Wasko, Janet. *Understanding Disney: The Manufacture of Fantasy*. Cambridge, MA: Polity, 2001.

Watson, Amy. "Coronavirus and TV Viewing." *Statista*, June 11, 2020. https://www.statista.com/statistics/1107040/broadcast-tv-viewer-increase-coronavirus-us/.

Wee, Valerie. *Japanese Horror Films and Their American Remakes: Translating Fear, Adapting Culture*. New York: Routledge, 2014.

Williams, Raymond. *Television: Technology and Cultural Form*. London: Fontana, 1972.

Wolcott, James. "Prime Time's Graduation." *Vanity Fair*, April 3, 2012. https://www.vanityfair.com/hollywood/2012/05/wolcott-television-better-than-movies.

Young, Paul. *The Cinema Dreams Its Rivals: Media Fantasy Films from Radio to the Internet*. Minneapolis: University of Minnesota Press, 2006.

Zakarin, Jordan. "Exploring the Whedonverse: Inside the Cult Hero Fame of 'Avengers' Director Joss Whedon." *The Hollywood Reporter*, April 24, 2012. https://www.hollywoodreporter.com/news/joss-whedon-whedonverse-cult-hero-avengers-buffy-firefly-314554.

Zakarin, Jordan. "Joss Whedon Writes Thank You Letter to Fans for Years of Support, 'Avengers' Success." *The Hollywood Reporter*, May 9, 2012. https://www.hollywoodreporter.com/heat-vision/joss-whedon-fans-whedonesque-avengers-thank-you-322483.

Zeitchik, Steven. "'Mulan,' Bellwether of a Pandemic, Is Off Disney's Calendar for Now." *The Washington Post*, July 23, 2020. https://www.washingtonpost.com/business/2020/07/23/mulan-coronavirus-postpone-disney/.

Zeitchik, Steven. "The Pandemic Will Make Movies and TV Shows Look Like Nothing We've Seen Before." *The Washington Post*, August 12, 2020. https://www.washingtonpost.com/business/2020/08/12/hollywood-pandemic-film-industry/.

INDEX